JAPAN UNDER CONSTRUCTION

JAPAN UNDER CONSTRUCTION

Corruption, Politics, and Public Works

BRIAN WOODALL

UNIVERSITY OF CALIFORNIA PRESS
BERKELEY   LOS ANGELES   OXFORD

100272

University of California Press
Berkeley and Los Angeles, California

The costs of publishing this book have been defrayed in part by
the 1994 Hiromi Arisawa Memorial Award from the Books on
Japan Fund with respect to *Encounters with Aging: Mythologies
of Menopause in Japan and North America,* published by the University of California Press. The Fund is financed by The Japan
Foundation from generous donations contributed by Japanese individuals and companies.

University of California Press, Ltd.
Oxford, England

Library of Congress Cataloging in Publication Data

Woodall, Brian.
    Japan under construction : corruption, politics, and public
works / Brian Woodall.
       p.   cm.
    Includes bibliographical references (p.) and index.
    ISBN 0-520-08815-8 (alk. paper)
    1. Public contracts—Japan. 2. Public works—Japan.
3. Letting of contracts—Japan—Corrupt practices.
4. Construction industry—Corrupt practices—Japan.
5. Political corruption—Japan. 6. Price fixing—Japan. I. Title.
HD3861.J3W66   1996
364. 1' 323' 0952--dc20   95-33484
                                              CIP

Printed in the United Sates of America
9 8 7 6 5 4 3 2 1

The paper used in this publication meets the minimum re-
quirements of American National Standard for Information
Sciences--Permanence of Paper for Printed Library Materials,
ANSI Z39.48-1984.

To Joyce, Leslie, and Melissa

Contents

Acknowledgments

In researching this book, I have drawn extensively on Japanese-language materials: newspaper reports, periodicals, industry association publications, and government documents. In addition, I conducted over one hundred open-ended interviews, primarily in 1987–1988 and in 1993–1994. Almost all of these interviews were conducted in Japanese, each lasting about an hour. I spoke with construction contractors, industry association officials, elected politicians and their aides, political party officials, government bureaucrats, newspaper reporters, and academics. Because of the highly sensitive, and sometimes sub rosa, nature of the subject matter, I cannot identify these individuals by name. For their willingness to answer sometimes naive questions and to assist in other ways, however, I owe a deep debt of gratitude.

At the time I undertook this study, sensible people warned me about the quagmire that lay ahead. They alerted me to the difficulties of handling the shadowy actors engaged in the complex and secretive process of rigging bids on public works projects. Others warned me about dealings with the government bureaucrats and legislators who also animate the policymaking stage in this heretofore strictly "domestic" domain. To my pleasant surprise, I found these warnings unnecessary. Indeed, with assurances that my intention was to analyze objectively the political economy of Japanese public works, these supposedly shadowy characters proved enormously helpful and astonishingly forthright. Some of these individuals went to amazing lengths to help me understand the rationale behind informal practices and behavior. For instance, more than five years before the general contractors scandal was splattered across the front page of every newspaper in Japan, self-confessed bid-riggers treated me to candid and enlightening accounts of Ibaraki Governor Takeuchi's "voice of heaven" in steering public works contracts to specific contractors.

I am also grateful to several institutions and many individuals, both in Japan and the United States. Financial support for a fruitful year of fieldwork in Tokyo during 1987–1988 was provided in the form of a Japan Foundation Dissertation Fellowship. Various grants and fellowships from the University of California at Berkeley supported the completion of my dissertation, and a Faculty Research Grant from the University of California at Irvine and sundry forms of research support from Harvard University helped in the lenthy transition from dissertation to book. I made the final revisions to the manuscript in Japan during 1993–1994 while on a grant from the Abe Fellowship Program of the Social Science Research Council and the American Council of Learned Societies with funds provided by The Japan Foundation Center for Global Partnership. Institutional and infrastructural support on two separate occasions was generously provided by the Institute of Oriental Culture at the University of Tokyo under the wise and good-natured sponsorship of Inoguchi Takashi.

Among the people who provided key introductions, suggestions, and comments on drafts are John Creighton Campbell, Robert L. Cutts, R. P. Dore, Bernard Grofman, Inoguchi Takashi, Chalmers Johnson, Kinjō Kunio, Kitō Makoto, Edward Lascher, Murakawa Ichirō, Masumi Junnosuke, Nagayama Keiichi, Gregory Noble, Okajima Shigeyuki, T. J. Pempel, Susan J. Pharr, Robert A. Scalapino, Thomas C. Smith, Ezra Vogel, Yakushiji Taizō, David Weinstein, and three anonymous readers for the University of California Press. Even though their generous suggestions were not always heeded, they made this a far better book than it could possibly have been otherwise. Dennis Encarnation kindly suggested the title. Valuable research assistance was provided by Toshiro Mochizuki, Emily McNeal, Kaye Yoshino, Matsui Mieko, and Steven Niwa. Kuniko Yamada McVey offered vital infrastructural support through the Documentation Center on Contemporary Japan, one of Harvard University's underappreciated research gems. The editorial efforts of Joanna Lieberman, Kaye Yoshino, and Amy Einsohn did much to improve the quality and clarity of my prose, while Sheila Levine, Scott Norton, and Betsey Scheiner guided the manuscript to publication.

Finally, I am extremely grateful to Saitō Hiuga and his wonderful family for the generosity and kindness they showered upon this American researcher and his family during the final stage of this book's completion. Joyce, my wife, has served as an ever-dependable and challenging sounding board for innumerable partially baked ideas, and she has provided a constant stream of support and encouragement. My daughters, Leslie and Melissa, did their best best to keep me from completing this book before its time.

Note on Conventions

Throughout the text, Japanese personal names are given in the common Japanese manner, with the surname followed by the given name. The only exception to this rule is made in the case of Japanese writers whose works are well known to Western readers. Most corporate names are given in the abbreviated form listed in the *Japan Company Handbook*, which includes all companies listed on the First and Second sections of the Tokyo, Osaka, and Nagoya stock exchanges, as well as many local market, over-the-counter, and unlisted companies. Macron marks are used except in cases where the word in question is widely familiar to Western readers (e.g., Tokyo and Osaka, instead of Tōkyō and Ōsaka).

Introduction

For three decades, U.S.-Japanese relations have been marked by a succession of disputes over Japanese exports of textiles, steel, automobiles, machine tools, semiconductors, flat panel display monitors, and consumer electronics. Japan's potential for overseas conquests in pharmaceuticals, biotechnology, and high-definition television has exacerbated these tensions, as has Japan's unwillingness to open its protected domestic markets in agricultural commodities, telecommunications equipment, and forestry products. Over the years, of course, the United States has issued various demands for "fairness" and "reciprocity." Nonetheless, it came as quite a surprise to many in 1986 when the United States began to mount an extraordinary effort to force Japan to open its domestic construction market to foreign bidders.

To be sure, Japan's domestic construction market was the largest in the world (valued at about ¥53.6 trillion a year), and it was expanding at an unparalleled rate. But given the size of the mounting bilateral trade imbalance—some $50 billion annually, about half of the total U.S. trade deficit—one would have expected Washington to focus attention on policies regarding automobiles and automobile parts, which accounted for about two-thirds of the trade imbalance, or perhaps on office machinery, the second-largest component of Japan's exports to the United States. The sudden burst of enthusiasm for penetrating Japan's domestic construction market was even more surprising in light of the U.S construction industry's seeming disinterest in Japan and the ignominious withdrawal, some twenty years earlier, of the last American firm to have been awarded a major Japanese public works contract.[1]

No one was more startled by the uproar than Japan's public works bureaucrats, who never would have imagined that domestic public works would occupy center stage in a major trade dispute with the United States. To their dismay, the dispute soon broadened, as Canada, South Korea, France, Britain, and China all weighed in, pressing their own demands for access to the Japanese construction market.

Eventually, the threat of additional U.S. retaliation—in the wake of a Congressional bill that excluded Japanese firms from selling goods and services for federally funded public works—compelled Tokyo to compromise, but not before the protracted conflict had come close to humiliating Japan's newly elected prime minister and his party. (For a chronology of these events, see Appendix A.)

The first question raised by these events is why the Japanese government allowed the apparently trivial issue of construction bidding procedures to jeopardize its continued access to vital U.S. markets, the destination of one-third of Japan's vast export product. As we will see, Japan's seemingly irrational economic behavior in this affair was, in fact, politically rational. For the pressures to open the domestic construction market threatened the interests of three sets of powerful political actors: construction contractors, public works bureaucrats, and career politicians, especially members of the Liberal Democratic Party (LDP).

Naturally, the construction contractors opposed any market-opening measures that would have provoked additional uncertainty in an already volatile industry. But the U.S. demands also threatened to undermine the occupational mission and postretirement prospects of Japan's public works bureaucrats and to imperil an important source of electoral advantage for career-minded politicians. Over time, pervasive networks of mutually beneficial links among Japanese construction contractors, government bureaucrats, and legislators had developed. Clientelism bound these diverse actors into a symbiotic embrace: Legislators exchanged political influence for campaign contributions and votes from construction industry clients, while bureaucrats leaked confidential information in return for postretirement sinecures with construction firms.

This spectacle prompts two more questions. First, How did Japan manage to sustain miraculous rates of economic growth in the post–World War II era despite the vast political pork barrel? And second, Why did the political, bureaucratic, and industrial actors involved in Japan's public works, by their continued collusion in price-fixing and bid-rigging, behave so differently than their counterparts in most other advanced democracies?

To answer these questions, we must examine the behavior of, and relations among, the legislators, government bureaucrats, and construction contractors who command Japan's public works subgovernment. In this introductory chapter I survey the analytical topography and introduce the theoretical framework that informs this study. Chapters 1 through 3 profile, in turn, the construction industry, the public works bureaucracy, and the career politicians of the Liberal Democratic Party, which dominated the Japanese legislature from 1955 until 1993. In chapter 4 I use the example of the construction system to explain how LDP politicians sought to exploit the party's formal and informal organizational structures—especially intraparty factions and policy tribes—for their electoral ends. In the concluding chapter I examine the way in which international forces shaped the calculus of self-interest on the part of the Japanese actors, the implications of Japan's simultaneous experience of economic growth and political clientelism, and the manner in which the principal institutions interacted to mold the behavior of elite actors.

The Dual Political Economy

Japan's grudging response to foreign pressure to pry open the domestic construction market must be viewed from a domestic vantage. The saying "first-rate economy, third-rate politics" refers to the paradoxical coexistence in Japan of world-class levels of economic performance in internationally competitive sectors, in contrast to wholesale inefficiency and political clientelism in certain politically vital domestic domains. Most scholars have focused on Japan's efficient and relatively unpoliticized internationally traded sectors and industries.[2] With an occasional caveat regarding the "cost side" of the Japanese model, these studies emphasize the positive aspects of the Japanese economic juggernaut and the industrial giants at its vanguard. The dysfunctions generated by the government's "economics first" strategy and the political inputs undergirding such a strategy in an advanced industrialized democracy have received less attention.

Several recent studies, however, have focused on the inefficient, highly protected, and patronage-ridden distributive sectors of Japan's political economy: the government-set rice price, the protection for small business, the official tolerance of a multitiered distribution system, the "non-policy" for land use, and a rigged public construction market. "After reviewing Japan's domestic policy sectors," Kent Calder (1988, 465) observes, "one begins to wonder both where the economic juggernaut so clearly visible to foreign competition could have come from and why domestic policy patterns so differ from the common generalizations about Japanese policymaking in internationally traded sectors." In Japan's domestic policy arenas, not only the policy outcomes but also the roles of the policy protagonists, the key pressure points, the preferred policy tools, and the mode of decision-making differ significantly from popular perceptions.

There is a systemic logic, however, to the behavior and interactions of elite actors in Japanese policymaking. Simply put, the behavior of policy protagonists is based on the incentives perceived to accrue from involvement in a given policy domain. As Theodore Lowi (1964, 688) argues, political interactions are determined by the type of policy at stake, so that for every type of policy there is likely to be a characteristic pattern of interactions among the central political actors. Or, in Aage Clausen's words (1973, 31), "Different alignments form as the policy content changes." The calculated pursuit of self-interest, in sum, prompts political actors to behave in characteristic ways in response to the varying incentives for involvement in different policy arenas. (Accounting for cross-national differences, however, demands an appreciation of the case-specific institutional infrastructure, a topic I address later in this chapter.)

In Japan, as in other advanced industrialized democracies, economic policy is forged in two fundamentally different policy markets. A *policy market* is the stage on which the key political actors meet and make key policy decisions. Out of the process of political exchange emerge the public policies that determine the allocation of economic and political benefits for the society. Policies for potential growth sectors, internationally competitive industries, and sectors deemed vital to the national interest emerge from what I call the *strategic policy market.* In this market, government bureaucrats and private sector elites act as the key policy protagonists, while elected politicians play a decidedly minor part. Meanwhile, the largest share of public policy decisions are forged in a highly politicized *structural policy market* encompassing domestic sectors in which the public is often the client. In these domains, elected politicians as well as government bureaucrats and private-sector elites play a direct and extensive role in policy formulation.

In this sense, the Japanese system is a dual political economy in which segmented policy markets generate separate but interactive "policy regimes" that operate under different equilibrium conditions. I refer to these segmented policy regimes as the *developmental state* and the *clientelist state.* Nevertheless, in any given arena, both policymaking and policy outcomes are likely to be an admixture of clientelism and developmental capitalism. This admixture is especially conspicuous in domains, such as telecommunications, where more than one government ministry and its parliamentary patrons contest jurisdiction. However, while few truly pure cases remain, especially since the mid-1970s, one can identify policy domains in which one or the other of Japan's "two states" predominates.

The Developmental State

The theory of the developmental state, pioneered by Chalmers Johnson (1982), has attracted widespread attention as an explanation for the phenomenal economic growth of Japan and East Asia's newly industrializing economies (e.g., Amsden 1989; Wade 1990). From this literature, we may distill three domestic conditions as crucial prerequisites to export-led, ultra-high-speed economic growth. First, protracted political stability creates an environment in which a meritocratic bureaucratic elite can play an active role in the policymaking process. Second, a system of government-business relations founded upon broad interaction and intensive bargaining imparts strategic vision to an economy driven primarily by the market-oriented calculations of the private sector. Third, a relatively equitable distribution of national wealth provides the social stability necessary to endure the stresses and strains imposed by an economic growth agenda that subordinates the interests of the general citizenry to those of private business.

Although the developmental state's actual contributions to Japanese economic growth are hotly contested,[3] these three conditions offer insights into the pattern of elite interactions that characterize policymaking in Japan's strategic policy market, where decisions concerning the broad architecture of the national economy and the course of development for the national industrial structure are forged. At the core of this policy market are policies designed to encourage growth in the high-growth "sunrise" sectors that have large potential spillover effects and in other industries deemed vital to the national interest.

In Japan these strategic policy domains are characterized by world-class rates of technological advancement, labor productivity, price-competitiveness, and economic efficiency. Of course, domestic politics determines which industries and sectors are deemed vital to the country's economic and security interests. For example, the development of commercially viable industries is the principal concern in Japan, whereas defense industries are deemed vital to the national interests of the United States.

Economic bureaucrats and private-sector elites are the protagonists in the formulation of strategic economic policy. As Edward Lincoln (1993, 4) explains, "Economic policy decisions in Japan emerge in a setting dominated by the central government bureaucracy and private sector firms. Depending upon the issue, politicians may also play an important role, although they are not consistently involved in all economic issues." The officials of the Ministry of International Trade and Industry (MITI) wield extensive powers, although administrators in other ministries, particularly the Ministry of Finance, also play key roles. The tradition of substantial autonomy inherited by this administrative elite dates back to the genesis of Japanese industrialization in the latter half of the nineteenth century (Johnson 1982, 35–82; Pempel 1982, 46–89). On this score, the situational contingencies of late development dictated the emergence of an activist state bureaucracy, which has, for "path-dependent" and historical reasons, continued to exert power in the policymaking process (see Sheridan 1993).

In the case of MITI, the ministry was given power, in the form of formal legal authorizations and informal "administrative guidance," to develop whatever industries it deemed critical to the health of the national economy (Johnson 1982). Aside from the policy domain of the Small and Medium Enterprise Agency, the lack of concrete distributive policy benefits insulated many of MITI's functions from partisan meddling. Fortunately for strategic economic policy, MITI offers few "opportunities for pork barrel politicking" (Okimoto 1989, 21; see also Campbell 1989, 130–33). From 1955 to 1988, MITI's annual budget averaged a minuscule 1.3 percent of the general accounts, only slightly more than the allocations of the markedly less prestigious Labor and Justice ministries.

Infrastructural power—the ability to formulate and implement policies through a process of negotiation, intimidation, and, mostly, compromise—prevails in the developmental state (Onis 1991). This is not meant to imply that the Japanese developmental state is or was a Stalinist-style totalitarian regime. As Richard Samuels (1987, 8–9) points out, the developmental state does not always get its way, and reciprocal consent has always characterized relations between government and business in Japan. However, aside from a few notable instances of private-sector defiance and policy failure, the majority of industrial policy outcomes have not diverged significantly from the state bureaucracy's objectives.[4] And although a form of market capitalism drives the economy, the state's role in the economic transformation has hardly been laissez-faire.[5] In particular, the state works with the private sector to create a macroeconomic infrastucture conducive to the development of strategic industries.

The developmental state employs a variety of policy tools to achieve its objectives. In Japan the tools of preference involve tariff, tax, and financial incentives. Specific policy tools include the waiving of import duties on designated machinery, accelerated depreciation and tax exemptions for R&D expenditures, low-interest policy loans for the introduction of designated foreign technology, and the creation of various government-business consortiums. In addition, the state provides

tax incentives and subsidies to support R&D activities, and it has established blueprints, in the form of "visions," for a future industrial
structure. The collaboration of government bureaucrats and private-
sector elites in formulating these visions resembles French indicative
planning (described best by Cohen 1969). Case studies reveal the
application of these strategic policy tools in a host of Japanese industries, including textiles, shipbuilding, steel, automobiles, semiconductors, computers, consumer electronics, and biotechnology. (See, e.g.,
Chida and Davies 1990; Johnson 1982; Genther 1990; Okimoto et al.
1984; Anchordoguy 1989; Yoshikawa 1987; Yoshino 1993.)

Nevertheless, largely because of Japan's miraculous rate of economic growth (as well as enormous trade and current accounts sur-
pluses), the role and power of the developmental state has atrophied
over time. In the late 1960s, MITI began surrendering many of its
formal powers and prerogatives. Meanwhile, many of the erstwhile
infant industries nurtured in the developmental greenhouse no longer
required nor desired further government assistance, by then perceived as meddling. But when formerly strategic sectors enter the
sunset stage of the industrial life cycle, the demands for government
protection and the incentives for meddling by legislative patrons grow.
Sectors such as textiles, coal mining, shipbuilding, and steel clearly
illustrate this phenomena. (See, e.g., Destler et al. 1979; Friman 1990;
Lesbirel 1991, esp. 1088–91; Peck et al. 1987.)

By the early 1990s, the only relatively pure forms of strategic policymaking could be found in sunrise industries such as biotechnology,
medical imaging, and future-generation computers. In such industries the knowledge-intensive character and scant employment held
little appeal for meddlesome politicians, who were more readily attracted to the immediate and tangible electoral rewards of distributive
policies. The role of elected politicians in strategic economic policymaking in Japan is thus broadly similar to the role played by Congress
in the politics of commercial R&D programs in the United States.[6]

The Clientelist State

Structural policy constitutes the bricks-and-mortar of economic policy.
The structural policy market concerns itself with state-owned enterprises, government spending on public works (as opposed to incen-

tives to private business), and the regulation of business activities. It also entails government procurement, distribution of the tax burden, setting of interest rates, balancing the budget, and policies to protect mature industries and to ease the decline for sunset industries (Clausen 1973). At the core of the structural policy market are distributive policies that are characterized by "the ease with which they can be disaggregated and dispensed unit by small unit more or less in isolation from other units and from any general rule" (Lowi 1964, 690). For instance, distributive policy benefits might be exchanged for the explicit or tacit promise of campaign support or postretirement careers for government officials.

Legislators, government officials, and special interests play the role of policy protagonists in the clientelist state. In the politics of Japanese public works during the period under scrutiny, the key parliamentary actors belonged to the Liberal Democratic Party, especially its influential public works caucus, known as the "construction tribe" (*kensetsu zoku*). The bureaucratic elite included upper officials of the ministries of Construction, Agriculture, Transport, and various other central government ministries and agencies. Because of the centrality of expenditures from the national budget, officials of the Ministry of Finance also played a role. The key special interest in this arrangement is the construction industry, with land developers and the real estate industry also figuring prominently.

As we will see, foreign pressure injected crisis into this normally tranquil policymaking arena. By threatening painful retaliation under a deadline for action, American *gaiatsu* (the term used by the Japanese media to describe the external pressure) altered the character and the pace of decision-making and drew additional actors into the policymaking process. These new actors included the mass media, opposition parties, the Foreign Ministry, MITI, the peak associations of big business, and public opinion. In addition, U.S. pressure altered the cost-benefit calculations of traditional actors, such as the large-scale general contractors, with their deep pockets, and the petty contractors, who are perpetually verging on insolvency.

Political clientelism is an interaction characterized by the selective allocation of distributive policy benefits by public-sector elites in exchange for the promise of solidarity and mutually beneficial inputs from favored private-sector interests. This exchange may involve government subsidies, official price supports and import quotas, targeted tax breaks, regulatory favors in the allocation of trucking routes, and other policy benefits. Three generic by-products accompany system-atized political clientelism: particularism, political corruption, and economic inefficiency. Let me define each of these in turn.

Particularism.   Particularism is the consistent granting of prior-ity to a small set of special interests at the public expense. From the perspective of democratic political theory, political clientelism ag-gravates the problems posed by the tension between "part versus whole" and "constituency versus nation" (Archer 1983, 378; Pennock 1979, 332, raises similar themes). As a nineteenth-century American legislator concluded, "Representatives of the people have, of a truth, secured appropriations for works in their own districts more to fur-ther their personal ambition than to promote the general welfare" (Emory R. Johnson, cited in Wilson 1986, 736). Motivated by personal ambition, legislators channel distributive policy expenditures into their electoral districts and thereby enhance their prospects for re-election. Naturally, constituents crave these outlays, since taxation dis-perses the financial burden of such public goods. Directly or indi-rectly, distributive policy benefits also serve the material needs of government bureaucrats and a host of special interests. Because these special interest groups often donate generously to political campaigns, legislators equate the public interest with that of the interest groups. These groups subsequently gain preferential access and distributive policy benefits. In short, as one Washington insider has conceded, "It's hard to say no to someone who gave you five grand" (quoted in Drew 1983, 77).

In the early 1990s, particularism prevailed in a number of Japan's distributive policy domains. Nowhere was it more striking than in agricultural policy, where Japan ranked markedly higher than the European Community and the United States in government assis-tance to producers and in the consumer cost of subsidizing those producers—and this notwithstanding a steep thirty-year decline both in agriculture's contribution to the gross domestic product and in the percentage of the workforce employed in agriculture.[7] Meanwhile, a host of government policies ensured access to capital, preferential tax treatment, and protection from competition from large retailers for the country's massive small business establishment. In addition, subsidies flooded narrow constituencies, particularly rural districts in which the LDP ruled supreme. (See, e.g., Calder 1988, 312–48; Upham 1989, 1993; Hirose 1981; Fukuoka 1985.) With regard to land-use policy, as Hasegawa Tokunosuke (1990, i) observes, "The greatest common measure in deciding actual policy is the sphere of interests of the various ministries and agencies (see also Fukai 1990; Nihon keizai shinbunsha 1990; Woodall 1992.)

In order to keep their particularistic interests on the government's agenda, the construction and real estate industries contributed massive amounts of money to the LDP and its candidates. Beginning in the late 1970s, the combined generosity of the two industries ranked first or second on the list of the LDP's most beneficent industrial donors (Hirose 1981; Ishikawa and Hirose 1989; Hrebenar 1986). A decade later, political contributions from the real estate industry increased while, perhaps not coincidentally, land prices soared (Nihon keizai shinbunsha 1990, 156). Precise contributions are impossible to calculate, because Japan's election finance laws do not require the reporting of donations of less than ¥1.5 million, but donations from the real estate and construction industries amounted to nearly 15 percent of the reported contributions to the ruling party in 1990 (*Asahi shinbun*, 6 Sept. 1991).

Political Corruption.   A second by-product of systematized clientelism is political corruption, which includes situations involving gain on the part of a public official, receipt of a benefit by a private citizen, or an improper nexus between the gain and the benefit (Thompson 1993, 369). Instances from the U.S. experience include the legendary "honest graft" of Tammany Hall's political bosses. Or as Fiorello La Guardia quipped, "Every time the city builds a school, a politician goes into the real estate business" (cited in Caro 1974, 328).

The formal authority exercised by public officials over the distribution of policy benefits grants a sometimes irresistible temptation to engage in corrupt behavior. So regularly does actual behavior deviate from the prescribed pathway in the Japanese context, that "formal institutions . . . often serve as a facade, giving legal sanction to what has already been decided by informal and covert techniques" (Ike 1972, 74). As Terry MacDougall (1988, 193) observes, "The politico-economic system of Japan is inherently corrupt. The combination of capitalists, power brokers, and government leaders known as 'Japan, Inc.' which produced an eye-popping rate of economic growth and catapulted a defeated island nation into the front rank of economic superpowers, cannot by its nature be anything but corrupt."

Italy's *Mani Pulite* ("clean hands") operation offers a most powerful lesson of the extent to which political corruption can pervade a governmental apparatus. The ongoing nationwide investigation, begun in 1992, has exposed a corrupt pyramid of infinite proportions, in which contractors paid billions of dollars a year to politicians in exchange for lucrative public works contracts. In the impoverished South, inflated contracts for public works were funneled to firms controlled by the Mafia, which reciprocated by delivering votes to those politicians who helped to sidetrack investigations into the activities of organized crime. Although the exposure of systematized political corruption was likened to "the invention of the umbrella"—because all Italians knew about the payoffs—the magnitude of the bribery was greater than anyone had assumed. Indeed, virtually every public contract was accompanied by bribes and kickbacks; even the contract for the maintenance of voting booths in Turin was awarded only in exchange for a bribe (*New York Times*, 8 June 1993). In order to secure a public works contract, contractors had to bribe strategically placed politicians to the tune of from 2 to 10 percent of the total value of the contract.

Conservative estimates fixed the grand total of such payoffs at over 80 billion lire (about half of Italy's enormous government budget deficit) during the course of the ten years preceding the exposure of the scandal. During the first year of the investigation, nearly 3,000 individuals were arrested or notified that they were under investigation, including senior executives of the country's largest private corporations and over 150 members of Parliament, among them four ex-premiers and a host of former cabinet members.

Japan's elected politicians are no strangers to political corruption. To cite but one example, an investigation into the Sagawa Kyūbin parcel delivery company in 1992 uncovered over $50 million in cash, untraceable discount debentures, and gold bullion stashed away in the office of LDP Vice-President Kanemaru Shin. Investigators discovered that most of the booty went to the LDP kingmaker by way of "gifts" and illegal political contributions from construction companies and the *yakuza,* the organized underworld (*New York Times,* 14 Mar. 1993; *Asahi shinbun,* 28 Mar. 1993; *Japan Times,* 31 Mar. 1993).

But the most notorious example of systematized political corruption involving Japanese elected officials was the *zenekon* scandal (the general contractors scandal), which erupted in the summer of 1993. Armed with evidence of Kanemaru's dubious dealings, investigators from the Public Prosecutors Office unearthed a labyrinth of illegal political contributions, bribery, and influence-peddling: Under an institutionalized system of bribery, contractors funneled money to politicians or their intermediaries in exchange for public works contracts. After a series of exposés by the mass media, bribery charges were brought against high-level officials of eight major construction companies, the former president of a land development company, and the head of a wood products firm. The mayors of Sendai City and Sanwa Town, the governors of Ibaraki and Miyagi prefectures, and a member of the Diet were arrested on charges of illegally using the powers of public office.

The corruption also pervaded zoning decisions and land-acquisition policies for public works projects. A noteworthy case is the Recruit scandal, which ultimately toppled the Takeshita cabinet in 1989. The influence-peddling came to light when a newspaper revealed that Komatsu Hideki, the deputy mayor of Kawasaki City, had profited handsomely from the sale of stock in the Recruit Cosmos Company. Komatsu, who was in charge of urban development for the city, had advised the Recruit conglomerate to purchase land for construction of a skyscraper in an area designated as Kawasaki Technopia. He also informed Recruit officers that the land values in that area were likely to soar following the planned deregulation of development there. Acting on this advice, Recruit immediately purchased the land and, in gratitude, the president of Recruit gave Komatsu a "gift" of 30,000 shares of stock, worth more than ¥100 million. (On the origins of the Recruit scandal, see Shiraishi 1990.)

Economic Inefficiency. A third by-product of political clientelism is economic inefficiency. The most egregious example of government-sponsored inefficiency in Japan is the price support system for rice, which forces consumers to pay more than six times the international market price for the staple of their diet. Conspicuous inefficiency also abounds in the health care industry, where the government procurement system permits pharmaceutical companies, distributors, and physicians to reap unjustifiable profits.

In the public works sector, the cost of paying off politicians is factored into the bids, and the result has been that the unit cost of private construction work in Japan far outpaces the cost in any other advanced industrialized country, including Italy (T. Satō 1992). The cost of kickbacks aside, pork-barrel politics leads to overspending for projects whose value is questionable except insofar as they enhance the electoral success of the politicians who vote them into being. As John Ferejohn (1974, 58) notes, "projects do not spring from some Zeus's head complete with a particular configuration of benefits. . . . In large part the benefit-cost ratio is determined by the essentially political nature of project choice." The mission-oriented mentality of the bureaucrats, the profit motive of the special interests, and the politicians' compulsion to build things in order to get reelected—these are the building blocks of what U.S. lobbyist George Pring has dubbed the "edifice complex" (Ashworth 1981, 124).

Among the losers are not only the Japanese taxpayers but the smaller construction companies, a point noted by an observer in the early 1980s:

A certain segment of contractors, politicians, and [government] officials glean an unjust profit. The self-defense of the construction industry and the Construction Ministry concerning the "theory of *dangō* [bid-rigging] as a necessary evil" is fallacious. If the bankruptcy of medium and small enterprises is to be avoided, an approach should be adopted that does not waste the taxpayers' money. In particular, the situation of divvying-up tax moneys by the parliamentary, bureaucratic, and business worlds definitely ought to be rectified.

("Kanagawa ken" 1982, 49)

Clientelism and Single-Party Dominance

There are obvious incentives for clientelistic meddling in policy benefits. In Japan these incentives are great because of the large share of the government's budget devoted to subsidies and public works. In the early 1980s, for example, England and France allocated about 4 to 6 percent of their respective budgets to various subsidies, the U.S. government spent 8 to 10 percent of the budget on such expenditures, and the former West Germany devoted 18 to 20 percent. In Japan, however, subsidies consumed nearly one-third of government outlays (Hirose 1981, 76). Government spending for public works projects was also disproportionately generous in Japan. In the early 1980s, the percentage of GNP that Japan devoted to public works spending was twice that of France and quadruple that of the United States (Calder 1988, 240). Although the Japanese government's total expenditures are relatively low (owing to smaller outlays for defense, education, and health), its fixed capital formation—concentrated in public works— far outpaces other advanced countries. In addition, public works expenditures account for nearly half of all loans administered under the Fiscal Investment and Loan Plan—Japan's so-called second budget (Sakakibara 1991, 59–61). And catastrophes like the 1995 Kōbe earthquake demand massive outpourings of government infrastructure investment. Indeed, the prinicipal means by which the Japanese government has promoted the emerging sectors has been by financing infrastructure to support the politically powerful construction and real estate industries (Calder 1993, 246).

Japanese legislative candidates instantly understood the electoral advantages of "bringing home the bacon." The Liberal Democratic Party (LDP), which had the good fortune to be the first party to gain a parliamentary majority in the postwar era, strategically utilized the distribution of public policy benefits to substantially remake the country "in its own image and likeness, in ways designed to benefit its supporters and weaken its opponents" (Pempel 1990b, 334). During its four decades of dominance in the legislature, the LDP "used the government resources that come with that majority to help its members win reelection. Once the LDP gained control of these government resources, other parties were severely disadvantaged under Japan's electoral rules" (Ramseyer and Rosenbluth 1993, 17). Preferential allocation of regulatory favors, subsidies, zoning decisions, incentives for industrial relocation, special tax concessions, and policies to protect small retailers—all these distributive policy benefits promoted the LDP's staying power.

Naturally public works figured prominently in the LDP's grand scheme, and the LDP's strength was founded upon "the skillful linking of public subsidies to the expansion of party power" (Hirose 1981, 15). While opposition party candidates offered competing ideological visions, LDP candidates provided constituents with tangible distributive benefits. An aide to a veteran LDP politician boasted that "when people want a bridge or a road built in their district, they come to us, not the socialists" (*San Francisco Chronicle,* 20 Dec. 1988). In this way, the LDP effectively utilized distributive policy benefits, rather than ideological appeals, to enlist the support of the growing "floating vote" of Japan's "new middle mass" (Rosenbluth 1993, 153; Murakami 1984, 202–29). The government deliberately increased spending on public works immediately before general elections (Kohno and Nishizawa 1990, 163) and, when confronted with the specter of electoral "crisis," the LDP "compensated" key claimants with strategically targeted policy measures (Calder 1988).

Japan's miraculous economic growth despite institutionalized political clientelism, and nearly four decades of uninterrupted single-party hegemony, upends the much-honored hypothesis that clientelism and its by-products inhibit economic development. Although various studies of developing countries and underdeveloped regions have offered evidence to verify this supposedly iron-clad law (e.g., Myrdal 1968), Japan appears to be a triumphant anomaly. Throughout this volume I will be taking a close look at the form and functions of Japan's clientelist state with the final goal of explaining the implications and potential exportability of Japan's dual political economy model.

Political Actors and Institutions

Though pursuing goals similar to their counterparts in other polities, political actors in Japan exhibit distinctly different patterns of behavior. For example: Competitors for public works projects willingly accept suboptimal profits by becoming co-conspirators in bid-rigging rings; the more efficient construction firms consistently forego potential profits and collude with less efficient rivals; some government officials perceive others, even colleagues posted to other sections of the same ministry, as principal adversaries; and LDP legislators construct expansive networks of personal support organizations that have no meaningful connection to the central party apparatus. These behaviors are not unique to Japan, but, compared to conditions in other advanced democracies, the uniformity and pervasiveness of price-fixing cartels in public works, the intensity and ubiquity of internecine battles pitting government bureaucrats against one another, are remarkable.

Moreover, Japan is unusual in that the LDP—the once seemingly perpetual ruling party—never possessed a well-structured base of grassroots support under the control of the party's organization. Instead, LDP candidates had to rely on personal campaign machines and extra-party organs for the electoral resources to pursue parliamentary careers. While intraparty factionalism is common enough in advanced democracies, nowhere was it as highly structured and prominent as in the LDP. Finally, LDP legislators and their constituents have voracious appetites for pork, but the allocation of the bacon is unusual in that the legislators do not channel the bulk of distributive benefits directly to their home districts.

To understand these and other characteristics of Japan's political actors, we must look to various institutions that shape and constrain interactions, and, as such, define the rules of the game in a policy domain (North 1990, 3). In most domains, one can identify a critical institution that most directly and powerfully affects the purposive political behavior of legislators, bureaucrats, and special interests. The critical institution for legislators is the electoral system, especially the method of voting and the number of representatives per district. For government officials, it is the civil service employment system, particularly those aspects dealing with recruitment, promotion, and retirement. When it comes to special interests, the critical institution depends on the particular type of policy at issue. For instance, the government procurement system shapes the patterns of interactions among equipment suppliers for government offices as well the interaction between those suppliers and the contracting agency. The critical institution for farmers tends to be government support policies, while specific tax and regulatory policies exert the most effect on the incentives of self-employed businesspeople. In general terms, the incentive structure of special interests in the politics of structural policymaking emanates from the key contact point between the state and civil society.

From 1955 to 1993 the patterns of behavior characteristic of Japanese public works' politics were largely the result of the interactive effects of three critical institutions: a government procurement system in which only a small pool of designated bidders received tenders, a civil service system that required government officials to retire at a young age and seek reemployment in the private sector, and an electoral system founded upon a single, nontransferable vote in "middle-sized" constituencies. The synergism created by these three institutions was colored by a fourth institution: the political party system, which was the quintessential case of a "one-party dominant regime" (Pempel 1990a). While other institutions played supporting roles, these critical institutions shaped the behavior of legislators, bureaucrats, and construction contractors into characteristic patterns. Decidedly secondary in influence was the impact of international forces on domestic politics, especially the ways in which the Japanese elite reacted to the pressure to reform these critical institutions.

This analysis rests in part on a simple assumption about human motivation: the foremost objective of most political actors is often the quest for a secure livelihood. For career politicians, this means reelection; for government officials, career and postretirement security. While the quest for personal security does not alone drive the actions of political actors—indeed, altruism, the desire to enhance one's reputation, and the simple lust for power also prevail—its role cannot be underestimated in explaining the behavior of protagonists in the policymaking process.

This quest for security of livelihood leads political actors to create formal and informal ties linking the parliamentary, bureaucratic, and industrial spheres into self-interest networks, variously termed "iron triangles," "webs of relationships," "whirlpools of activity," "subgovernments," "distributional coalitions," and "circles of compensation." For their part, legislators enact policies that favor particularistic interests in civil society, especially those groups and individuals that supply blocs of votes and political contributions. Government officials readily respond to requests that hold the prospect of lucrative postretirement positions. While vested-interest networks exist in all advanced democracies, they tend to be more institutionalized in countries such as Japan, in which a stable, well-defined political elite dominates. As underscored by the Japanese response to U.S. pressure in the construction rift, any threat to the stability and survival of clientelist networks inevitably meets determined resistance.

Rival Approaches

To date, the debate among learned observers has focused on the question of whether Japanese bureaucrats or elected politicians dominate the policymaking process. The most unequivocal statement of the bureaucratic-dominance thesis holds that "the elite bureaucracy in Japan makes most major decisions, drafts virtually all legislation, controls the national budget, and is the source of all major policy innovations in the system" (Johnson 1982, 20). The opposing contingent, however, asserts that "real bureaucrats . . . administer in the shadow of the LDP" (Ramseyer and Rosenbluth 1993, 120). Yet other observers adopt a middle ground in arguing that policymaking is dominated by a coalition of politicians and bureaucrats.[8]

By conceptualizing Japan as having a dual political economy, however, one is better able to attend to how the policymaking roles of legislators, bureaucrats, and special interests vary according to the type of policy at issue. Bureaucrats and private-sector elites wield dominant sway over affairs in the strategic policy market—in which only a handful of politicians have either the incentive or the expertise to play more than a cameo role—while politicians play a leading, and in some cases, *primus inter pares*, role in the subgovernments that dominate the politics of structural policymaking. In addition, greater numbers of legislators tend to be attracted to those policy sectors employing large numbers of workers over a broad geographical area. Furthermore, roles change over time. From the end of World War II through the mid-1970s, Japanese government bureaucrats played a major role in a broad range of policy arenas. But since then their powers and prerogatives have steadily declined, while those of elected politicians and private-sector elites have increased.

A second advantage of viewing Japan as a dual political economy is that this approach illuminates the political and economic functions of the "industrial dualism" prevalent in developed and developing countries alike.[9] The theory of the dual economy asserts that every economy "must be analyzed in terms of two relatively independent sectors: a modern, progressive sector characterized by a high rate of productive efficiency and economic integration, and a traditional sector characterized by a backward mode of production and local self-sufficiency" (Gilpin 1987, 66). While industrial dualism clearly prevails in Japan, there is also a dual structure of political relations among the leading actors in the two separate but interactive policy regimes. And, contrary to the theory of industrial dualism, which posits that market forces and internationalization will eventually lead to the incorporation of the traditional sector into the modern sector, my framework emphasizes the clientelization of erstwhile sunrise sectors as they gerontrify and as the incentives for political intervention and the demands for government protection increase. In Japan, market forces and international factors began to dismantle clientelist structures in policy domains like agriculture, small business, and construction, even as clientelism emerged in depressed manufacturing industries such as coal mining, shipbuilding, and steel.

My approach also provides a balanced explanation for the puzzling fact that in Japan economic growth has coexisted with political clientelism. In order to understand how the LDP delivered both public goods as well as private goods during its protracted legislative hegemony, one must look beyond the role of the ruling party to the often-times independent role of the government bureaucracy in the formation and implementation of industrial policy.[10] The interactions between the majority party and high-level bureaucrats are quite complex and intricate, in part due to the bureaucracy's historically elite status and relatively wide-ranging role in the policymaking process. Overall, the Japanese bureaucracy bears a greater likeness to the French *grand corps* than to the U.S. federal bureaucracy or the patronage-ridden civil service in Italy.

Other theories that purport to explain the unique character of Japanese political behavior fall into one of three categories: "culturalist theories," the "policy-determines-politics" approach, and "institutionalist theories." The respective strengths and shortcomings of each class warrant brief attention here.

Proponents of culturalist theory ascribe the behavioral patterns of Japanese political actors to various aspects of Japanese culture and tradition, such as the penchant for "groupism" and harmonious human relations. Culturalists have argued that the *dangō* system of bid-rigging, ministerial loyalty, the personal support organizations of legislative candidates, and LDP factionalism are all products of Japan's political culture. Although social structure and tradition surely influence behavior to some degree, the amorphous term "culture" suggests that some sort of omnipresent apparition mysteriously guides the behavior of Japanese political actors. Culturalist explanations also suffer from farsightedness in that they often involve an obsessive search for a distant historical precedent when, in fact, practices and organizational forms are actually rather new and are changing. Finally, the tautological tendencies of culturalist explanations inhibit cross-cultural comparative analysis, even though rigorous cross-cultural analysis is the only way to deduce which aspects of behavior are culturally derived.

Most forcefully articulated in Theodore Lowi's seminal work, the "policy-determines-politics" approach rises from a typology of public policies: constituent policies, redistributive policies, regulative policies, and distributive policies.[11] The beauty of this approach lies in its intuitive sensibility and elegant simplicity: the nature of politics in the policymaking process depends upon the type of policy. In distributive policy, for instance, logrolling is the characteristic mode of interaction, while the principal decisional locus is supposed to be the legislative committee. While this approach offers important clues into the politics of the policymaking process, it suffers in the translation, since the politics of policymaking around the world are enacted in unanticipated ways (Sartori 1970, 1984). For instance, although Congressional committees are the principal locus of distributive policymaking in the United States, the LDP's Policy Affairs Research Council was the legislative center of distributive policymaking in Japan during the LDP's heyday. Thus analysts must attend to the interactive effect of different configurations of political institutions, such as the political party system and electoral structures, on the politics of the policymaking process.

Institutionalist theories come in various forms, and my argument aims to contribute to this school of thought. Here, however, it is crucial not to oversimplify by focusing solely on the nature of any single political institution.

One institutionalist theory that has gained some currency is the "legislative delegation approach."[12] Working from the premise that "Japanese political actors rationally maximize subject to institutional constraints," Ramseyer and Rosenbluth (1993) construct a tight argument that turns on "implicit agency contracts" between voters and legislators, LDP backbenchers and party leaders, LDP leaders and bureaucrats, and LDP leaders and judges. The strengths of this approach lie in its conceptual elegance and its links to a broad comparative literature. Nevertheless, it seems to ignore a central question: Aside from the path-dependent and historical reasons for the important role played by the bureaucracy in policymaking, why do influential Japanese politicians waste so much time and money currying the favor of these bureaucrats, rather than simply command them and fire them if they do not comply? And if bureaucrats really are mere lapdogs, why do key LDP corporate backers provide costly sinecures for retired government officials? Clearly, the system of incentives and rewards must be more complex than the legislative delegation approach allows.

Instead of attempting to demonstrate that policymaking in Japan is dominated *either* by autonomous state bureaucrats *or* by elected politicians, my dual political economy approach draws attention to the fact that the roles of legislators, bureaucrats, and private-sector elites differ according to the type of policy at issue. Within a given policy domain, critical institutions forge the elite's self-interested behavior into characteristic and predictable patterns. Thus elite behavior can best be understood as a product of institutions and their interactive effects, rather than as a cultural artifact.

Summary

By focusing on patterns of elite interaction in the politics of public works, the core chapters of this book constitute a case study of a crucial policy domain within Japan's clientelist state. Throughout, I seek to answer three broad questions. First, Why did the workings of Japan's domestic construction market become the subject of such a heated, protracted, high-stakes dispute between Japan and the United States? The goal here is not only to understand why the United States was so insistent and Japan so adamant but also to examine the domestic ramifications of the shifting power structure in the world political economy.

Second is the question of how Japan sustained rapid economic growth despite systematized political clientelism. Here, the contrast with Italy—the other advanced industrialized democracy most rife with clientelism—is instructive in assessing the potential exportability of the Japanese model. What can emerging democracies in Eastern Europe or the newly industrializing economies of East Asia learn from the Japanese and Italian experiences?

Finally, what does the recent burst of reform in Japan tell us about the conditions prerequisite to political reform and the consequences of such reform for entrenched patterns of political behavior? Again, parallels with the Italian case—with particular reference to the *Mani Pulite* investigations and the collapse of legislative hegemony under the Christian Democratic Party—provide insights into the conditions and consequences of political reform in an advanced industrialized democracy.

One

Construction Contractors and the Calculus of Collusion

In January 1986, the local press in Osaka carried an inconspicuous article detailing the plans of the Kansai International Airport Corporation (KIAC) to invite bids on contracts for the construction of a levee. The article came to the attention of Keith Bovetti, a commercial counselor in the U.S. Consulate in Osaka. For over a year, Bovetti had been working to generate interest among American firms in Japan's increasingly lucrative service sector, which included public works and third-sector construction projects. Along the way, KIAC informed Bovetti that foreign companies could not bid on the project outright; they could only join Japanese firms as subordinate partners. This news did not rest well with him, for he feared that failure to break through at Kansai might inhibit future efforts of U.S. firms. To alert American firms of the bidding, Bovetti sent a translation of the newspaper article to the Commerce and International Trade Agency in Washington. Later, he dispatched a translation of the bidding requirements and procedures. Eventually, some forty-three American companies registered with the KIAC.[1]

Rather than providing a cheerful end to a short drama, this incident generated a protracted trade dispute. The conflict centered around the U.S. demands for "fairness" and "reciprocity," and Japan's refusal to reform its government procurement system. Vitriolic rhetoric and promises of retaliation issued forth from both shores. U.S. Assistant Commerce Secretary H. B. Goldfield, in testimony before a Senate subcommittee said, "It's very clear that the Japanese want to protect their own industry. At the same time, they want to participate in our open market. Mr. Chairman, that just isn't fair" (quoted in Auerbach 1986). Meanwhile, the USTR threatened to invoke Section 301 of the 1974 Trade Act.° Adding vigor to these threats, Alaska's Senator Frank Murkowski and Texas Congressman Jack Brooks sponsored a bill banning Japanese firms from participating in federally funded public works in the United States. The bill passed by near unanimous margins in both houses.

Undaunted, a procession of Japanese spokesmen staved off the foreign adversary. Officials from the Ministry of Construction and the Ministry of Transport staunchly defended the government procurement system. Politicians uttered similar refrains. Transport Minister Hashimoto Ryūtarō (1988) argued that foreign firms interested in bidding on public works must first accumulate a "number of years" of experience in Japan's private construction market. Pressure group officials and business leaders also took the fore. Ishikawa Rokurō, then president of Kajima Corporation and head of the Japan Chamber of Commerce and Industry, maintained that

Since public works are financed by taxpayers, it is important to ensure that they are carried out efficiently and that the work is up to standard. Thus [in Japan] bids are only accepted from designated contractors—contractors who have proven their ability to do the job right. Within this group, the lowest bid is chosen and a contract is signed. This is the designated competitive tender system—a system adopted in many countries throughout the world. If a foreign company wants a contract for a Japanese public works project, it should follow the Japanese rules.

("Conductor of Commerce" 1988)

° Section 301 of the Trade Act of 1974 requires the USTR to investigate complaints by private parties concerning barriers to fair trade in individual product markets. However, retaliation is not required in the event that a barrier is identified. Super 301 of the Omnibus Trade and Competitiveness Act of 1988 was designed to add teeth to Section 301 by providing retaliatory remedies in the case of unsatisfactory progress in removing unfair trading practices. Under Super 301, once the USTR cites a country as an unfair trading partner and names specific barriers, the removal of those barriers must be negotiated within eighteen months. If the negotiations do not prove satisfactory, the U.S. government can impose sanctions on imports from the offending country.

Why did the Japanese government allow this matter to exacerbate relations with its most important trading partner? Despite the pronouncements of the apologists for Japanese policy, the rationale for the formal procurement system was to protect not Japanese taxpayers, but an institutionalized system of bid-rigging known as *dangō* ("agreement by consultation").

Although explicitly proscribed by the Accounting, Anti-Monopoly, Criminal, and Construction Industry laws, most public works contracts in Japan come about through shadowy *dangō* arrangements. Evidence of bid-rigging has been reported in virtually every locality and most public corporations. A headline in a major Japanese daily proclaimed: "Majority of Large-Scale National Projects Decided Through 'Dangō'—¥1.8 Trillion Divvied-Up by 'Friendship Club' of 170 Major Contractors" (*Yomiuri shinbun,* 3 Dec. 1981). Likewise, a construction company official casually noted that most contracts for public works during the course of the past several decades had been decided beforehand through *dangō,* a practice that he views as "routine work" in the construction industry ("Ōte kensetsu" 1982). As a newspaper reporter observes, "The Japanese archipelago lies in the midst of a sea of *dangō* (*Asahi shinbun,* 29 Aug. 1993).

Though the term *dangō* benignly denotes "consultation" or "conference," its actual meaning is reflected in its many aliases, which include "adjustment," "resolution through discussion," "tendering pact," "shady cartel," and "discussion for adjusting the exchange of information and communications." "Above and beyond the act of collusion among those submitting bids for a project, the term 'dangō' denotes prior mutual consent in determining the successful bid" (Nawa 1987, 34). Less formally, *dangō* is an "independent arrangement" among contractors to decide the successful bidder, or the contractors' practice of "neatly dividing up and parceling out their construction market by a 'gentlemen's agreement.'"[2]

Ironically, an instance of bid-rigging emerged in a project connected with the construction of the aforementioned levee at the Kansai Airport. Following the exposure of the collusive accord in a Lower House Budget Committee meeting in September 1989, the Japan Fair Trade Commission issued a cease-and-desist order against six construction companies that composed the Marine Land Reclamation

Construction Association, an illegal cartel that conspired to set the price of soil needed for reclamation. This collusive action allegedly produced a skimmed profit in the neighborhood of ¥5 billion, a portion of which supposedly went to influential politicians.[3]

Achieving and sustaining a collusive system, it is important to note, is enormously difficult. Indeed, the literature on cartel theory overflows with lists of "conditions," "factors," and "obstacles" that block the path to successful collusive action.[4] For instance, John McMillan (1991, 204) uses the *dangō* system to illustrate the three "difficulties" that must be overcome for successful price-fixing to occur: creating a mechanism for dividing the spoils, self-enforcing the agreement, and eliminating competition from new entrants.

Building upon this literature, I propose that successful and sustained collusive action demands the fulfillment of five necessary and sufficient conditions. First, it is essential to delineate the membership of the conspiratorial arrangement. Second, barriers must be erected to prevent opportunistic outsiders from undercutting the agreed-upon price. Third, since conspiratorial agreements are not legally enforceable, compliance must be secured through informal means. Fourth, there must be a mechanism for apportioning the benefits and costs of collusive action. And, fifth, a successful collusive system must have the means of evading or coopting the government's antitrust watchdogs in order to survive for an extended term. Moreover, in an increasingly interdependent international economy, the patterns of collusive behavior must evade trade monitors in other countries.

The fulfillment of these conditions poses such obstacles to successful and sustained collusion that the vast majority of documented attempts have been short-lived. As we will see, these five conditions were satisfied under the *dangō* system. And, as one would expect, the equilibrium of collusive action was destabilized by the increased public scrutiny generated by the *zenekon* scandal and the imposition of U.S. pressure for institutional reform. By exerting pressure, the United States underscored the drastically divergent interests and capabilities of Japan's technologically advanced large-scale general contractors as compared to its petty contractors.

But before examining how the collusive *dangō* system operates, we need to understand something of the nature and history of Japan's construction industry.

Profile of a Two-Tier Industry

The Japanese construction market is the largest in the world. In 1992 Japan's construction investment as a percentage of gross national product (18.2 percent) was the highest among advanced industrialized countries, exceeding England (12.4 percent), Germany (11.7 percent), France (10.8 percent), and the United States (8.5 percent) by a wide margin. On a per capita basis, construction spending in Japan ($3,480) was double that in the United States ($1,630) and in the European Community ($1,690). From 1984 to 1989, the Japanese construction market expanded by 27 percent—ranking second only to late-developing Spain among Western nations—and between 1987 and 1993, the Japanese market expanded by nearly 50 percent. Construction investment in 1993 was estimated to be just under ¥90 trillion, compared to ¥2.5 trillion in 1960. Throughout this period, government spending on construction played a significant role, accounting for over one-third of total construction investment, on average.[5]

Other measures of growth include the number of construction firms and construction workers. In 1955, for example, there were fewer than 62,000 registered construction contractors; by March 1992, there were 522,450 licensed contractors registered with the Ministry of Construction. And whereas the construction industry employed 4.7 percent of the country's workforce in 1955, by 1980 construction workers outnumbered individuals employed in farming and forestry. In 1992 Japan's 6.2 million construction workers represented 9.6 percent of the workforce—a rich source of campaign support for ambitious legislative candidates, as we shall see.

During the 1980s stagnant domestic demand impelled many Japanese construction firms to look overseas for new markets. (The "ice age" in domestic construction, a product of the worldwide oil shock of the late 1970s, lasted until 1986 and slowed the average annual increase in public and private investment in construction from 21 percent a year, between 1970 and 1978, to 0.01 percent a year, between 1978 and 1986.) As a presence in overseas markets, Japanese firms rose from a seventh-place ranking in 1981—behind American, South Korean, French, West German, Italian, and British contractors—to second place in 1989. Though U.S. firms retained first place in the international rankings, their margin of preeminence declined precipitously, from $478 billion in 1981 to $181 billion in 1989. And Japanese construction companies made great inroads in the North American market, winning 40 percent of the overseas orders in North America in 1987. Much of this work serviced the construction needs of long-time Japanese clients who invested in North America during the frenzy of foreign direct investment that followed the appreciation of the yen after the 1985 Plaza Accord. Japanese contractors also made impressive gains in the construction markets of Southeast Asian countries by providing design and consultancy services for large-scale projects, many of which were funded by generous Japanese foreign aid (Chittiwatanapong 1992).

Apart from its size and rate of expansion, the most striking facet of Japan's construction industry is its two-tier structure. At the top are a small number of large general construction contractors, the major *zenekon*; at the bottom are more than 500,000 small firms.[6] The largest *zenekon* possess the technological capability to design and construct innovative skyscrapers, factories equipped with "clean rooms" for the assembly of sensitive high-technology products, fast-breeder nuclear reactors, and even projects for outer space, and they are among the world's leaders in the building of tunnels and underground facilities, the use of robots in construction, and the use of prefabricated modular devices transported directly to the construction site. In 1991 four of the five largest construction companies in the world were Japanese (Levy 1993, 24). In contrast, the multitude of small-scale firms, many of which are inadequately capitalized, possess technical capacities only slightly superior to those of medieval builders (Watanabe 1982, 272). Be it in urban Yokohama or rural Shikoku, many workers at construction sites still don the traditional garb—billowing knee-length trousers and boots split into two parts between the big toe and the other toes—and shinny up flimsy wooden poles, rather than modern ladders.

The elite of Japan's general contractors are the Big Six: Shimizu Corporation, Taisei Corporation, Kajima Corporation, Takenaka Corporation, Ōbayashi Corporation, and Kumagai Gumi (see Table 1). Together, the aggregate net sales volume of these six firms exceeded ¥10.3 trillion in 1993. Collectively, they employed more than 73,000

TABLE 1. *Major* Zenekon

	Original Name (Year Founded)	1993 Sales (¥ millions)	1993 Work-force
Big Six			
Shimizu Corporation	Shimizu Kata (1804)	2,168,285	11,951
Taisei Corporation	Okura Gumi Shokai (1873)	1,980,309	13,926
Kajima Corporation	Kajima Kata (1839)	1,954,704	14,679
Takenaka Corporation	Takenaka Fujinoe (1610)	1,598,105	10,900
Ōbayashi Corporation	Ōbayashi Yoshigoro (1892)	1,519,982	12,574
Kumagai Gumi	Kumagai Tasaburō (1902)	1,078,615	9,392
Others			
Fujita Corporation	Fujita Ichirō (1910)	849,783	5,954
Toda Corporation	Toda Toshinoe (1881)	753,459	6,176
Hazama Corporation	Hazama Gumi (1889)	663,272	5,407
Tōkyū Construction	Tōkyū Kensetsu Kōgyō (1959)	618,814	4,848
Satō Kōgyō	Satō Gumi (1862)	615,541	5,793
Nishimatsu Construction	Nishimatsu Keisuke (1874)	602,575	5,347
Mitsui Construction	Mitsui Kensetsu Kōgyō (1941)	582,461	5,056
Inoue Kōgyō	Inoue Yasusaburō (1888)	575,330	605
Penta-Ocean Construction	Mizuno Gumi (1896)	521,922	5,238
Kōnoike Construction	Kōnoike Gumi (1871)	493,573	4,486
Tobishima Corporation	Tobishima Fumijirō (1883)	460,422	4,317
Aoki Corporation	Burudōzaa Kōji (1947)	347,469	3,455
Okumura Corporation	Okumura Taihei (1907)	344,057	3,799
Zenitaka Corporation	Zenitaka Yoshizō (1887)	306,833	2,755
Asanuma Corporation	Asanuma Gumi (1892)	292,143	2,659
Andō Corporation	Andō Kata (1873)	261,905	2,484
Nakano Corporation	Nakano Gumi (1892)	108,788	948
Magara Construction	Magara Yōsuke (1910)	106,871	1,088
Odakyū Construction	Nomura Gumi (1869)	104,110	1,213
Matsui Construction	Matsui Kakuzaemon (1586)	93,088	889

SOURCES: *Japan Company Handbook* (1994); *Yakuin shikihō* (1993); *Nikkenren nijūnenshi* (1987); and Nakamura (1982, p. 77).

full-time workers. In 1993 Shimizu, which reported sales of ¥2.17 trillion, held the top spot for sales, while Kajima employed the largest number of workers (nearly 15,000). Each of the Big Six administer extensive overseas branch offices and subsidiaries, and several own or hold substantial interests in domestic affiliates specializing in road paving, residential land development, and other construction services.[7]

Beneath the elite six are the "quasi-large-scale" general construction contractors. In 1993 Fujita Corporation, Toda Corporation, Hazama Corporation, Tōkyū Construction, and Mitsui Construction had the largest sales volume in this second tier. Nishimatsu Construction, Satō Kōgyō, and Tobishima Corporation were among the leaders in large-scale civil engineering works. A group of a dozen or so firms, including Penta-Ocean Corporation, Kōnoike Construction, and Aoki Corporation round out this second tier of large *zenekon*. Although smaller in terms of revenues and workforce than the Big Six, these second-tier *zenekon* possess the technologival sophistication to construct super-high-rise buildings, clean rooms, offshore energy developments, computerized buildings, and urban redevelopment projects. All of these firms are active internationally, and some of them—notably Nishimatsu, Penta-Ocean, and, especially, Aoki—realize a major share of their sales in overseas markets. In the case of Aoki, overseas markets accounted for nearly one-third of the firm's sales during 1993.

Beyond this small circle of major *zenekon* are more than half a million small firms, and the gulf between the two groups is wide indeed. In 1991, for example, construction firms capitalized in excess of ¥100 million (0.09 percent of registered firms) took in over half of all revenues from completed projects, while firms capitalized between ¥50 million and ¥100 million (1.16 percent of registered firms) reaped about 8 percent of the revenues from completed projects. In contrast, roughly 80 percent of the registered construction firms were capitalized at under ¥10 million, and nearly 40 percent of all construction firms were individually owned and operated. These petty contractors operate in a Hobbesian world, lacking modern machinery, stable management systems, or cozy ties with major banks. In 1982, for example, nearly three-fourths of bankruptcies reported among construction firms involved contractors capitalized at ¥10 million or less

(Nakamura 1982, 104). In order to survive, many of these contractors depend on the prepayment system for privately as well as publicly funded projects, whereby contractors routinely receive 20 to 40 percent in advance.

Subcontracting is more prevalent and more multi-layered in Japan's construction industry than it is, for example, in the United States. On any project, "a carpenter subcontractor may subcontract rough framing to a second-tier subcontractor, who, in turn, might subcontract roof joists to a third-tier subcontractor who, in turn, may hire a fourth-tier subcontractor to distribute the joist" (Levy 1993, 14). These subcontractors tend to have lower skills and offer relatively lower wages and fewer employee benefits. Frequently, firms at the very bottom tier of these subcontracting networks employ a substantial number of unskilled illegal aliens, many of them from other Asian countries ("Demand Grows" 1988). Although some formerly small-scale firms, such as Chisaki Kōgyō of Hokkaidō and Fukuda Corporation of Niigata, managed to expand and to establish substantial regional or nationwide operations, most tend to remain small, local concerns.

Historical Development of the Industry

To understand Japan's construction industry, one must first view it as the product of a historical evolution that reaches back to the seventh century, when Japan's earliest builders constructed the Hōryūji, the world's oldest remaining wooden building. Japan's first construction firm, the forerunner of Matsui Kensetsu, was established in 1586 by Matsui Kakuzaemon, who was commissioned to build a castle for the lord of the Kaga Domain (today's Ishikawa Prefecture). Not until the Edo period (1603–1867), however, when the capital was moved from Kyoto to Edo (the present-day Tokyo) did the building trade expand greatly. By the seventeenth century, Edo had become the world's largest city, perhaps the first to boast a population surpassing one million, and there was a great demand for carpenters to build estates for feudal lords and shops for the growing merchant class.

Subsequently, in the Meiji period (1867-1912), under the slogans "rich country and strong military" and "increase production and promote industry," the government launched an infrastructure program that produced the country's first true construction contractors, and the Japanese construction industry began to shed its guildlike existence (T. Maeda 1988, 81). In the early Meiji period, "many of today's leading contractors came into existence, thanks to the multitude of government orders" for administrative offices, railroads, and riparian works (F. Hasegawa 1988, 5). Also during this period, foreign engineers from Britain, Holland, Germany, and the United States introduced Western construction techniques to Japan. These efforts brought forth the Western-style Tsukiji Hotel, built by Shimizu Kisuke II in 1867, and the British First Mansion and the American First Mansions, constructed by Kajima Iwakichi to house merchants in Yokohama's foreign settlement. (Nakamura 1982, 72).

The Finance Law (*Kaikei Hō*) of 1890 decreed that companies would win contracts for nationally funded public works projects through open competitive tendering. Under this law, during the late Meiji period and into the Taishō period (1912–1926), "even firms without experience or the power of trust were able to secure contracts simply by submitting the lowest bid" (T. Maeda 1988, 84). During this period of open competition, Ōbayashi Gumi, one of today's Big Six, was established. Ironically, the open, "democratic" bidding procedures mandated in the Finance Law were not substantially revised until 1922—the high tide of the period of "Taishō Democracy"— when the construction industry succeeded in pressuring the government to establish a system of designated competitive tendering. According to one observer, this institution was motivated by the fact that

blood letting orders [*shukketsu juchū*], collusion, and conflict among contractors had become an everyday occurence. This [situation] spawned the emergence of professional "fixers" [*dangōya*] who served as intermediaries and go-betweens. Moreover, the custom of paying a certain percentage of the tendering cost to other firms came into existence. For these reasons, the government began assessing the accomplishments of firms and designating trustworthy contractors to bid on projects.

(Nakamura 1982, 107–8)

Japan's construction industry grew with the country's imperialist expansion. Preparations for the Sino-Japanese War of 1894–95 sparked a boom in military-related works as well as railway and electric power projects. In 1900 Kajima Gumi supervised construction of a railway line linking Seoul and Inchon in Korea. Shortly thereafter, three Japanese firms—Ōkura Gumi (the forerunner of Taisei Construction), Ōbayashi Gumi, and Hazama Corporation—combined to build a 440-kilometer-long stretch of the Trans-Formosa Railroad. However, the overseas advance that began in earnest during the late Meiji period was not always a blessing for the Japanese construction industry. In the midst of preparations for war with Russia in 1904, railway lines were constructed connecting Pusan with Seoul and Seoul with Sinuiju. Owing to allegedly inadequate and inaccurate information provided by the client, the firms that participated in this project suffered financial losses and, in some cases, bankruptcy (Hippo and Tamura 1988, 60). Still, the overseas advance continued, and Japanese firms constructed various railway lines, including the Pusan-to-Dalien link of the South Manchurian Railway, as well as hydroelectric projects and mining facilities in the puppet state of Manchukuo. By 1941 Japanese contractors were constructing roads and military works throughout all of occupied China and in various parts of Southeast Asia. At home, the war mobilization led to the disbanding of construction industry associations in favor of the Army's Military Authority Cooperative Association (Gunken Kyōryoku Kai), the Naval Facilities Cooperative Association (Kaigun Shisetsu Kyōryoku Kai), and, in the closing days of the war, an umbrella organization known as the Wartime Construction Team (Senji Kensetsudan).

The aftermath of war provided a setting for corporate reform and rapid growth. As part of the Occupation's trust-busting program, for instance, the Ōkura *zaibatsu* dissolved, and the Ōkura Gumi became the Taisei Construction Company. Other firms, such as Kajima and Shimizu, took the opportunity to modernize their corporate names by dropping *gumi* ("group" or "gang"), a feudalistic-sounding term often associated with organized crime syndicates. During the first decade of the postwar era, the construction industry benefited from the domestic reconstruction boom. The peak in domestic orders came in 1947; three years later, an additional boost was afforded by the admission of Japanese firms to the Okinawa market. There, joint ventures linked major Japanese contractors with Morrison Knudsen, the Bechtel Group, Pomelroy, Kiewit, and other U.S. construction companies. In addition, war reparations, beginning with the building of a hydroelectric station in Burma in 1954, provided a springboard for recapturing overseas markets.

The construction industry built the infrastructure for the Japanese economic miracle. In this regard, the Ikeda cabinet's New Industrial Cities Policy offered incentives that benefited contractors throughout the country. The Tanaka cabinet's program to "remodel" the Japanese archipelago bequeathed a similar, albeit ephemeral, bounty. In the meantime, the construction industry reaped handsome rewards from preparations for the 1964 Tokyo Olympics and the 1970 Osaka World's Fair, as well as from the flood of public investment during the "era of highways" in the 1960s and '70s. Indeed, the industry rode a continuous wave of expansion until the onset of the "ice age" in the wake of the oil shocks in the late '70s. In the mid '80s the government inaugurated a program to expand domestic demand and construction began to boom in the late '80s. But this boom was short-lived, as demand in the private construction market collapsed in the wake of the bursting of the "bubble" economy and the shock waves generated by the *zenekon* corruption scandal at the outset of the '90s.

Dangō as a Collusive System

As mentioned earlier, the first condition necessary to sustain effective collusive action is the delineation of the membership of the conspiratorial ring. Deciding on the optimal size of a price-fixing cartel is a complex problem. The larger the number of actors who stand to benefit from collusive action, the smaller the share of the gains from the action that will accrue to each. Moreover, the larger the group, the higher the transaction costs involved in orchestrating effective bargaining. The illegal nature of the undertaking requires members of the group to bargain until they agree how to share the costs and benefits, and again the difficulties in orchestrating collusive action increase as group size increases. Creating a conspiratorial ring broad enough to satisfy the interests of all potential spoilers is also a fundamental problem. For example, if all but one firm in a competitive arena agrees to a higher price, then the hold out firm stands to reap large profits by selling its product at a lower price. This generally has the effect of undercutting the cartel by driving the fixed price down to a competitive level. (Olson 1982, discusses these problems.)

In the case of Japanese public construction, two institutional devices facilitate the task of delineating a conspiratorial ring. The first is a highly structured system of industry associations at both the national and local levels. Close contact among executives of various firms, commonly facilitated by membership in industry associations, provides opportunities for greater communication, allowing participants to resolve standards of acceptable market conduct.[8]

The second, more direct facilitator of collusive action is the Japanese government procurement system. Government procurement systems come in three generic forms. In an "open competitive tendering" system, all qualified parties submit bids, and the contract goes to the firm making the lowest responsible bid. This procurement system operates in nearly all of the projects administered by the U.S. Army Corps of Engineers, and, since early 1994, in contracting for extremely large-scale public works projects and consultancy services in Japan. Under a second system of government procurement, for projects that demand highly specialized expertise, or during times of emergency, a specific firm might be awarded a "discretionary contract." This system functions in a portion of contracts granted at all levels of government in both the United States and nationally authorized projects in several Western European countries. In Italy, as exposed by the *Mani Pulite* investigators, discretionary contracting was the preferred procurement system for public works projects, especially in the South, where three-quarters of public works contracts were not put out to tender. According to a Milanese business executive, "They would just write their names on pieces of paper and draw them from a hat. First one out would win the first contract, second one the second, and so on" (*New York Times*, 3 March 1993).

In spite of reforms in 1994, the bulk of government procurement in Japan corresponds to a third type, "designated competitive tendering system," or "select competition" as it is known in Great Britain. In the case of projects administered by the central government, firms wishing to bid must reveal sources of funding and operational capacity. Until 1988, when intense U.S. pressure effected a minor modification, a devious catch-22 required that all would-be bidders undergo assessment based on the results of construction work during the previous two years within the Japanese market (Ministry of Construction 1988, 37–47). Of course, foreign firms had no recent record of performance in the Japanese market and were thus barred from bidding. Yet even after complaints from foreign governments suceeded in extracting modest reforms, foreign participants remained excluded from cozy *dangō* arrangements, and they were forced into joint ventures as junior partners or blackballed by vital subcontractors.

Under the Japanese government's procurement system, ten "qualified" firms are generally invited to submit bids for a public works project. The contract is then awarded to the firm submitting the lowest responsible bid judged according to the government's confidential ceiling price. In this way, the procurement system limits potential conspirators on a project to the small pool of designated bidders. Not surprisingly, construction contractors and their political patrons, who staunchly seek to limit the number of firms designated to submit bids, value this institutuional apparatus. When the government doubled the number of firms invited to bid, in response to a media campaign following a 1981 bid-rigging scandal in Shizuoka Prefecture, pressure groups in the construction industry immediately initiated efforts to reverse the policy. Their principal effort was to promise substantial campaign contributions to influential members of the LDP's "construction tribe," one of the groups of "policy specialists" in the party. By the end of the following year, these tribalists—led by legendary political broker Kanemaru Shin—succeeded in restoring the status quo ante (Itasaka 1987, 74–75).

Thus, the Japanese system affirms the general rule that mutual recognition of interdependence among evenly matched firms in a well-defined market breaks down when the number of members exceeds ten or twelve (Posner 1970). As one student of collusive action observes, "a smaller number of firms reduces conspiratorial transaction costs by limiting the number of encounters needed for communications" (Haar 1983, 30–31). For example, a ring that has 10 members will comprise 45 one-on-one relationships, but doubling the ring to 20 more than quadruples the constituent pairs to 190, an extremely challenging and expensive coordination problem. By defining and limiting the pool of potential conspirators, the Japanese government procurement system only simplifies the coming together of collusive contractors.

The second condition for sustaining a successful price-fixing ring rests in the group's ability to exclude outsiders, both to maintain each member's share of the profits and to shut out spoilers who might un-dermine the accord by charging a lower price (see, for example, Kuhl-man 1969, 69–82).

As we have seen, the government procurement system itself re-stricts the circle of "competition" to a small subset of firms who are invited to submit bids for public works projects. In many cases, as the *zenekon* scandal revealed, the meddling of elected politicians influ-ences which firms will receive a designation to bid. Construction firms that fail to cater to the appropriate bureaucratic and political parties risk being shut out of future bidding.

Thus, gift-giving is pervasive. Most competent business managers know the birthdays, hobbies, and other particulars of key government officials, politicians, and their administrative assistants (Jin 1989; Min-ami 1981, 17). Outpourings of generosity occur most frequently at midsummer and year's end, the customary gift-giving seasons in Ja-pan. (A Ministry of Construction bureaucrat told me of his amaze-ment upon witnessing the bountiful harvest of gifts reaped by senior officials in the Road Bureau as compared with the paltry takings of those in bureaus with fewer distributive benefits to dole out.) During the 1970's, a public works scandal in Fukushima Prefecture uncovered a massive pyramid of corruption in which contractors used gifts and campaign contributions to court prefectural government officials, party and interest group leaders, local politicians, and even the pre-fectural governor (Yoshida 1984). At the national level, large-scale general contractors routinely funnel contributions to influential poli-ticians. The Sagawa scandal revealed that as many as twenty of Japan's largest construction contractors donated up to ¥20 million each year over a number of years to LDP Vice-President Kanemaru Shin (*Asahi shinbun*, 10 Apr. 1992). Finally, as in the United States, the mass me-dia frequently features accusations of outright bribery involving con-tractors and public officials—generally local and municipal adminis-trators. Of the one hundred or so bribery scandals each year in Japan, over half involve construction firms (Iinuma 1987).

Political influence, known as the "voice of heaven" (*ten no koe*), often influences the selection of the anticipated low bidder. As a local contractor observed, "when the 'voice of heaven' comes down and the process of *dangō* is completed, for all intents and purposes the win-ning bidder has been decided and designated competitive bidding be comes a mere ceremony" (*Asahi shinbun*, 31 Aug. 1993). In Ibaraki Prefecture, Governor Takeuchi Fujio allegedly intervened an average of six to seven times a month on behalf of some thirty construction firms (ibid., 18 Dec. 1993).

Large transfers of money tend to accompany the articulation of heaven's will. Kanemaru's heavenly voice allegedly fetched a kickback of 5 percent or more of the contracted price of the public works project. More typically, influential politicians—particularly members of the LDP's construction tribe—receive a "back margin" of 1 to 3 percent of the cost of the project (Jin 1989, 86). For example, Mayor Ōyama Masahiro of Sanwa Town in Ibaraki Prefecture allegedly received ¥14 million in "gratitude money" from Hazama Corporation, the company constructing a ¥140-million sports center in his jurisdiction (*Asahi shinbun*, 20–21 July, 10 Aug. 1993).

From a contractor's perspective, funneling kickbacks to politicians is a necessary "insurance fee" to secure designation to bid for especially desired public works projects. As the *zenekon* scandal revealed, large contractors awarded letter grades to legislators based upon their perceived influence. Not surprisingly, construction kingpins like Kanemaru, Takeshita Noboru, and Ozawa Ichirō received the highest marks and, hence, the largest contributions. At the local level, contractors in Ibaraki coined the term "Takeuchi pilgrimage" to refer to the courtesy calls they paid, hefty bundles of cash in hand, to persuade the governor of the virtue of their cause (Sanger 1993a).

The cost of active complicity rendered by government bureaucrats is difficult to tally. Instances of outright bribery, especially among officials of the central state bureaucracy, are seldom proven. Officials at the Ministry of Construction, for example, are commanded to "neither accept cash nor women" (Honda 1974, 198). One bureaucrat, Kyōsaka Motoji, former director of the ministry's Hokuriku Regional Bureau, failed to heed this dictum and was arrested in 1977 on charges of accepting substantial gratuities from contractors in exchange for favoritism in deciding lists of designated bidders (Kanryō kikō kenkyūkai 1978, 74–77). Indirectly, however, the cost of bureaucratic mediation is embodied in sinecures for retired officials—known as "descent from heaven landing spots." Indeed, firms employing ex-bureaucrats not only benefit from their technical competence, but also appear to be privy to strategic information leaks concerning the government's "confidential" ceiling price.

Since sub rosa arrangements cannot be formalized in a legally binding contract, enforcing the terms of the collusive accord is a third hurdle for a collusive ring. The members of the cartel have a mutually profitable course of action—loyal adherence to their agreement—yet each member faces a strong incentive to depart from that course, to cheat. If all cheat, however, the profitable agreement breaks down, and all suffer. Thus effective collusion demands recognition of the destabilizing effect of secret price-cutting and the creation of procedures to force compliance to the agreed-upon accord.[9]

In Japanese public construction, the need to mete out selective incentives creates a role for industry associations and, on occasion, the organized underworld. In all, there are more than one hundred formal industry associations registered with Japan's Construction Ministry. The most prominent are the Japan Federation of Construction Contractors and the Japan Civil Engineering Contractors' Association. But the actual task of meting out selective incentives falls to the myriad of informal "fellowship clubs"—known as "*dangō* organizations"—such as the Tokyo-based Management Harmony Society (Keiei Konwakai), the Tōhoku Construction Industry Conference (Tōhoku Kensetsugyō Kyōgikai), and the Saitama Saturday Society. For the most part, these groups sponsor breakfast meetings with influential politicians and arrange golf outings intended to foster a chummy atmosphere in which to exchange information about public works projects. On occasion, however, such groups also punish wayward members.

A firm that violates the bid-rigging agreement—a transgression known as *dangō yaburi* (meaning "to break the *dangō*")—is ostracized from the industry association and barred from participating in future collusive accords (Minami 1981, 45, 76). As a local construction industry official in Yamanashi observed, "If a different company tried to get a contract by entering a low bid, it would be kicked off the list of designated bidders for future projects" (Blustein 1993a). Naturally, enforcing this sort of negative selective incentive requires the cooperation of the government authorities who determine the pool of designated bidders. Firms engaging in iterated games of bid-rigging "lend" co-conspirators the opportunity to win a contract in exchange for the right to "borrow" the contract for a future project. From the Fukushima scandal emerged a ledger detailing the lending and borrowing activities of th prefecture's electrical contractors' association over an extended period (Yoshida 1984, 168). A schematic of the bid-rigging system of the Saitama Saturday Society, a local industry association, is shown in Figure 1.

Strong disincentives for whistle-blowing also facilitate self-enforcement. The practice of lifetime employment for career employees at large firms makes it irrational for employees to blow the whistle on collusive accords. And the risk of retaliation in a setting defined by a

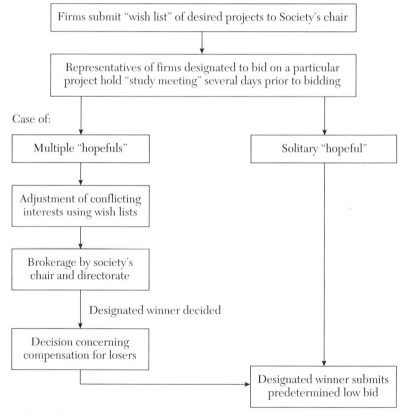

Figure 1. The Saturday Society's Scheme for Bid-Rigging on Public Works
SOURCE: Asahi shinbun, 31 Jan. 1992.

highly regimented system of trade associations discourages whistle-blowing on the activities of competitors. When it does occur, it often takes the form of an anonymous tip from a disgruntled insider. A reporter assigned to the press club at the Ministry of Construction told me that anonymous telephone calls to the newspapers—particularly the *Asahi Shinbun*, a vocal critic of the *dangō* system—increased perceptibly during the "ice age" of curtailed public construction investment, from 1978 to 1986.

Finally, on occasion, collusive rings utilize coercive incentives to secure compliance. For example, an instance of bid-rigging on a municipal road contract in Shizuoka City came to the attention of the authorities after an infuriated co-conspirator hit a local construction company boss over the head with a metal chair. The incident occurred when the victim voiced displeasure with a particular *dangō* arrangement (Schoenberger 1989). Gangsters (*yakuza*) occasionally help enforce selective incentives. In Sakato City in Saitama Prefecture, a contractor desperately desired the contract for an agricultural waterworks project. Several days prior to the date for submitting bids, he telephoned representatives of the other firms designated to bid on the project and attempted to arrange a meeting at a local eatery. Unnerved by the unfolding *zenekon* scandal, most of the other contractors refused the invitation. As a last resort, the contractor hired two thugs, with ties to a well-known gangster organization, to intimidate the contractors who had declined to collude. When word of *yakuza* involvement reached the mass media, the bidding was suspended, and the overzealous contractor and the gangsters were arrested (*Asahi shinbun*, 25 Nov. 1993).

The fourth hurdle for a cartel is devising a mechanism for parceling out the gains (Olson 1982, 20–23). Because of the high transaction costs imposed by the need for consensual bargaining, firms may demand a disproportionate share of the gains from the collusive action in return for their cooperation. Threats to hold out, in turn, will not be credible unless they are sometimes carried out. Reaching agreement on apportioning the costs and benefits may thus take an extraordinary amount of time, and often a broker is needed to orchestrate the accord and create an acceptable formula.

As investigations in the *zenekon* corruption scandal revealed, for a

number of years, officials of certain large-scale general contractors allegedly parceled out public works projects in the various regions
(K. Matsumoto et al. 1993). For example, a senior executive in Ōbayashi Corporation's Osaka office served as broker in rigging bids for the
construction of a levee at Kansai International Airport (Kōsei torihiki
iinkai 1990, 33–36). And a retired Construction Ministry bureaucrat
allegedly performed brokerage in rigging bids for air conditioning and
sanitation contracts in offices built for the Ministry of Justice and the
Public Prosecutor's Office (*Asahi shinbun*, 25 Nov. 1987). On occasion, a particular broker will acquire almost mythical powers. Uera
Sukemasa, one-time president of Tobishima Corporation, was supposedly so powerful and politically well-connected that he determined
the disposition of any public works project he chose (*Asahi shinbun*,
24 Oct. 1993). Similarly, Kimura Hitoshi came to be known as the
"Emperor of the *Dangō* Association" for dam construction. After retiring from a senior post at Taisei Construction, Kimura unabashedly
admitted to drawing up a "list of *dangō* for dams" specifying contracts
for planned projects over the course of a decade (*Asahi shinbun*,
2–19 Feb. 1982).

Brokers also devise a formula to apportion the benefits and costs of
the collusive action. Commonly, this artifice involves the funneling
of an agreed-upon portion of the revenues from a rigged contract,
known as "*dangō* money," from the designated winner-to-be to the
other firms in the cartel (Minami 1981, 40, 52, and 62). Frequently,
an informal agreement concerning the disposition of subsequent contracts effects a compromise. The bid-rigging for a project to dismantle
an old factory in Tokyo's Shinagawa District combined several meth-
ods. In return for agreeing to submit the low bid of ¥49 million, Gotō
Dismantling Company allegedly promised to pay ¥3 million to each of
the other four conspirator firms and to assist a co-conspirator in obtaining the contract for an upcoming project ("Doboku gyōkai" 1979).

The system allegedly employed by public works contractors in Kawasaki City provides further insights into how benefits may be appor-
tioned. To avoid undercutting the predetermined winning bid, representatives of designated firms wishing to win the contract regularly
met to work out an acceptable compromise. When such discussions
failed to produce a viable modus vivendi, representatives convened

an "adjustment meeting" at the office of the Kawasaki Construction Contractors' Association. If this meeting did not conclude in a suitable accord, a vote or the drawing of lots decided the predetermined low bidder. Over the course of time, this informal process became routinized (*Asahi shinbun,* 5 Oct. 1993). In Kawasaki, as elsewhere, forcing the bidding to go through several rounds before the prearranged "chosen one" magically triumphs commonly conceals a collusive agreement.

The "shady joint venture" (*ura jointo*) is another popular tool for apportioning the fruits of collusive action. The system employed by contractors in Chiba Prefecture illustrates this practice. Following the designation and bidding processes, the contract for a public works project goes to firm 1 as the "nominal" low bidder (*meigi*). As the prime contractor, firm 1 is expected to allocate segments of the project to specialized subcontractors. However, in a shady joint venture, the prime contractor tosses the contract as an extralegal "curve ball" (*marunage*) to firm 2, nicknamed the "padded mitt" (*anko*). Firm 2 then proceeds to throw a curve to firm 3, and firm 3 tosses the ball to firm 4. As nominal prime contractor and subcontractor, firms 1 and 4 can lay just claim for services rendered. But, in a shady joint venture, firms 2 and 3 also receive payment for service charges, even though neither submitted the low bid or performed any work. According to a local contractor, half of all civil engineering works in Chiba Prefecture involved shady joint ventures of this sort (*Asahi shinbun,* 7 Aug. 1993). A documented instance of a shady joint venture emerged in the bidding for a riparian project in Ibaraki Prefecture in 1978. In that case, a local company submitted the low bid of ¥1.86 billion, while two large-scale Tokyo-based construction firms divided more than two-thirds of the contracted amount. Following a decade of legal maneuvers, the conspirators were "punished" with suspended jail sentences (*Asahi shinbun,* 8–31 Nov. 1981).

The fifth, and final, problem for a cartel is evading criminal prosecution and the probing eye of government antitrust regulators. Success here requires active or passive complicity on the part of public works bureaucrats, often motivated by pressure from influential legislators and other concerned political actors. Given the increasing levels of international interdependence and aggressive unilateralism, the survival of collusive accords often depends as well on the apathy or ignorance of trade monitors in other countries (see Keohane and Nye 1977; Bhagwati and Patrick 1993).

In Japan's public construction arena, the supposedly confidential government-set ceiling price for public works provides temptations for officials from the contracting ministries to engage in collusive behavior. The reemployment of large numbers of retired officials in the private sector creates strong incentives for preferential leaks of confidential information. Firms employing retired officials somehow acquire an uncanny ability to divine the government's ceiling price. A survey of major projects undertaken in the mid-1970s concluded that those firms that hired ex-officials submitted bids that were 99.92 percent of the supposedly confidential official estimates (Yamamoto 1975, 138). The amazing calculation skills of Japanese contractors were also displayed in the bidding for the six stages of the ¥1.44-trillion Trans–Tokyo Bay Highway. There, in each instance the winning bid was 99.7 percent of the government ceiling price (McGill 1994, 9).

A case involving the Hokkaidō Development Agency (HDA), an organ under the purview of the prime minister's office, offers additional evidence of the connection between retired government officials and strategic leaks of confidential information. Present and former officials of the HDA's Development Bureau admitted that virtually every public works contract handled by the bureau during the preceding quarter of a century went to firms employing ex-officials of the HDA. Prior to the deadline for bidding, the government's secret ceiling price was leaked, and the majority of the leaks seem to have emanated from the bureau's eleven branch offices, which designate which firms will be allowed to submit tenders. The implicated officials sought to justify their actions by claiming that had they not done what they did, local firms would have been victimized by the onslaught of giant Tokyo-based construction companies (*Yomiuri shinbun,* 2 Mar. 1992).

Another factor facilitating the institutionalized system of collusion is passive complicity on the part of government actors. As a newspaper editorial asserts, "In Japan it seems that government agencies, when commissioning contracts on public works projects, not only look the other way but also create conditions that make it easy to fix bids" (*Asahi shinbun*, 6 Oct. 1989). Government complicity includes weak penalties and lax enforcement of the antimonopoly law: "The Japan Fair Trade Commission (JFTC) does not enforce the law in a manner which could be characterized as vigorous or even adequate by U.S. standards" (Wolff and Howell 1992, 57).[10]

The *dangō* system has not only enriched individual politicians but also benefited the LDP as a national force. Along with small business and farmers' organizations, the constructon industry serves as one leg in the LDP's grand coalition, and it has consistently ranked at or near the top of the ruling party's list of financial benefactors. Knowledge-able observers estimate that half or more of the LDP's total contri-butions come frm the construction industry. In the midst of the *ze-nekon* scandal, for instance, the president of Taisei Construction publicly admitted that his company alone made ¥8.6 billion in illegal political contributions between 1990 and 1993 (*Asahi shinbun*, 19 Oct. 1993). Such generosity has bought the construction industry "influence from top to bottom. The steel makers have it only at the top, but construction is strong at the very base of the pyramid" (Has-egawa Tokunosuke, in Schoenberger 1989).

For tax purposes the construction firms lump most of these illegal contributions under "unaccounted-for expenditures." Under Japanese law, companies can avoid providing detailed explanations for such ex-penditures by paying higher taxes. According to the National Tax Administration Agency, the construction industry typically accounts for 60 to 75 percent of all unaccounted-for expenditures claimed by firms capitalized at ¥100 million or more. During 1992, for example, the tax returns of large-scale construction firms included ¥43.8 billion in such outlays, nearly three-quarters of the nationwide total of ¥59.5 billion. Between 1990 and 1991, three major general contractors—Shimizu, Taisei, and Kajima—reported ¥150 billion in unaccounted-for expenditures (*Asahi shinbun*, 8 Apr., 31 Aug., 10 Sept., 30 Dec. 1993). And while officially reported political contributions remained relatively unchanged between 1985 and 1991, "shady political dona-tions" nearly doubled.

To generate funds for under-the-table contributions to influential politicians, some contractors founded dummy companies that they billed for overhead expenses. Other firms formed large pools of "be-hind-the-scenes money" from incremental miscellaneous expenses si-phoned from networks of branch offices. General contractors also or-dered subcontractors to submit inflated bills for their services and compelled them to kick-back a portion of the money to the general contractor. For example, between February 1991 and January 1992, one subcontractor reportedly channeled around ¥50 million to several general contractors; the kickbacks amounted to almost 1 percent of the subcontractor's annual profits (*Asahi shinbun*, 29 Oct., 8 Nov. 1993).

In short, the *dangō* system is entwined in the mechanisms of po-litical power in Japan's economy. Construction contractors reap in-flated profits, government officials glean administrative power and postretirement security, and legislators harvest political contributions and campaign support. The losers, of course, are the taxpayers: by various estimates, bid-rigging and political payoffs inflate the cost of public construction in Japan by 30 to 50 percent.[11] And inflated bids have been estimated to produce between 16 and 33 percent of the construction industry's total revenues—somewhere between $50 bil-lion to $100 billion annually (McMillan 1991, 201). As noted earlier, the *dangō* system also creates incentives for bribery, graft, and other forms of corruption. Organized crime is believed to control or influ-ence nearly one thousand construction firms (Schoenberger 1989; H. Itō 1987, 58–68; Kaplan and Dubro 1986). Even the cost of pri-vate-sector construction is higher in Japan than in any other advanced industrialized country. Although labor costs for construction in the United States are almost double those in Japan, the unit cost of build-ing a suburban office building is nearly three times greater in Tokyo than in Chicago.[12]

The Logic of Collusive Action

We must not overlook the advantages of the *dangō* system as an alter-native to the myopic drive for immedite and maximal profit in situa-tions of free competition. In this sense, the system allows companies to take a longer view in selecting and pursuing a business strategy, relying all the while on collusive accords for a "fair share" of the market. Because of its sensitivity to cyclical economic downturns and to the effects of "lumpiness"—the large size and sporadic frequency of transactions—construction is an industry in which "collusive conduct is as natural as competition" (Erickson 1969, 98). Since the costs of idle capacity are high in this capital-intensive industry, acquiring a large contract at the outset of the building season can often make or break a company. Such cash-flow considerations are all the more significant in the Japanese case, since a substantial portion of the contracted amount is paid in advance.

Given the costs of retaining employees under Japan's lifetime employment system, it is rational for large-scale general contractors to sacrifice potential profits by adhering to a system of collusive action. Workers in subcontracting firms then bear the costs of cyclical economic downturns. And, for entirely different reasons, the system is rational from the perspective of subcontractors. As Takeuchi Yoshio, an official of the Kansai International Airport Corporation notes, "the Japanese subcontractors would be ostracized if they worked with foreigners. They may be able to eat once with a foreign boss, but it's all over for their relationships with Japanese companies" (Schoenberger 1989). Seen in this light, the *dangō* system represents a mutual insurance system for firms in a volatile industry.

Yet the *dangō* system also serves a set of broader interests and functions. Despite a pervasive network of cartels in public construction, the overall quality of Japan's social infrastructure is impressive. In comparison with Italy, where subways, highways, urban transport projects, and other public works were paid for but never built, the state and quality of Japan's public infrastructure is relatively high. Although one might anticipate widespread negligence and venality, instances of shoddily constructed highways, tunnels, and other public structures are remarkably rare. The bidding is rigged, but the contractors uphold high standards of accountability in meeting the exacting government specifications. Indeed, the 1995 Kōbe earthquake inflicted the bulk of its devastation on older structures built to less stringent government specifications.

Moreover, inasmuch as the *dangō* system props up the overstaffed and technologically backward firms that constitute the massive underside of the industry, the cartels may be seen as a de facto proxy for

Japan's underdeveloped social welfare and unemployment programs ("Ōte kensetsu" 1982, 55; Minami 1981, 71 and 104). Some observers estimate that as many as one-third of Japan's more than half a million licensed construction firms would go bankrupt if the government abolished institutionalized bid-rigging (Schoenberger 1989). That the *dangō* system facilitates political stability, social equality, and mutual reciprocity in government-business relations helps to explain the paradox of Japan's phenomenal and sustained economic growth in a pervasive system of political clientelism.

As long as Japan's public constructon market remained insulated from foreign competition, the intricate system of bid-rigging functioned relatively smoothly. It provided the selective incentives required to induce ratonal individuals to engage in otherwise irrational action. And, notwithstanding the imposition of a variety of limited and conditional reforms beginning in 1988, collusive behavior continues to characterize Japan's public construction market. Simply stated, the *dangō* system functions because Japanese political institutions provide ways of circumventing the potential obstacles to successful, sustained collusive action. Specifically, the designated bidder system helps determine the members of bid-rigging cartels, while blocking entry by would-be spoilers. Industry associations enable the self-enforcement of illicit accords and the apportionment of the benefits and costs of collusive action, while lax enforcement and weak penalties for antitrust violations do little to deter bid-rigging.

This precarious, but relatively stable, equilibrium received a jolt when the U.S. government sought to gain market access for U.S. contractors in the bidding for construction projects at the Kansai Airport. From the Japanese point of view, the opening of the lucrative domestic construction market would not only invite competition from foreign firms but also upset the bid-rigging cartels by introducing competition among domestic firms. In response to this threat to the *dangō* system, government officials, legislators, public works bureaucrats, and the large construction companies all had an enormous stake in resisting any efforts to reform the government procurement policies, no matter how painful the sanctions proposed in Washington, D.C.

Two

Public Works Bureaucrats Under Siege

In November 1987 bilateral negotiations concerning bidding and participation in the Kansai projects stalled when Japan refused to comply with the U.S. demand for modifications of the government procurement system for public works. An article in the *Nikkei Shinbun* asserted that "each country has unique aspects to its system for bidding and contracting for projects, and the matter of deciding participation is not one that should be handled in Japan-U.S. negotiations" (6 Nov. 1987). Japanese negotiators maintained that a multilateral forum was the appropriate medium in which to address the problem. Pointing to the existence of substantial domestic obstacles, an upper-level official at the Ministry of Construction (MOC) stated that any change in the system would render it "necessary to reach a consensus among the various government agencies—beginning with the Construction Ministry—that administer public works in Japan" (ibid.). The bilateral talks reached a stormy impasse and then collapsed as barbed statements from concerned parties on both sides—fortified by strongly worded editorials in the mass media—elevated the issue into a "problem of liberalization of the construction market." Journalists termed the dispute "construction friction" (*kensetsu masatsu*).

Why did the Japanese government allow an issue such as access to construction contracts to become a major source of friction with its largest trading partner? One analyst concluded that the ministries involved in the dispute, primarily the construction and transport ministries, were basically interested in "protecting their client industries and preserving the public works bidding system so crucial to their relations with industry and politicians" (Krauss 1989, 12).

Although partially correct, this observation overlooks the narrower, more personal motives that shape the behavior of government bureaucrats. For while bureaucrats serve the public interest and the interests of their clients, they also serve their own interests—which include the attainment of status and prestige, job satisfaction, power, financial compensation, promotion, and postretirement security.[1] And when formal organizational objectives or procedures hinder the maximization of personal security objectives, bureaucrats will often resort to informal means of conducting business. To protect their personal interests, bureaucrats may, for example, endeavor to forge ties to elected politicians and special interest groups. Or bureaucrats may focus on expanding their agency's jurisdictional turf and budget.

In this chapter, I examine how and why the behavioral patterns of Japanese public works bureaucrats came to assume their distinctive form. Pervasive interministerial sectionalism, one of the defining characteristics of Japanese public bureaucracy, is an important facet of this behavior. The system of reemploying retired government officials in the private sector, public corporations, and in national elective politics also affects the motives and behavior of Japan's public works bureaucrats. Before exploring these matters, however, we need to look at the bureaucrats themselves. In the case of MOC officials, the protagonists of this chapter, it is essential to understand the contrasting purposes and perspectives of two distinct "species" of public works bureaucrats, the generalists and the technical specialists. Although U.S. pressure to pry open Japan's construction market endangered the interests of both species of public works bureaucrats, it was more threatening to the security of the technical specialists' livelihood—particularly to the future of the engineers who provide design services.

The Public Works Bureaucrats

The central headquarters of the Ministry of Construction (Kensetsu-shō or MOC), located in Tokyo's Kasumigaseki District, stands at the apex of a bureaucratic network whose nationwide embrace links the country's center and periphery. With its control over 8 to 14 percent of Japan's general accounts budget and a quarter of total allocations of the Fiscal Investment and Loan Plan (the "second budget"), MOC is among Japan's most powerful disbursers of public funds. Even officials of the Ministry of Finance, the vaunted "bureaucrats of the bureaucrats," concede that the relative power of MOC and the other spending ministries has increased in recent times (pers. interview). Public works expenditures, the "treasure mountain" under the bailiwicks of MOC and other spending ministries, account for nearly one-third of the Japanese government's general accounts budget.

Despite being nicknamed "Kasumigaseki's money-power gang," MOC's bureaucratic officers suffer from a lingering sense of inferiority. In the popular perception MOC is considered a "third-rate ministry"—or, optimistically, an "ultra-second-rate-ministry"—in contrast to the Ministry of Finance and the Ministry of International Trade and Industry (MITI). Reputed to be among the most politicized of Japan's central governmental ministries, MOC is allegedly a "politically driven pork barrel" for the Liberal Democratic Party. Some political commentators even go so far as to claim that the ministry became the exclusive preserve of the LDP faction commanded successively by Tanaka Kakuei, Takeshita Noboru, and Kanemaru Shin.[2] In the wake of the reforms of 1993, some believe Ozawa Ichirō, who seceded from the LDP and founded the Shinsei Party, became the political master of MOC. The *zenekon* scandal dealt a severe blow to MOC's prestige, prompting one publication to claim that, for the moment, the ministry had "the worst reputation among government agencies" (Ōmiya and Group B 1993, 136). Moreover, MOC is relegated to the secondary category of a "project ministry"—or "contracting ministry"—compared with the more prestigious "policy ministries." Efforts to convert MOC from a "tinkering agency" into a "thinking agency" have done little to alter its reputation. Nonetheless, the ministry plays the part of "godfather" to Japan's gargantuan construction industry, wielding powers that are said to be relatively greater than those possessed by MITI over its private-sector clients (S. Matsumoto 1974, 134–35).

MOC's Structure and Mission

Created in the postwar era, MOC is an offspring of the Home Ministry (Naimushō), the most powerful and prestigious agency of the prewar state, which was dismantled as part of efforts by the Supreme Commander of the Allied Powers to remove "militaristic" vestiges from the governing order. Established on 10 July 1948, MOC inherited the organizational structure and functions of the Civil Engineering Bureau (Doboku Kyoku) of the Naimushō. Under the post-Naimushō system, MOC was to administer the tasks of reconstructing and maintaining public-sector facilities, supervising infrastructure development, and overseeing public works projects.

Although the Naimushō was disbanded and its powers distributed to other ministries (e.g., Labor, Home Affairs, Health), only a small fraction of ex-officials of the defunct ministry (most of whom were attached to the police apparatus) were purged. The Occupation officials who disbanded the Naimushō, it seems, "had no inkling of the breadth and depth of its institutional memory and the force it would retain long after its demise" (van Wolferen 1989, 361). Thus MOC was run and staffed by members of the old Civil Engineering Bureau, who soon earned the sobriquet "domestic bureaucrats" (*naimu kanryō*)—a term denoting their supposedly myopic attitude vis-à-vis international affairs—a nickname that continues to stigmatize MOC officials today. Indeed, MOC was so insulated from the buffeting of foreign pressure that it was not until the spring of 1987, in the midst of the Kansai Airport crisis, that the ministry established an Office for International Planning.

The Law for the Establishment of a Ministry of Construction (*Kensetsushō Setchi Hō*) spells out the formal functions and organizational structure of MOC. Those functions include (1) national land and regional planning; (2) city planning; (3) administration of projects concerning rivers, coastline, erosion, canal, and flood prevention; (4) management of roads and tramways; (5) supervision of the Japan Highway Corporation; (6) construction of housing and preparation of residential land; (7) supervision of the Housing Finance Corporation and the Japan Housing Corporation; (8) supervision of the construction industry; (9) building and repair of public edifices; (10) the survey of land and adjustment of maps; and (11) the conduct of research on matters related to civil engineering and architecture.

At the time of its establishment, MOC was composed of seven headquarters bureaus—a Minister's Secretariat, General Affairs, River, Road, City, Building, and Special Construction—and six regional construction bureaus (Tōhoku, Kantō, Chūbu, Kinki, Chūgoku-Shikoku, and Kyūshū). Forty years later, the number of headquarters bureaus was reduced to six (the Special Construction Bureau having been absorbed into the Minister's Secretariat), and two regional construction bureaus were added (one for Hokuriku, and the creation of separate organs for Chūgoku and Shikoku). MOC also oversees the Geographical Survey Institute, the Public Works Research Institute, the Construction College, and other auxiliary organs. Thus MOC's formal administrative structure extends into virtually every locality of the country except Hokkaidō and Okinawa, which are administered by separate agencies under the auspices of the Office of the Prime Minister.

In 1992 MOC's nationwide organizational network included 8 regional construction bureau offices, 232 work offices, and 654 branch work offices. A typical regional construction bureau is divided into six departments (General Affairs, Land Acquisition, River, Road, Public Buildings, and Planning), which are, in turn subdivided into two to six sections. Each of the twenty or so sections has a central work office and five or six branch work offices scattered throughout its region.

MOC's "Two Species"

At the time of its creation, MOC's internal sections, affiliated organs, and local branches employed slightly less than 6,000 individuals. The ministry's workforce rose precipitously up through the mid-1960s, to more than 35,000 names, but it has declined steadily ever since, standing at 24,490 officials in 1992. Like officials in all central state ministries in Japan, MOC's officials fall into two distinct categories, depending on whether they entered the ministry after passing the Class A or the much less demanding Class B segment of the Higher-Level Public Officials Examination. The former are referred to as "career" officials, while the vastly more numerous latter group is known as the "non-careers" (*non kyaria*). What most differentiates the two groups of bureaucrats is the nature of their respective promotional tracks: career officials are eligible for promotion to the top administrative posts within the ministry, whereas their noncareer counterparts are not.

The elite status of MOC officials is indisputable. Like their counterparts in Japan's other central state ministries, the vast majority of MOC's career bureaucrats are graduates of the country's most prestigious educational institutions. It is said that aspiring officials with both intellect and connections gravitate to the Finance Ministry, while those having only the former become construction bureaucrats (van Wolferen 1989, 119). Though MOC usually falls behind the Finance Ministry, MITI, and the Economic Planning Agency in its attempt to woo the elite university graduates, it does quite well compared to the other spending ministries. In 1987, for example, 44 percent of MOC's 263 upper-level officials hailed from the University of Tokyo (Tokyo Daigaku, or Tōdai) and 21 percent from the University of Kyoto (Kyoto Daigaku, or Kyōdai), both universally acknowledged as the country's premier institutions of higher learning (*Kensetsushō meikan* 1988).

With respect to their elite status, Japanese government bureaucrats have much in common with the *grand corps* of the French civil service and little in common with the patronage-ridden Italian state bureaucracy. Like their French counterparts, Japanese officials are recruited from the country's most prestigious educational institutions by way of a rigorous examination system. In addition, the Japanese bureaucracy, like the French executive branch, plays an important role in initiating and drafting public policies. In Italy, in contrast, there is an increasing trend toward the "southernization" of the bureaucracy: though the South accounts for only about one-third of the total population, it produces about 70 percent of all civil servants and over 80 percent of the highest-ranking civil servants. Furthermore, it is estimated that between 1973 and 1990 nearly 60 percent of those who aquired permanent posts in the Italian government bureaucracy were recruited without entrance examinations, and that many civil service postings were secured through selective appointments by Christian

Democratic politicians (see Cassese 1993). While there are sporadic reports of LDP meddling in bureaucratic personnel matters, Japanese officials continue to be a meritocratic elite whose policymaking roles and functions warrant attention.

There is an old Japanese saying: "He who is not a graduate of Tō-dai's Law Faculty does not become a bureaucrat." Although somewhat less applicable today than in previous times, the traditional "doctrine of law faculty omnipotence" continues to characterize the general state of affairs for career-level personnel in the central state bureaucracy. But unlike other ministries, MOC allows both administrative generalists and technical specialists the opportunity to assume the top administrative post—thus the ministry's nickname "technical heaven" (Jin et al. 1981, 201).

MOC's "administrative officials" (*jimukan,* or *jimuya*) are generalists, most of whom are graduates of law or economics faculties. The "technical officials" (*gikan,* or *gijutsuya*), who constitute about 60 percent of all MOC officials, possess specialized skills acquired from training in engineering, architecture, and other technical fields of study. Compared to their counterparts in commissioning agencies in the United States, MOC's technical specialists perform a larger share of the design services involved in public works projects. A typical entering class of new staff includes some fifteen generalists and between sixty-five and eighty specialists, about half of whom have been schooled in civil engineering. While technical specialists outnumber administrators in the regional construction bureaus, local branches, and auxiliary organs, the administrative generalists predominate in the upper-level bureaucracy at MOC's Kasumigaseki headquarters.

Some observers liken MOC to a niche inhabited by "two species" or to "two government offices inside a single government agency." Indeed, relations between the species are not always cordial, and there is an ever-present undercurrent of "factional conflict" (Honda 1974, 193). On occasion, members of the opposing camps have refused to acknowledge one another in the corridors of the ministry's headquarters (Y. Itō 1978, 67). However, when schisms appear within a camp— such as rifts between civil engineers and city planners —they serve to forge alliances between the technical and administrative officials at the bureau or section level (pers. interview).

Two Ladders to the Top

The story of how the technical specialists came to alternate with generalists in occupying MOC's foremost leadership position is enlightening. Before World War II technical officials in the Civil Engineering Bureau were not promoted above the rank of section chief in the ministry's headquarters or head of the civil engineering department in its prefectural branches. The clique of Tōdai Law Faculty graduates, particularly those in the powerful River Section, repeatedly fended off the efforts of specialists to achieve loftier posts. After the war, during the U.S. Occupation, the economic stabilization measures mandated in the Dodge Line placed a high priority on the construction of a modern network of roads. In fact, General Douglas MacArthur's first directive upon landing in Japan was to order the repair of roads linking Atsugi, Yokohama, and Tokyo (Nishioka 1988, 1). Civil engineers in the Road Section, such as Iwasawa Tadayasu, who secured an appointment to the post of Road Bureau chief, seized upon the opportunities that such a shift in priorities presented.

With the disbanding of the Naimushō, technical specialists united in the drive to have one of their own installed as administrative vice-minister (*jimujikan*), the highest career civil service position in a government ministry. These efforts might well have been fruitless had it not been for the Occupation officials' preference for "scientific administration" (for which, presumably, officials with a technical bent would be valuable assets). Moreover, the new ministry was created during the brief reign of the Socialist-dominated cabinet of Katayama Tetsu (1947–1948). Cabinet member Nishio Suehiro vociferously opposed the appointment of Ōhashi Takeo, a former police official and heir apparent, to the vice-minister's post because, Nishio claimed, Ōhashi had victimized him when Ōhashi served as chief of the Okayama police. And so, on 10 July 1948, Iwasawa became the first technical specialist to succeed to the vice-ministership, a triumph that inspired other technicians—notably the "Kyoto University Gang of Four"—to seek employment with the fledgling ministry.[3]

Though it may have been bloodless, the coup by MOC's technical officials was not uncontested. An experience recounted by Kobayashi Yosaji, an MOC official during Iwasawa's tenure and later the president of Nippon Television Company, illustrates the mood at the time: One evening, Kobayashi, then chief of the documents section of the Minister's Secretariat, paid an unnanounced visit to Iwasawa's private residence, where he was greeted at the door by the vice-minister's wife. At the sight of an unfamiliar face, and without an instant's hesitation, she asked, "Are you a specialist or a generalist?" Kobayashi was left with the distinct impression that had he confessed to being a generalist, he would have been ordered to go around to the servant's entrance (Kanryō kikō kenkyūkai 1978, 28).

Upon Iwasawa's retirement in March 1950, Nakata Masami, a generalist, was appointed to the post of vice-minister, initiating what has become an unwritten, but inviolable, law at MOC, that the top post alternates between technical and administrative officials—usually changing hands every two to three years (see Appendix B). Yet an element of bitterness persists among generalists concerning this system. From their vantage, some of the technicians who assume the vice-ministership are "technical fools," officials with specialized training and shallow administrative experience (pers. interview).

On their way up the ladder in MOC, generalists and specialists pursue separate paths. A new generalist typically serves a one- or two-year apprenticeship in the Kasumigaseki headquarters, where he or she will be promoted to chief clerk and deputy section chief. (These are the highest posts to which noncareer officials may aspire.) After serving several years in these posts, the generalist is dispatched outside the capital as section chief in one of the regional construction bureaus or "loaned" to a prefectural or municipal government. After two to four years in the hinterland, the now-seasoned generalist is summoned back to Kasumigaseki to serve as deputy section chief. He or she then proceeds through a succession of regular promotional steps—specialist official, planning specialist, and subsection chief— leading to the post of section chief. At this juncture, the official has amassed about two decades of experience at MOC, and a fair number of colleagues from the entering class will have already left government service. From this point on, the competition for promotion to the top positions in the ministry intensifies. The most fortunate generalists advance to the post of chief in one of four key sections (Personnel, Documents, Finance, and Policy) in the Minister's Secretariat, and then to deputy-director and director of the Minister's Secretariat, Economic Affairs, or Housing Bureau. When the worthiest generalist secures the position of vice-ministership, the others remaining from his or her entering class resign shortly thereafter in order to give the new vice-minister unquestioned seniority.

For MOC technical specialists, in contrast, the first assignment, after a brief stint at ministry headquarters, is to a regional construction bureau. After eight or nine years of gradually moving up the administrative hierarchy, the technician is transferred to Kasumigaseki, where he or she feels very much like a "freshman in the headquarters office." A series of promotions at headquarters is followed by another assignment to a regional construction bureau, this time as an upper official. With luck, the technician is recalled to Kasumigaseki to become chief of the Planning Section of either the River or the Road Bureau. The technical bureaucrat deemed the "flower" of the entering class is eventually promoted to the post of vice-minister for engineering affairs (*kensetsu gikan*). And, under the alternating scheme, this technician may advance to the vice-ministership.

Thus the career tracks of generalists and technical specialists are entirely discrete except for the alternation in the vice-ministership. No crossover occurs, for example, at the second highest posts in the respective career ladders, deputy vice-minister for administration and vice-minister for engineering affairs. Generalists invariably stand at the head of the Minister's Secretariat, Economic Affairs (dubbed the "Construction Industry Bureau"), and City Bureaus, while specialists lead at the River and Road Bureaus. The lone exception to this rule is the directorship of the Housing Bureau, where generalists and technicians constitute almost equal shares of the bureau's rank-and-file. However, inasmuch as an architect has never ascended to the top post at MOC, specialists regard the post of Director of the Housing Bureau as a promotional cul-de-sac. (Upon appointment to this post, Mihashi Shin'ichi is said to have behaved as if he had been fired rather than promoted to a directorship within the ministry.)

While a balance of power prevails in the uppermost posts in MOC's head office in Kasumigaseki, the relative presence of generalists is most apparent in the middle echelons of ministerial leadership. Meanwhile, technical specialists—who wield greater influence in budgetary matters—dominate the upper administrative posts in the ministry's regional construction bureaus, auxiliary organs, and local branch offices.

Politics and Personnel: The Kōno Tempest

Atop the formal hierarchy of MOC are two politically appointed officials, the minister and parliamentary vice-minister of construction. These individuals, however, generally maintain their distance and do not attempt to meddle with MOC's unwritten personnel laws. The one exception to this tradition was Kōno Ichirō, minister of construction during the second and third Ikeda cabinets (1962–1964), whose brazen meddling in the personnel system temporarily upset the balance of power at MOC.

Upon assuming office, Kōno is rumored to have told the assembled hierarchy of the ministry: "Forget about the past. Those who cooperate with me, stay. Those who won't cooperate, oppose [my orders], or are incompetent, leave" (Kanryō Kikō Kenkyūkai 1978, 30). He then proceeded to do as he wished, ignoring the supposedly inviolable precepts of the delicately balanced personnel system. In one action, he demoted Maeda Kōki, then director of the City Bureau, to the relatively insignificant post of director of the Government Buildings Bureau (since downgraded to a department under the Minister's Secretariat), instead of promoting Maeda to the top post in the Housing Bureau for which he had been groomed. The alleged reason for this demotion was Maeda's failure to greet Kōno properly when the two crossed paths in a ministry washroom. As it turned out, the extremely nearsighted Maeda happened not to have been wearing his eyeglasses at the time of the happenstance encounter. When Kōno realized his error, he had Maeda promoted to director of the Housing Bureau, a waystation on the fast track to the vice-ministership, a post Maeda ultimately secured (ibid. 31–33).

Kōno also shattered MOC's unwritten covenant by insisting on the appointment of generalists to the directorships of the Kantō and Chūbu Regional Construction Bureaus. But his most controversial act was the rare interministerial transfer of three of his generalist disciples from the Police Agency into high-level posts at MOC. In one stroke, Kōno not only breached the etiquette of noninterference and the wall between generalists and specialists but also reignited the enduring grudge between the civil engineering and police wings of the old Home Ministry, the Naimushō. MOC officials, many of whom had begun their careers in the Home Ministry, were nonplused, to say the least, at finding themselves once again in the midst of police officials, and several offered their resignations in protest (ibid, 30–31). Among those who retired were the vice-minister for engineering affairs and the director of the Road Bureau. After Kōno's own departure, the delicate informal balance between generalists and technicians was quickly restored.

Several observers have depicted Japan's government bureaucrats as minions cowering in the shadow of their legislative overlords (e.g., Ramseyer and Rosenbluth 1993, 110–12; McCubbins and Noble 1993, 15–16). But the Kōno tempest raises doubts about such analyses. While cabinet ministers do, in fact, wield formal authority over promotions, evidence from MOC and other ministries suggests that the exercise of such authority is the rare exception and not the rule. As a temporary "visitor" in the ministry, a cabinet minister finds it difficult enough to attain even moderate competency in policy matters, let alone delve into personnel. Another deterrent to personnel matters is that those bureaucrats who are promoted as a result of political meddling often find that their career advancement suddenly slows down when the parliamentary patron leaves the minister's chair (pers. interview). At any rate, instances of politicians meddling in bureaucratic personnel decisions are rare enough to become front-page news when they do occur. Aside from the Kōno tempest and several legendary episodes at MITI, there have been few documented cases of significant partisan intervention in bureaucratic promotions.[4]

Public works bureaucrats, on the other hand, have candidly admitted in interviews to showing favoritism in promoting the careers of politicians who cooperate in securing passage of policy and budgetary proposals. Often this favoritism takes the form of giving advance notice of a policy decision to a politician, enabling the preferred legislator to be the first to claim credit. Other times preferential treatment is given in bidder-designation decisions for public works projects. Bureaucrats can also delay or divert projects supported by meddlesome politicians; they can withhold or distort information; and they can take significant liberties in the implementation of policy. As politicians the world around have discovered, bargaining with bureaucrats is often more effective than attempting to maximize control over their activities.

Personnel "Loans"

MOC's hub-and-spoke administrative network spreads outward from Tokyo to nearly every district in the country. In addition, MOC exerts considerable informal influence over the construction bureaucrats at the prefectural and municipal levels. The principal medium for the exercise of this influence is the institutionalized practice of temporarily "loaning out" (*shukkō*) midcareer MOC officials to local bureaucracies and public corporations. Among high-level headquarters officials in 1987, more than two-thirds of the generalists and 41 percent of the specialists had been loaned-out at some point in their career (*Kensetsushō meikan* 1987). These officials typically spend from two to four years as departmental or section chiefs attached to prefectural or municipal bureaucracies. The generalists serve in a diverse range of administrative areas, while specialists tend to be clustered in civil engineering posts.

MOC also "loans" midcareer officials to public corporations, particularly those under the ministry's jurisdiction. In October 1987, for instance, 43 MOC officials were on loan to public corporations. (By way of comparison, the Ministry of Labor had loaned out 45 employees; Agriculture, 25; and MITI, 23; *Amakudari hakusho* 1988, 306.) Of the 16 on-loan officials attached to the Hanshin Superhighway Corporation in 1987, half were midcareer MOC bureaucrats, the rest hailing from prefectural and municipal governments in the Kansai area.

The Roots of Sectionalist Rivalry

Given MOC's size, multiple missions, and hub-and-spoke structure, and given the natural propensity of any bureaucratic organization to devolve into turf battles over budget and resource allocations, one is not surprised to learn of rampant jurisdictional conflicts involving the ministry. Such sectionalism, indeed is one of the most important structural characteristics of Japanese bureaucracy and government, and the sectionalism at MOC is so deep-seated and pronounced that the agency has been described as a grab-bag of "bureaus with no ministry" constructed upon a handful of "sections with no bureau" (Jin et al. 1981, 202–3). There is, for example, an ongoing rivalry between the Street Section and the Parks and Greenery Section of the City Bureau, and the City Bureau and the Housing Bureau regularly tangle over questions of jurisdictional authority and budgetary primacy vis-à-vis the construction of residential housing in urban areas (pers. interview). Naturally, tensions increase during periods of fiscal restraint, as in the late 1970s.

The classic case of MOC sectionalism is the ageless battle between those who administer the country's rivers and riparian works and those in charge of roads. In prewar times, the overseers of river administration were so ascendant that the Home Ministry's River Section was called the "star" of the ministry. Throughout the first decade of the postwar era, the River Section maintained its preeminence, and budgetary allocations for riparian works and flood control exceeded expenditures on roads. These priorities were understandable in that the war coupled with several destructive typhoons had left the country's river works in a pathetic state demanding immediate repair. Moreover, a disproportionately large share of MOC's administrative vice-ministers, particularly in the 1950s and 1960s, were individuals who rose through the ranks of the officialdom of the River Bureau. Since the mid-1950s, however, the balance of power has tilted in favor of the Road Bureau. This shift may reflect a logical redefinition of priorities after the taming of flood hazards, but prescient political entrepreneurs like Tanaka Kakuei also recognized the vast political benefits of sponsoring legislation that bolstered the road administration. Today, the battle between the two bureaus continues to seethe, although in recent years the stature of the Housing Bureau has increased relative to both.

In addition, MOC, like all central state government ministries and agencies, frequently finds itself entangled in interministerial warfare. For instance, a long-simmering sectionalist feud over issues of zoning and road construction in rural areas has created enduring enmity between MOC and the Agriculture Ministry. Any proposal to build a dam is virtually guaranteed to spark interministerial conflict involving, inter alia, the Finance Ministry, as the guardian of the public purse; the Health and Welfare Ministry, as the sentinel for drinking water; the Agriculture Ministry as the champion of water for agricultural irrigation; MITI, as the spokesman for industry; and MOC, as the authority on building things. Another noteworthy example of a protracted interministerial sectionalist feud arose over efforts to solve the problems of heavy traffic and air pollution in metropolitan areas. At various times during this dispute, lasting from the mid-1960s to the mid-1970s, the belligerents included the Transport Ministry, MITI, MOC, the Public Safety Commission, and the Police Agency.

Sectionalist rivalry in the circumstances surrounding the so-called Three Road Laws (*dōro sanpō*) has come to define the contours of postwar road administration and budgetary politics in this important arena.[5] Since prewar public works priorities had relegated roads to a low status relative to railroads and water works, the postwar era began with a road system comprised of "washboard roads" (*dekoboko michi*), "muddy paths" (*nukarumi michi* or *doronko michi*), and "rattletrap byways" (*onboro dōro*). In 1948 the U.S. Occupation officials, intent on expunging militaristic undertones from the Road Law of 1919, oversaw preparations to create a new framework for road administration. Naturally these efforts captured the interests of the officials of MOC's Road Bureau, whose motto was then, as now, encapsulated in the lyrics to the ministry's "Utopia Song": "asphalt blanketing the mountains and the valleys . . . a splendid utopia."

Introduced in the first session of the Diet following the end of the Occupation, the Road Law (*Dōro Hō*) of 1952 was presented as a parliamentarians' bill rather than as cabinet-sponsored legislation. The core components of the law provided for the creation of a nationwide network of two types of trunk roads, an expanded framework of subsidy assistance, and a base from which MOC could petition the Finance Ministry for relevant budgetary allocations. Tanaka Kakuei, then a young parliamentarian, correctly perceived the political benefits of an ambitious program of road-building and championed the new law. Almost immediately, a jurisdictional battle erupted between the Ministry of Agriculture and the newly established Ministry of Construction. Meanwhile, within MOC, the River Bureau sought to cling to its "star" status by staving off the rising momentum of the Road Bureau.

The same Diet session deliberated on the Special Measures Law for Road Facilities (*Dōro Seibi Tokubetsu Sochi Hō*) and approved it on 31 May 1952. In essence, the Special Measures Law created a pool of financing to be generated from a system of toll roads. While tolls for some bridges and ferries had been levied in prewar times, a faction within the Road Bureau clung to the belief that roads ought to be free; they were overruled, and the Road Bureau recommended toll status for the Kan'mon Tunnel, which links the islands of Honshū and Kyūshū. This proposal generated a clash between MOC and the Finance Ministry, which was loath to see a whittling away of its jurisdiction over budget allocations. A feud also arose between MOC, the Ministry of Transport, and the trucking industry, which, for obvious reasons, objected to toll roads. The Special Measures Law, however, was enacted and the Mie Highway became the country's first toll road. Four years later, the creation of the Japan Highway Corporation (Nihon Dōro Kōdan) ushered in the era of high-speed toll expressways.

The Temporary Measures Law Concerning Financial Resources for Road Facilities Expenses (*Dōro Seibi Hi no Zaigento ni Kansuru Rinji Sochi Hō*)—the third legislative pillar of postwar road administration—was passed in the summer of 1953, after stormy and protracted deliberations; once again, Tanaka was among the chief proponents. The Temporary Measures Law proposed to increase assistance to local government bodies, establish a system of five-year plans for road construction, and impose a gasoline tax that would be earmarked for the building and maintenance of roads. The mention of an earmarked gasoline tax provoked a reprise of the battle between MOC and the Finance Ministry, with the latter vigorously denouncing the creation of a pool of financial resources outside its control. Meanwhile, the Transport Ministry found itself in a quandary: it was eager to partake of the benefits of an improved and better-maintained network of roads, yet it opposed a tax that would displease the trucking industry. In the end, the law passed and the first five-year plan for road facilities was announced in June 1954.

Yet the sectionalist feuds spawned by the Three Road Laws did not subside with their legislative enactment. Over time, MOC has feuded with MITI over an automobile weight tax; a series of "gasoline tax wars" pitted MOC against MITI and various other ministries; and MOC has jousted with the Transport Ministry over the railroads. Deliberations on tax reforms touched off a major contretemps between MITI and MOC in spring 1988. Angered that petroleum products alone were subject to a new consumption tax, the oil refinery and retail industries—backed by their ministerial overlord, MITI—petitioned for a reduction in the gasoline tax. MOC's Road Bureau countered that any cuts in gas tax revenues would seriously impair road improvement and maintenance. MOC officials also asserted that the pricing policy of MITI and the petroleum industry—not the tax system—was to blame for the high price of gasoline at the pump. (Tokyo motorists pay three times as much for gasoline as New Yorkers and twice what motorists in Frankfurt pay.) As this sectionalist warfare reached a crescendo, combatants included members of the LDP's Tax System Committee, as well as powerbrokers on the Commerce Committee and Construction Division of the LDP's Policy Affairs Research Council. For its part, the road camp targeted some forty-two parliamentarians for persuasion and *nemawashi* (briefing or, literally, "root binding"), and mobilized ten top officials of the Road Bureau along with 550 heads of local authorities in the effort. Although MOC and its forces won this particular battle, no one believes the war is over.

In sum, sectionalism permeates the government bureaucracy in Japan. And at times, enterprising parliamentarians, particularly members of the conservative parties, join the fray. If they are on the winning side, they may receive a bonus of sorts from the victorious ministry. For example, MOC repaid a number of parliamentarians who generated support for its cause with enduring and mutually rewarding ties to the ministry. In addition, some of these politicians went on to become members of the LDP's construction tribe, as we shall see in chapter 4.

Descent from Heaven

Career civil servants in Japan usually retire between the ages of 50 and 55, and this "descent from heaven" (*amakudari*) takes one of several forms.[6] The most common course is to launch a "second career" at a private firm, generally a firm within the bailiwick of the ex-official's home agency. Another form of *amakudari*, known as "side-slip," involves lateral migration into an upper administrative position in a public corporation. A third form of *amakudari*, sometimes termed "position exploitation," involves the pursuit of a second career in elective politics through the exploitation of ties to organized interest groups. Less popular paths include descent into positions in trade associations, think tanks, nonprofit organizations, and, recently, advisory positions with foreign firms.[7]

Amakudari is primarily a postwar phenomenon. In the prewar era, bureaucrats tended to retire later, and many were appointed to the House of Peers. Moreover, most considered it beneath the dignity of a servant of the emperor to descend into the private sector (Johnson 1974, 958). By and large, the Japanese system of *amakudari* has less in common with America's "revolving door" phenomenon than with the French government bureaucrats' *pantouflage*—migrating from the civil service to positions in private-sector firms, public corporations, and elective politics.[8]

The practice of early retirement emerged as a result of three factors: the guarantee of lifetime employment for career officials, the need to differentiate among university cliques (particularly the large number of Tokyo University alumni), and, most importantly, the seniority system of personnel promotion (Johnson 1974, 960). Since, in most cases, only one member of an entering class eventually attains the post of vice-minister, each naming of a new vice-minister prompts a series of resignations; at MOC, for example, unsuccessful aspirants in the vice-ministerial race are expected to resign within two years after the ascent of a classmate. Moreover, along the way, officials with nebulous prospects for the top spot often receive a "tap on the shoulder" and a request to "clear a pathway" for those junior officials who are on the fast track.

In addition to providing top bureaucrats with postretirement security, the reemployment system spreads bureaucratic expertise throughout the private and public sectors and facilitates government-business interaction. As we will see, *amakudari* is not simply a mechanism for enhancing bureaucratic dominance of private-sector firms, nor simply a device used by firms to capture or co-opt the government bureaucracy. Both of these views have an element of truth, but *amakudari* is more complex. The flow of "descended angels" from the government bureaucracy into private business, public corporations, and elective politics serves as an adhesive element in the formation of enduring policy networks. As a glimpse at the "transfer routes" of retired MOC bureaucrats shows, *amakudari* promotes the ties that bind bureaucratic, legislative, and private-sector elites into a concrete triumvirate commanding Japan's public works domain. Additionally, retired upper officials continue to play a key role in policy and personnel decisions in their former ministries.[9]

Amakudari *to Construction Firms*

MOC tends to rank second to the Finance Ministry among the country's central state agencies in the number of its former officials who find reemployment in private-sector firms. The construction and real-estate industries provide the majority of landing spots for MOC's ex-officials, many of whom alight into positions as "advisors" to such firms. In most cases, the final posting within the bureaucracy determines an ex-bureaucrat's level of reemployment at a construction firm. For example, an official retiring at the level of bureau chief in MOC's central headquarters could expect to descend into an executive director post (with a good chance of eventually becoming company vice-president), while a former regional bureau chief would likely secure a managing director slot with a construction company. This custom only increases the bureaucrats' incentive to maximize promotional possibilities during their truncated careers in government service.

From the vantage of a public works contractor, the benefits of employing former bureaucrats are by no means trivial. The "descended angels" attended elite schools and have considerable expertise and information, but many close observers doubt that these qualifications are as important to the new employers as the connections and personal networks these former officials command. For MOC is in the position to give what is called "candy" to favored contractors who employ its retired bureaucrats, treats like preferential decisions on bidder designations or leaks concerning the government's ceiling price for public works projects. As a former president of a general contracting company explains, "There is a thing called a souvenir project (*omiyage kōji*). It involves the Construction Ministry's gift of a project [to a particular contractor] in order to secure an *amakudari* spot for a retired official. There is talk that such projects have been worth as much as one billion yen" (*Asahi shinbun*, 16 Nov. 1993). So it makes good sense for public works contractors to employ someone with friends who work in the "candy store." In the words of one observer: "with regard to public works, in the final analysis connections to the contracting agency are important. For that reason [firms] energetically scout out retired upper officials" (Minami 1981, 25).

Over the years an informal head-hunting system has emerged to satisfy this demand. The process begins when a firm that hopes to hire an "old boy" sends what has come to be known as a "requisition for spare parts" to the Personnel Section of MOC's Minister's Secretariat. These so-called spare parts—or, more correctly, "spare employees"— are bureaucrats nearing the age of retirement. The request for spare parts implores MOC to "pass along an honorable official to this humble company" (*Asahi shinbun*, 16 Nov. 1993). In this regard, MOC's Personnel Section functions as an outplacement agency for its retiring officials. Indeed, until the increased scrutiny aroused by the *zenekon* scandal, the Personnel Section prepared and sent out documents requesting specific conditions of employment for descending bureaucrats. Companies wishing to employ former MOC officials had to promise that their salary would be commensurate to that of their final ministerial posting, and provisions were also made for elite bureaucrats to receive such fringe benefits as a company car, personal secretary, and a private office.

The personnel rosters of upper management in Japan's major construction firms reflects the pervasiveness of *amakudari*. In 1993, for example, former MOC officials held the posts of president of Kajima Corporation, chair of Sumitomo Construction, and vice-president of

Tobishima Corporation. According to a survey taken by Tokyo Commercial Research, 363 of the 2,021 officials (or 18 percent) of the 61 large general contracting firms listed on the Tokyo Stock Exchange in 1992 were former officials of government agencies or quasi-public corporations. Of these, 55 were ex-officials of MOC, while 44 were descendees from the Japan Highway Corporation, and 36 had retired from the Japan Housing Corporation (*Asahi shinbun,* 16 Nov. 1993).

A report issued in the early 1980s revealed that "imported personnel" with backgrounds in the public service filled the top nine positions at Kajima Corporation ("Kensetsu gyōkai" 1982, 179). By way of contrast, Takenaka Corporation, another of the Big Six, had a long-standing policy of not importing "old boys" from MOC, a rule that allegedly contributed to the company's relatively paltry harvest of public works contracts (Minami 1981, 29). Not surprisingly, firms employing large numbers of former public works bureaucrats tend to derive a relatively large share of their revenues from government contracts. In 1981, for instance, the top officials of the five largest civil engineering contractors included 52 ex-officials, more than two-thirds of whom had descended from careers in MOC (*Amakudari hakusho* 1982, 90–94). The system is replicated at the prefectural and local levels as well (Yoshida 1984, 220).

MOC's retired upper officials, particularly the technicians, are in such demand that a popular saying holds that there are "seven suitors for each daughter," and a successful contractor will boast of having "won the shōgun's daughter" (Honda 1974, 197–98). And the dowry these brides bring their grooms is access to information on confidential government projects. As an official of a major construction firm admitted, "The estimated cost for a public works project is always contracted at the maximal budgetary level. Since a bureaucrat will lose his job if he does not use the full budget, he will leak information to contractors. In many cases the bid will come in at 98 to 99 percent of the estimated cost" (*Shūkan gendai,* 1 May 1982, 57). By tacit agreement, each firm that takes in one of MOC's "old boys" is guaranteed at least one large-scale public works project (Asano et al. 1977, 29–30). Since the revenues from a single major project, such as the construction of a dam or a highway, may be sufficient to ensure the solvency of a firm for up to a decade, the benefits of this "welfare pension in-hand project" system far outweigh the salaries a company pays the ex-officials.

Over the years, a host of cases have come to light involving dubious links between retired bureaucrats and the awarding of public works contracts. Instances have been reported in such diverse locales as Hokkaidō, Kagawa, Ishikawa, Miyagi, Nagano, Niigata, Ōita, and Toyama prefectures (Y. Itō 1978, 67; Minami 1981, 108; Yamamoto 1975, 138–39). In Hiroshima Prefecture, for example, on 15 December 1974, Kumagai Gumi emerged as the lowest bidder in the competition for a project to widen a road in Fukuyama City. The ¥162.7-million tender submitted by the firm was exactly the same as MOC's confidential estimated cost of the project. Only a few months earlier, a former director of MOC's Fukuyama Project Office had "descended from heaven" into a position with the company, a coincidence that prompted a local contractor to assert that it is "clearly impossible to imagine that information did not pass into the hands of Kumagai Gumi" (Jin et al. 1981, 196).

One study of large construction firms that employ considerable numbers of former government officials reported the following correlations (Jin et al. 1981, 179):

Company	% of Top Officials Coming from Government	% of Revenues Derived from Public Works Projects
Tobishima Corporation	24%	63%
Mori Gumi	40%	72%
Tokura Construction	35%	75%
Fukuda Corporation	70%	70%

The most striking case concerned Totetsu Kōgyō, a firm with strong ties to the since privatized Japan National Railways Corporation: former government officials counted for fully 80 percent of the firm's 24 top management posts, and public works contracts represented 80 percent of its total revenues (ibid. 140).

Amakudari is not the exclusive reserve of former central state bureaucrats and major construction contractors. In fact, retired bureaucrats at the prefectural and municipal levels also descend into positions with local construction contractors. For instance, some 124 employees of the 60 firms belonging to the "Hama Yūkai" (Yokohama Friendship Association) were retired officials from the Yokohama City government. These ex-officials allegedly acted as a pipeline for "informal information" pertaining to municipal public works projects (*Asahi shinbun*, 19 Sept. 1993). Table 2 summarizes the reemployment situations of ex-officials of the Tokyo Metropolitan government.

Amakudari to private-sector firms is controversial and demands for reform have been voiced over the years. In August 1993, as the *zenekon* scandal was widening, MOC announced that its officials above the rank of section chief (or department head among regional construc-

TABLE 2. Amakudari *Patterns of Ex-Officials of the Tokyo Metropolitan Government*

Final Government Posting	Year	Amakudari Destination	Position
Director, Construction Bureau	1979	Tobishima Corporation	Executive director
Inspector, Road Bureau	1979	Mitsui Construction	Advisor
Deputy Director, Road Bureau	1979	Hazama Corporation	Advisor
Secretary, Road Bureau	1980	Kyoritsu Construction	Advisor
Secretary, Housing Bureau	1981	Muramoto Construction	(unclear)
Head, Minami New Town Development Headquarters	1981	Asakawa Gumi	Business director
Inspector, Port Bureau	1979	Kajima Corporation	Chief engineer
Head, Tokyo Bay Office, Port Bureau	1979	Shimizu Corporation	Advisor
Manager, Port Bureau	1980	Ōtaki Kōmuten	Business manager
Construction Director, Port Bureau	1980	Ōbayashi Corporation	Business manager

SOURCE: Minami (1981, 25–27).

tion bureau officials) would exercise "self-restraint" (*jishuku*) with regard to reemployment with general construction contractors until the resolution of the scandal. A number of prefectural governments quickly followed suit and announced reform measures aimed at stemming the flow of confidential information to construction firms (*Asahi shinbun,* 11 Oct. 1993). In addition, the public outcry aroused by the *zenekon* scandal forced MOC to announce that its Personnel Section would no longer specify the conditions of employment, such as the use of company cars and private offices, for officials seeking reemployment in construction firms. I will discuss the consequences of these modest and impermanent institutional modifications in the concluding chapter.

"Side-Slipping" into Public Corporations

For retired MOC officials who are reemployed in the public sector, the preferred course of action—especially for the generalists—is termed "side-slip descent from heaven" (*yokosuberi gata amakudari*), reemployment in upper administrative positions in quasi-governmental corporations, foundations, financial banks, and similar organs. It is said that more than one-third of the top positions in these public entities are "hereditary" in that their occupants tend to come almost exclusively from the ranks of retired government officials, particularly those from the agency which oversees the corporation ("Tokken kanryō" 1982, 81). Between 1971 and 1987, the government ministries from which the largest number of retired officials side-slipped into public corporation posts were MITI (885), Agriculture (668), Finance (591), and MOC (525; *Amakudari hakusho,* various years).

It is not much of an exaggeration to refer to the positions assumed by these former high-level bureaucrats as sinecures. The posts—president, vice-president, member of the board of directors, and auditor—usually entail few duties other than ceremonial functions and bring an annual salary well in excess of $100,000, a healthy sinecure indeed. And all the more so with a generous retirement allowance.

MOC is in the enviable position of controlling some forty-one "progenitor posts" in a dozen public corporations.[10] Once secured, these posts are jealously guarded. If a suitable candidate cannot be found among a ministry's annual crop of "descending angels"—a situation referred to as "human resource insufficiency" or a shortage of "bullets"—the inevitable result is interministerial personnel warfare. For example, a sectionalist battle ensued after the resignation of Nanbe Tetsuya, a former director of MOC's Kantō Regional Construction Bureau, from the post of president of the Japan Housing Corporation. Due to a shortage of ammunition, MOC was forced to relinquish control over the post to an "old boy" from the Finance Ministry (Zakai tenbō shuzai gurupu 1978, 61–63).

Another aspect of this type of *amakudari* is called "spinning washtub personnel," which captures the fate of the many ex-bureaucrats for whom reemployment is not a once-in-a-lifetime proposition; in extreme cases, descent from heaven occurs five or more times. Those former bureaucrats who travel from one reemployment post to another are known as "migratory birds" (Jin et al. 1981, 199–200). In the lore of the Ministry of Construction, "Migratory Bird Number One" was Housing Bureau Director Mihashi Shin'ichi, who retired in 1968 and peregrinated through six posts in five separate public corporations.

What distinguishes side-slip *amakudari* from the other forms is its highly institutionalized nature. In fact, side-slipping *amakudari* is so structured and "hereditary" that it is possible to predict with a high degree of accuracy the active bureaucrat who is most likely to descend into a given post. Ministries and agencies jealously protect the posts perceived as their own, even as they constantly seek to "colonize" new territories.

Descending into Elective Politics

Within MOC, an old saying holds that "those who have no place to go [after retirement] become MPs," and indeed MOC is well represented in the Diet. In particular, the Diet's Upper House "reemploys" many former high-level officials of the River Bureau, who have relatively few *amakudari* landing spots in private or public corporations. Like other ministries, MOC engages in the practice of "gilded promotion," whereby junior officials with designs on elective political careers are promoted ahead of their cohort group. In many cases, officials occupy the gilded post only briefly, generally a matter of months or even weeks, before retiring from government service (*Asahi shinbun*, 21 Oct. 1993). These gilded promotions enable the aspiring legislators to impress voters and industry groups by citing the high-status position at which they retired.

Among former MOC officials who choose a second life in the parliamentary realm, technicians far outnumber generalists. For in retirement the technical officials are able to convert their years of contact with local contractors into political backing and campaign contributions from the construction industry. And the former technicans are attractive candidates for elective office owing to the clout they wield at their former agency.

Notably, all of the MOC officials who descended into second careers in elective politics between 1950 and the summer of 1993 joined the LDP or one of its conservative forerunners. (During the tumultuous 1993 general elections, four "old boys" joined Ozawa Ichirō's Shinsei Party, and another was elected under the banner of the Kōmeitō.) Over two-thirds of the MOC retirees chose to join the LDP faction headed by former Prime Minister Tanaka and later led by "construction tribalists" Takeshita Noboru and Kanemaru Shin.[11]

MOC's might in national elective politics was first demonstrated in 1950, when former Vice-Minister Iwasawa successfully campaigned for a seat in the Upper House. Following his lead, MOC's next four vice-ministers also opted to descend into the political world. This string of victories culminated in the election of Yoneda Masafumi as the top vote-getter for the Upper House election in 1959. The parliamentary success of retired MOC officials is easy to explain: MOC's control over the country's massive public works budget, as well as the ministry's "godfather" status vis-à-vis the country's half a million construction companies and more than six million workers, naturally attracts campaign contributions and votes.

Informally, MOC supports the campaigns of its former upper-level officials with an organizational weapon known as the Construction Machine (*kensetsu mashiin*). The Construction Machine was especially efficacious in securing seats for candidates running under the national constituency system in the Upper House prior to the reforms of the early 1980s. Among the informal rules of the game was a two-term limit that ensured a place for a new MOC candidate every six years (Jin et al. 1981, 188–89; Minami 1981, 141–46). Coordination of the system fell to MOC's deputy vice-minister for administration, who carefully divided up the expansive field of construction industry votes by segmenting the country into eastern and western blocs. Each bloc was then designated to favor one or the other of the MOC candidates.[12] The task of making sure that local construction interests voted for the desired candidate fell upon the shoulders of the directors of the regional construction bureaus and the heads of MOC's numerous work offices. It is rumored that the promotional future of these two groups of officials depended on their ability to target the construction vote for the designated candidate, and that these officials issued veiled threats of withholding public works funding when visiting local districts in which opposition party candidates were believed to wield substantial support among construction contractors (Jin et al. 1981, 201).

MOC is also said to indirectly influence elections in the localities by way of its power over the "on loan" appointments of midcareer officials to serve as heads of the civil engineering departments in prefectural and some municipal governments (van Wolferen 1989, 117). The presumption here is that these on-loan officials influence the voting behavior of members of the myriad of local-level construction industry associations. In addition, some have argued that public construction spending increases in the prefectures represented by former MOC officials. A case in point is the sudden jump in public construction appropriations that accompanied the election of Imai Isamu, a former director of the Shikoku Regional Construction Bureau, to a Lower House seat representing the Ehime Third District. From a ranking of forty-second among Japan's forty-six prefectures (excluding Okinawa) in 1972, Ehime Prefecture moved steadily upward in the national rankings to the twentieth slot in 1977. A similar blessing is alleged to have been bestowed upon Ōita Prefecture in 1979, following the election of former Kyūshū Bureau Chief Tawara Takashi to a Lower House seat representing the prefecture's Second District.

Some MOC officials pursue elective careers in local, rather than national, politics. In autumn 1993, for instance, twelve descended angels from MOC or the National Land Agency were serving as prefectural governors or mayors of major cities. Among them, the governor of Gifu Prefecture was a former director of the City Bureau, while the mayor of Yokohama was a retired vice-minister. MOC was hardly alone among government agencies in dispatching ex-officials into second careers in local elective politics. In October 1993 nearly 60 percent of all prefectural governors were either ex-government bureaucrats or former officials of government entities. Of course, this total would have included an additional name, that of Takeuchi Fujio, a former director of MOC's City Bureau, had he not been forced to resign as governor of Ibaraki Prefecture in the midst of the *zenekon* scandal. The ensuing investigations revealed the widely underestimated power of local authorities to exercise the "voice of heaven" in the designation of firms to bid for public works contracts. Indeed, it was said that Governor Takeuchi's power was "rather close to that of a king" (*Asahi shinbun,* 21 Oct. 1993).

"Construction Friction"

When the U.S. government began to demand changes in Japan's government procurement system, the media in Japan labeled the imbroglio "construction friction." But "friction" would seem to be an understatement. That the Japanese government was willing to suffer economic sanctions in order to protect its procurement system illustrates the power of the MOC bureaucracy and its allies in the Japanese business world and the parliamentary realm. In resisting the U.S. ultimatum, the government bureaucrats involved in Japan's public works administration demonstrated that they were willing to fight to protect their interests, no matter what the cost to the national economy. As Sahashi Shigeru, a former vice-minister at MITI, once remarked, "bureaucrats are officials of the various ministries before they are the servants of the nation" (in Johnson 1975, 7). Had he pressed this logic a bit further, however, he might have added that Japan's bureaucrats are rational, self-interested individuals before they are officials of the various ministries.

Most imperiled of all bureaucratic interests in the bilateral construction friction were the interests of the engineers and technical specialists in MOC and other contracting agencies. As Maureen Smith, a U.S. Commerce Department official, pointed out:

We recognize the fact that the commissioning entities in Japan have very substantial design staffs. This means that large elements of the design work would not be open to bidding of any kind, and that it basically would be done in-house. Now the logical extension of this concept is that American or foreign companies can be and often are excluded from the design stage, or, if you will, "designed out."

(Brooks 1990, 13–14)

Analysts in Japan understood the message perfectly: "The demands of the U.S. side to open the construction market amount to an ultimatum for the Japanese government to surrender its monopoly over the performance of engineering services in favor of utilizing America's own massive engineering construction contractors" (K. Maeda 1990, 136).

As the case of the public works bureaucrats illustrates, important implications flow from the goal-oriented behavior of Japanese government bureaucrats. For example, the sectionalism that pervades Japan's bureaucracy derives more from officials' quest for security via budget aggradizement and expansion of administrative turf than from elements of the national culture, though the latter are emphasized in much of the literature. The pursuit of security is also reflected in the informal ties and policy networks binding bureaucrats, private-sector clients, and parliamentarians into a symbiotic embrace. In this regard, diverse organizations—such as the numerous deliberative councils (e.g., *shingikai, kondankai*) and government-sponsored think tanks (e.g., the Research Institute on Construction and the Economy)— have been established to facilitate public-private cooperation and consultation. Similarly, the various forms of "root-binding" (*nemawashi*) reinforce informal ties between bureaucrats and their patrons in the parliamentary world, particularly members of the relevant "policy tribes."

As we have seen, the patterned behavior of Japanese government bureaucrats is shaped by the civil service employment system, particularly the practice of early retirement whereby former officials are reemployed in the private sector, public corporations, and in elective politics. While the system facilitates interaction between the government and civil society, it also provides strong incentives for particularistic, and sometimes corrupt, behavior on the part of supposedly neutral government officials. Such activities include strategic leaks of information concerning the confidential government ceiling price for public works projects. (It is impossible to believe that the systematic ability of firms employing ex-bureaucrats to submit bids identical to or within a fraction of a percentage point of the ceiling price is coincidental.)

In the final analysis, therefore, the intransigence of the government bureaucrats toward U.S. pressure to modify the government procurement system for public works was rooted in a pervasive sense of crisis. Changes of the sort demanded by the United States threatened to erode the administrative turf and promotional possibilities of the public works bureaucrats. Particularly threatened were the technicians in the contracting agencies, especially MOC, who perceived the U.S. assault as a challenge to their virtual monopoly over basic design services. Moreover, any change in the status quo threatened to undermine the reemployment system, which is essentially an informal extension of the career ladder for Japan's government officials.

Yet if the conflict over bidding for projects at Kansai Airport upset the bureaucrats, it also cast a shadow of gloom over elected politicians, particularly those in the long-preeminent LDP, many of whom believed that their political careers depended on claiming credit for the preferential allocation of structural policy benefits. And so we now turn to the plight of the career politicians.

Three

The Career Politician and the
Phantom Party's Invisible Feet

In early January 1988, on the eve of his first visit to the United States as prime minister, Takeshita Noboru faced a pair of thorny bilateral trade disputes, both of which were deeply enmeshed in domestic politics. One altercation, the incessant stream of American demands that Japan further open its agricultural market, had intensified in late December, when the Takeshita government rejected a dispute panel's ruling that Japan's import quotas on certain food categories violated the General Agreement on Tariffs and Trade. Anxious about the U.S.-Japan negotiations on beef and the looming specter of American demands to liberalize Japan's protected rice market, Takeshita wanted to defuse the controversy as expeditiously as possible.

The second dispute, of course, was the ongoing battle over Japan's system of public works tendering and government procurement. Both houses of the U.S. Congress had passed sweeping resolutions and the U.S. Trade Representative had announced a ban on Japanese firms' participation in federally funded public works construction. Hoping to avoid a disastrous maiden mission to Washington and to prove his ability to fill the shoes of his predecessor, former Prime Minister Nakasone, Takeshita wanted to at least temporarily resolve these disputes.

The construction issue provided the opportunity for Takeshita to demonstrate the extent to which his reputed sway in domestic political circles could produce international diplomatic benefits. As a former minister of construction and leading figure in the LDP's "construction tribe," Takeshita had at his disposal a considerable store of latent capital in this policy arena. He realized, however, that even with his extensive network of personal connections which extended to the uppermost echelons of the construction industry and the government bureaucracy, he would still meet obstinate resistance if he pressed for compliance with the U.S. demand to modify the bidding system. Moreover, such resistance would not be confined to the construction industry and the public works bureaucracy. As a Japanese journalist observed, "An even more formidable obstacle in the [way of] rule changes would be politicians in his own Liberal Democratic Party, who covet hefty pork barrels and want to protect the [massive] market" (S. Itō 1988). Thus in attempting to resolve the dispute, Takeshita stood to encounter some of the stiffest opposition from members of his own party, whose political careers depended on support from the construction industry.

Career politicians were not a new species in Japan's parliamentary ecosystem; they had been crossing the red carpet of the National Parliament Building since prewar times. But since the 1970s career politicians had entered national elective politics in greater numbers and had assumed upper-leadership positions in larger proportions than ever before. By the late 1980s a generation of ambitious officeholders whose chief concern was winning the next election had come to dominate the LDP. And many of these career politicians depended on the construction industry for campaign contributions and a stable base of voter support.

Campaign contributions and voter support are the prerequisites for any political career, but in postwar Japan there have been some unusual twists. For one, the cost of pursuing a political career in Japan is exorbitantly high, more so than in most advanced democratic polities, and the financial burden has grown more onerous over time. Second, the LDP, though the predominant party for almost four decades, never had more than a sparse and fluctuating corps of registered party activists. Between 1975 and 1988, for example, the LDP's rank-and-file membership fluctuated wildly, from half a million to nearly six million. Moreover, intraparty rivalry was fierce, with the chief electoral rival of an LDP candidate often being another LDP candidate. One LDP legislator has likened this rivalry to warfare: "Look at the men from the same districts. They're terrible. They can't even talk pleasantly to each other in the Diet. That's because there is usually a serious war between them" (in Thayer 1969, 119).

Despite the high cost of running for office and the low level of grassroots support, the LDP managed to maintain its hegemony because its candidates were able to pull together personal support networks. A pillar of most of these networks was the construction industry, the employer of nearly one-tenth of the country's workforce and a massive reservoir of campaign contributions. It was the construction industry, in other words, along with the farmers and self-employed shopkeepers, that forged ties between candidates and constituents. It was competition for construction industry support that fueled the intraparty rivalries. And it was loyalty to the construction industry that guaranteed LDP opposition to any efforts to modify the public works procurement process.

The Phantom Party's Head

From its founding in 1955 until its stunning fall from grace in 1993, the Liberal Democratic Party occupied the commanding position in Japan's parliamentary arena. In the twelve general elections held between 1958 and 1990, LDP candidates won over 45 percent of the popular vote and more than 55 percent of the seats in the Lower House. (In comparison, in the eleven elections for the Chamber of Deputies held between 1946 and 1987, Italy's long-dominant Christian Democratic Party managed to secure only 39 percent of the popular vote and 42 percent of the seats.)[1] Furthermore, between 1955 and 1993 LDP MPs filled nearly every cabinet post, and all fifteen prime ministers during the period came from the ranks of its party leaders. Unlike single-party dominant regimes in Sweden, Israel, West Germany, and Italy, the LDP never shared power in a coalition, aside from a brief, incestuous liaison with the New Liberal Club, an offshoot party that subsequently disbanded and rejoined the parent organization. The thirty-eight years of LDP rule represents the longest uninterrupted period of conservative dominance in a contemporary democracy, making Japan the world's preeminent example of a "predominant party system" (Sartori 1976, 192–201).

However, despite its protracted hegemonic rule, the LDP had the frailest of grassroots support bases. In the words of a party worker in Hiroshima: "The Liberal Democratic Party is a ghost. It has no feet" (in Thayer 1969, 85). Compared to mass-based domestic rivals such as the Kōmeitō and the Japan Communist Party (JCP), the LDP has had a relatively weak local-level organization and relatively few registered party loyalists. From its inception the LDP has been a parliamentarians' party, with a small, elite membership of elected representatives at the helm of virtually all party activities and decision-making. This group constitutes the visible head of this "phantom party" but—in keeping with the traditional Japanese image of ghosts—the party lacks "feet," having only a modest grassroots membership and a loosely structured contingent of affiliated local politicians.

The MPs who have played such a central role in the LDP are by and large career politicians, people for whom politics is a permanent vocation rather than a temporary avocation. Over the course of the twentieth century, legislatures worldwide have evolved from part-time amateur bodies into full-time professional bodies, and a host of advanced industrialized democracies, including Britain, Italy, Sweden, Germany, New Zealand, and the United States, have witnessed the advent of the career politician.[2] This phenomenon corresponds with Weber's prophecy that the "professional politician" would emerge as the central figure of modern democratic politics (Gerth and Mills 1958, 77–128). In Japan, as in other advanced industrialized polities, politics has become, more than in the past, a job for people who prefer it to any other line of work (Ehrenhalt 1991, 20).

The rise of the career politician as the leading actor on Japan's legislative stage has been accompanied by the increased salience of constituency service.[3] There is the presumption that constituents tend to support candidates who appear to be responsive to their interests. If this assumption is true, one would expect to find the gradual ascendancy of legislators whose background characteristics would render them more likely to adopt constituency-oriented "home styles" (Fenno 1978). For example, all other things being equal, voters would tend to prefer an established local politician to an ex-government official who had no record of sensitivity to district-level interests.

In Japan the influx of career politicians into the legislative arena attests to the role of political institutions in determining the criteria of electoral success. For instance, as discussed later on, a revision of the campaign finance law accelerated the trend toward ever-increasing numbers of "hereditary" politicians in the ranks of Japan's conservative legislative elite.[4] Just as political institutions shape political systems, so too political careers shape political institutions (Hibbing 1991, 405).

The Rise of the Career Politician

Throughout the period of LDP dominance, the vast majority of the party's legislators entered national elective politics via two broad occupational routes. First, as we saw in the previous chapter, former high-level government officials descended into the parliamentary arena from positions in the central state bureaucracy. Second, local elected politicians have ascended to the national parliamentary arena after building supportive coalitions at the grassroots level or after serving apprenticeships as staff assistants for a member of parliament. Until the 1970s, the descending angels played a disproportionately visible role in party affairs, especially in the uppermost leadership stratum. However, after the 1970s the numbers of former bureaucrats among LDP backbenchers as well as party leaders steadily decreased, and the grassroots politicians became progressively more dominant. This shift seems to have been the product of a broader demand for candidates able to provide a greater range of constituency services. Experienced in local elective politics and sensitive to the needs and interests of constituents within the district, grassroots politicians were the logical candidates to satisfy the electorate's desires.

One way to trace the increase in career politicians is to look at the trends in the age at which legislators enter national elective politics and the age at which they assume positions of party leadership, since candidates who consider politics as a primary career will tend to enter national elective politics at an earlier age and remain longer than their amateur predecessors. Between 1955 and 1992 successive classes of LDP backbenchers have been younger, even as there has been a steady gerontrification among party leaders, LDP legislators, and Lower House MPs as a whole. During this period the mean age of conservative backbenchers has fallen from 50 to 46, while party leaders are four to six years older on average than their predecessors. In other words, while LDP backbenchers are entering the political ring at a younger age, they need to labor longer in order to ascend to the coveted positions of formal legislative influence.

Longitudinal trends in the age at which legislators who rose to the level of cabinet ministers were first elected to the Lower House also illustrate the rise of career politicians in Japan. Between 1955 and 1971 approximately half of all cabinet appointees were older than 45 when first elected to the national parliament. But between 1972 and 1976 about 70 percent of cabinet appointees were younger than 45 when first elected, and since then this figure has not dropped below 60 percent.

It is also revealing to look at the age of LDP backbenchers in each of the pre-Diet occupational routes (descending from the ministries or ascending from local politics). The mean age of descending angels upon entering the Diet dropped from 54.5 in 1958 to 46.8 in 1990. Moreover, the number of high-ranking ex-officials among the LDP backbenchers has declined since the early 1960s (see Figure 2). Relative to the average LDP backbencher, former local politicians tend to be older, while ex-staffers tend to be younger. Lacking both the ties to powerful organized interests that ex-bureaucrats often wield, as well as the benefits of "inheriting" a proven personal campaign machine, the majority of local politicians have to invest more time in constructing personal bases of local electoral support. In contrast, since a substantial share of former staffers are the offspring or close relatives of MPs, they tend to make their bid for a place in the national parliamentary ring at an earlier age than either the local politicians or the ex-officials.

The average tenure of LDP legislators in national elective politics has also been increasing. For example, LDP legislators who left the Lower House between 1958 and 1963 had served on average nearly 15 years, while those who left between 1983 and 1990 had served on average nearly 30 years. The number of terms legislators serve before securing a coveted position as cabinet minister or one of the top posts in the LDP's leadership has also climbed, from an average in 1956 of over 5 terms, to nearly 10 terms in 1976. The institutionalization of

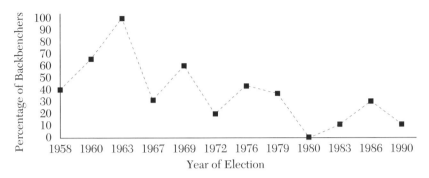

Figure 2. High-Ranking Ex-Officials Among LDP Backbenchers, 1958–1990

SOURCES. Based on data from various years of *Kokkai benran; Jinji kōshinroku;* and *Asahi senkyō taikan.*

the LDP's promotional ladder is also exemplified by the sharp decline in the number of first-term cabinet appointees who had served fewer than four electoral terms. Between 1965 and 1993 only two Lower House members were "singled out" (*batteki*), as compared with nineteen in the 1950s (Satō and Matsuzaki 1986, 39–47).

The influx of "hereditary politicians" is another indication of the rise of the career politician. In the 1990 elections, 38 percent of all LDP backbenchers and 50 percent of all LDP leaders were hereditary politicians.[5] Over time, a Lower House seat has come to be viewed as a family heirloom, the supportive constituency as a family-owned business, and control of each as something that an incumbent can transfer to a designated successor. Of course, members of political families have always benefited from opportunities to meet influential people and glimpse the inner workings of government. Should they choose to seek office, they will have broader name recognition than candidates from less distinguished families. In Japan, more importantly, these scions inherit an organized and tested campaign machine. First, the key supporters and officials of these personal campaign organizations tend to be more willing to shift their allegiance to an incumbent's designated heir rather than to an outsider. These insiders also know that the hereditary politician will inherit fully formed pipelines of political money (Igarashi 1986, 112). This advantage is all the more significant because a large share of campaign contributions are drawn from business sources headquartered in Tokyo and other metropolitan areas, which may be far from the home district. The bequest system serves both sides: campaign contributors enjoy a longer time horizon to reap benefits from their political investments, and hereditary politicians can take advantage of the political capital accrued by their forebears.

To the extent that more LDP MPs have come to consider politics as a primary career, they must focus on enhancing the security of their incumbency. The principal activities to this end are constituency service, credit-claiming, and distributive pork, particularly public works projects that can be strategically targeted. In order to build reliable bases of grassroots support and causeways for channeling the enormous flows of political funds needed to sustain a successful political career, many LDP MPs, as the *zenekon* scandal revealed, bartered their legislative influence.

The Invisible Feet of the Phantom Party

To win election and reelection, LDP candidates needed loyal constituents in their districts and continuous flows of campaign funds. Since the party itself did not supply adequate amounts of either, candidates had to develop personal support networks. By promising to supply particularistic constituency services, a candidate could attract constituencies that would be loyal to the specific candidate rather than to the party. This phenomenon, termed the "personal vote" (Cain et al. 1987), is not unique to Japan. As one U.S. Congressman observed, "If we depended on the party to get elected, none of us would be here [in Congress] today" (in Mayhew 1974, 26–27). Examples of the Japanese construction industry's role in the scheme illustrates the nature of this mutually beneficial relationship during the era of LDP legislative hegemony.

Kōenkai

A *kojin kōenkai* (or *kōenkai*) is a candidate's personal support organization. While not unknown in prewar Japan, *kōenkai* in their present form did not become widespread until the postwar period.[6] In the early 1990s one Japanese voter in every seven had an affiliation with a candidate's *kōenkai* (Watanuki 1991, 70–71). An association of supporters outside the formal party organization, the *kōenkai* is "a mechanism through which a number of benefits . . . are distributed to members in exchange for support for the candidate at election time" (Watanuki 1967, 67). In essence, a *kōenkai* is an umbrella organization under which many smaller support groups, managed by local politicians, link the candidate with constituents at the grassroots level. There are two basic types of *kōenkai:* those that organize the vote and those that act as channels for political contributions.

Kōenkai come in various sizes and are not unique to LDP candidates. Perhaps the largest *kōenkai* of all time is the "Bokuyūkai," which boasted 150,000 members, of Ōno Banboku, a powerbroker in the early days of the LDP. More modest in size, though not in exposure, is former Prime Minister Tanaka's "Etsuzankai," which during its heyday consisted of 313 local chapters and 95,000 members (Fukuoka 1985, 25). The *kōenkai* of a veteran Lower House MP from Kyūshū was more typical in size, embracing some 20,000 members, only a quarter of whom were registered party members. When asked why so few of his supporters were formally affiliated with the party, the MP responded that if the rest of them were to become formal party affiliates, it would cost him ¥60 million a year in membership fees (pers. interview). Apparently, then, at least in some districts, *kōenkai* members are not expected to pay their own party dues.

Kanemaru Shin, the one-time "don of all dons" in the public works arena, developed a *kōenkai* that had eighty-nine branches dispersed throughout eight regional blocks. The vote-gathering "Kushinkai" claimed the allegiance of over three-quarters of the municipal mayors and six of the prefecture's thirty assemblymen. It is said that long-time Governor Mochizuki Kōmei, had close ties to the kingmaker—ties that allegedly paid huge dividends in the form of public works projects to construction contractors, who in turn reciprocated by funneling political funds to the governor. As the Sagawa scandal revealed, construction firms channeled large flows of money into the "Kenshinkai," Kanemaru's local fundraising organ. For example, many of the more than six hundred construction firms affiliated with the Yamanashi Prefectural Contractors' Association routinely contributed to the Kenshinkai. The expectation was that local contractors would "donate" as much as 5 to 10 percent of the total amount of a public works contract to Kanemaru in gratitude for his political brokerage.[7]

One function of a *kōenkai* is to act as a transmission belt for communicating the needs and interests of its members to the candidate. As a Lower House representative commented, interaction with *kōenkai* members permits politicians to monitor public opinion continuously.[8] Such clientelism is not unique to Japan. Similar observations abound in the literature on Italian politics under the Christian Democrats, where clientelism was said to be "an efficient and effective way through which the political allegiances, preferences, and demands of citizens are brought to weigh on public policies" (La Palombara 1987, 59). More importantly from a candidate's point of view, such organizations mobilize voter turnout and provide pipelines of political money. Perhaps the paradigmatic illustration is Tanaka's Etsuzankai, with its vote-gathering apparatus in the Niigata Third District and a nationwide fundraising network (Matoba 1986, 163). Former Prime Minister Takeshita, a Tanaka protégé, is said to have controlled a network of 10,000 fundraising *kōenkai*, each of which extracted ¥10,000 in monthly membership dues. A typical Tokyo-based fundraising *kōenkai* of a typical LDP candidate collects between ¥10,000 and ¥50,000 in monthly dues from each corporate member (Fukui and Fukai 1992, 6–7).

In return for these monthly contributions, *kōenkai* constituents expect their representatives to intercede on their behalf in matters such as securing jobs, arranging marriages, mediating with government agencies, securing government subsidies, and a host of other personal affairs; how the representative votes on matters of national interest are of little concern. One need not spend a great deal of time in a *kōenkai* office to see just how much time and effort candidates and their staff devote to catering to constituents' personal needs: "It is something analogous to caring parents giving sweets to their children" (Kyōgoku 1987, 228). In particular, claiming credit for the preferential allocation of public works projects is an effective means for parliamentarians in Tokyo to bond with local political elites and constituents. The *kōenkai* newsletter gives each candidate an opportunity to claim credit for building cultural halls and schools, and channeling subsidies and other policy benefits into the district.[9]

The Pillars of Influence

In the 1990 general elections there were 130 Lower House districts. The largest prefectures, Tokyo and Osaka, had 11 and 9 districts, respectively, while the 9 smallest prefectures had a single district each. All but the smallest district (Amami Islands) elected a multimember delegation. The number of votes needed to win election ranged from 44,154 (Tokyo Eighth District) to 147,112 (Fukuoka First District), with the average being 80,000.

Within an electoral district, each candidate has a circle of those citizens and organized groups whose support is expected at election time. This constituency, however, cannot be taken for granted, lest they be stolen away by a rival. For example, in order to ensure its hegemony, the LDP would run multiple candidates in virtually every electoral district. In the 1990 general elections the LDP made multiple endorsements in over 90 percent of the Lower House races. In addition, a large number of conservative candidates ran as independents. For most LDP candidates, then, the strongest rival was another LDP candidate or a conservative independent.

As we have seen, the *kōenkai* work to solidify the candidates' "hard" constituency. Here, local politicians play a key role, and the *kōenkai* of a typical LDP MP is estimated to hold the loyalty of five or six prefectural assembly members, three to fifteen municipal council members, and ten to twenty local influentials. At its zenith, for example, Tanaka's Etsuzankai included 13 of the 20 prefectural assemblymen, 26 of the 33 municipal mayors, and nearly half of the 756 municipal assemblymen representing precincts in the Niigata Third District (Fukuoka 1985, 28). The *kōenkai* of Fukaya Takashi, a conservative MP representing the Tokyo Eighth District, claimed to have the support of a ward mayor, 22 ward assembly members, and 2 members of the metropolitan assembly (Fukui and Fukai 1992, 7).

Frequently, flows of questionable money bolster the ties that bind local elites to a particular candidate. For example, Yamaguchi Takehira, an influential member of the prefectural assembly and head of the LDP's Ibaraki Prefectural Federation, reportedly received payments of ¥20 million twice annually for his services to Governor Takeuchi's political machine. (A portion of the funds were said to come from a cache stored in a cardboard box in Takeuchi's official residence.) Takeuchi, it is assumed, expected that Yamaguchi would use the money to grease the appropriate wheels and facilitate passage of desired bills by the prefectural assembly. Yamaguchi also served as an intermediary between the governor and the construction contractors (*Asahi shinbun*, 29 Nov. 1993).

In another case, one of the key supporters of Miyagi Governor Honma Shuntarō was Moriya Mitsuo, the owner of a wood products company who was known as the "political merchant of Miyagi." Prior to the gubernatorial election in February 1993, Moriya—an official of the LDP's prefectural federation—allegedly helped to raise over ¥1 billion from construction contractors for Honma's campaign fund. Ultimately, Moriya was arrested for his role as middleman in an illegal contribution of ¥20 million to Governor Honma from Taisei Corporation, which hoped to win contracts for the construction of a ¥61-billion cancer treatment center and a ¥102-billion sports facility in Miyagi Prefecture (*Asahi shinbun*, 28 Sept., 30 Sept., 5 Oct. 1993).

Local construction contractors are frequently active in the *kōenkai* of LDP candidates, supplying office space, campaign vehicles, workers to answer telephones, and, of course, vast sums of money. For example, Kajima Corporation reportedly "donated" nine employees as administrative staffers to the former director of the Economic Planning Agency, Hiraizumi Wataru, at a cost to Kajima reportedly in excess of ¥50 million in annual salaries for the on-loan staffers (*Asahi shinbun*, 30 Oct. 1993). Contractors and groups organized within construction industry associations also provide campaign support for descended angels from MOC. In May 1991, for example, Ozawa Ichirō and Kanemaru Shin reportedly arranged a meeting involving executives of major construction companies on behalf of former MOC bureaucrat-turned-legislator Inoue Takashi. The executives understood that the purpose of the meeting was to solicit their assistance in enlisting new party members and paying these new members' ¥4,000 annual dues. The firms agreed to assist in enlisting 20,000 new members and cooperate in paying the ¥80 million in membership fees (*Asahi shinbun*, 9 Sept. 1993). These new members are known as *kisetsu tōin* (seasonal members) or *niwaka tōin* (sudden members) because they are rounded up only at election time.

Candidates eager to expand their *kōenkai* actively court general contractors who have close ties to multiple levels of subcontractors. In return for their support, these contractors expect preferential treatment and political brokerage in the awarding of public works contracts. In Yamanashi during the 1980s, for example, there was said to be a direct correlation between a construction firm's cash and non-cash campaign contributions to the victor in the gubernatorial campaign and that firm's subsequent share of prefectural public works contracts (Yonemoto 1987, 226–28, 230).

Another example: Some sixty construction firms in Akita Prefecture divided themselves into four separate *kōenkai*, one for each LDP MP representing a district in the prefecture. Among other things, the companies supplied office staff and workers to hang campaign posters (*Asahi shinbun*, 30 Sept. 1993).[10]

The innermost circle of a candidate's machine consists of relatives and trusted friends, who can be counted on for unconditional support. One senior LDP legislator traced his "private franchise" to a group of former classmates from a prestigious local high school (pers. interview). On occasion, the insiders overstep the bounds of legality. In his biography, one-time public works doyen Amano Kōsei (1986) recalls standing with tears in his eyes outside the jail where his wife was detained on charges of violating elections laws on his behalf. During the *zenekon* scandal the wife of the governor of Ibaraki reportedly accepted a melon box containing ¥5 million in cash from Hazama Corporation and then, when questioned by investigators, steadfastly denied any recollection of the incident (*Asahi shinbun*, 6 Aug. 1993). During the 1970s Fukushima public works scandal, a mayor's spouse and confidants dutifully stuffed cash into envelopes to be used to buy the electoral support of local influentials (Yoshida 1984).

Given the construction industry's nationwide reach and political clout, it is not surprising that ties to the industry figure prominently in the innermost circles of many LDP candidates. Indeed, a number of LDP politicians headed up construction firms prior to entering national elective politics. For instance, Kumagai Tasaburō, former Upper House councilor and one-time director general of the Science and Technology Agency, held the posts of president and chairman of the internationally active Kumagai Gumi. Matrimonial ties have also linked many LDP politicians to the construction industry. Aside from founding his own construction firm, Tanaka Kakuei married the daughter of the head of Sakamoto Gumi, a major general contractor; Ozawa Ichirō and the younger brother of Takeshita Noboru each wed daughters of Fukuda Tadashi, chairman of Fukuda Corporation, the largest general contractor in Niigata Prefecture; one of Takeshita's daughters married the son of public works powerbroker Kanemaru Shin, while Takeshita's other daughter married a scion of Takenaka Corporation, one of Japan's five largest construction companies.

Yet perhaps the case of Upper House member Shimojō Shin'ichirō best exemplifies the bonds that may form between the construction industry and the inner circles of LDP candidates. To begin with, Shimojō hails from a political family: his grandfather held a seat in the prewar House of Peers, and his politician father once served as education minister. He also married into a political family, that of Ishikawa Rokurō, a former Transportation Ministry official, ex-president and chairman of Kajima Corporation, and one-time head of the powerful Federation of Economic Organizations (Keidanren). Ishikawa, moreover, was the son-in-law of the legendary Kajima Morinosuke (former head of Kajima Corporation, three-term Upper House councilor, and one-time director general of the Hokkaidō Development Agency). Kajima's other son-in-laws were MP Hiraizumi Wataru (which helps to explain the generous donation of nine all-expenses-paid staffers from Kajima) and Asami Takeo, a former MITI official and brother of a former chairman of Keidanren. Other past and present influentials on the Kajima family tree include the son-in-law of former Prime Minister Nakasone. For Shimojō, matrimonial ties to the Kajima clan—nicknamed "Kajima of Politics" (*Seiji no Kajima*)—created an instant personal constituency with links to the highest levels of the country's political, government, and corporate worlds.

A Costly Career

Maintaining one or more *kōenkai* is essential for political success but is also very expensive. Some first-term MPs assume their seats bearing over a million dollars in debt (Fukui and Fukai 1992, 5–6). A candidate's major expenses include salaries for administrative assistants and clerical staff, gifts for constituents on ceremonial occasions, and the costs of mailing and office supplies. In addition, a candidate is expected to pay for festive gatherings, outings to resorts, and a host of other activities involving *kōenkai* members (Curtis 1971, 132). A typical backbencher spends about ¥120 million a year, and as much as eight times that amount in an election year.[11]

Candidates know that public financing provides some assistance, and the LDP's Treasury Bureau, called the "kitchen," doles out an additional increment. Faction bosses or senior members of the faction also supply funds. But these three sources combined account for less than a third of the cost of a political career.[12] Thus candidates must rely on their own wits and fundraising skills. Clearly, there is a considerable incentive to barter political influence, in the form of constituency servcies, for financial support from corporate donors.

For many candidates, the construction industry represents a lucrative and convenient source of such support. Of the 480 legislators responding to a newspaper survey taken in October 1993, almost half (223) admitted to accepting political contributions from construction firms (*Asahi shinbun*, 31 Oct. 1993). However, legally reported political donations pale in comparison to the construction industry's "shady" contributions. It is estimated that from the mid-1980s until 1992, when the Sagawa scandal surfaced, at least ¥10 billion a year in illegal political contributions from major general contractors found its way to the personal vault of former LDP Vice-President Kanemaru (ibid., 10 Sept. 1993). In the *zenekon* scandal, the mayor of Sanwa Town was accused of receiving ¥14 million in bribes in return for preferential intervention in the awarding of public works projects. Meanwhile, police arrested Miyagi Governor Honma Shuntarō, Ibaraki Governor Takeuchi, and Sendai Mayor Ishii on charges of taking illegal contributions of ¥20 million, ¥85 million, and ¥130 million, respectively (ibid., 28 Oct. 1993).

The situation is different in the case of senior party leaders. Party leaders tend to be less preoccupied with the electoral motive, and their long incumbency affords them access to expansive networks of government and corporate contacts. As a legislator ascends the LDP's seniority ladder, the number of pipelines to financial backers in the corporate world grow more numerous, and eventually these pipelines supply far more money than needed to cover the leader's political ex-

penses. At that time, an aspiring party leader begins to distribute
money to junior members of the faction in hopes of building a personal power base within the faction and the party. An oft-mentioned
aspect of former Prime Minister Tanaka's legendary political perspi-
cuity is the money distribution pyramid he fashioned within his faction. Rather than handing out all the money himself (and increasing
the likelihood of an investigation), Tanaka directed certain of his corporate backers to funnel funds to specific senior members of the faction, who were then expected to distribute money to the faction's
rank-and-file. Nakasone put a similar system into operation in his
faction. Junior members of a faction also receive regular installments
from one and, in some cases, two "quasi-bosses" (*jun bosu*), senior
politicians who have aspirations of someday taking over the faction
(pers. interview). A successful takeover was engineered by *jun bosu*
Watanabe Michio after faction leader Nakasone stepped down in the
midst of the Recruit scandal.

The Role of Electoral Institutions

The cost of pursuing a career in Japanese electoral politics has dramatically outpaced both inflation and increases in the size of the electorate over the years. In the early 1960s the average legislator spent
¥5 million a year; by the late 1970s the average soared to around ¥100
million; by the late 1980s the figure was ¥120 million (Togawa 1961,
47; Hrebenar 1986, 62–63). A large portion of this surge can be attributed to institutional factors, specifically, the use of an electoral system based upon a single, nontransferable vote within districts that
elect multimember delegations.[13] In the 1990 general elections, 130
"middle-sized" districts elected 512 members of the Lower House,
and all but one district elected between two and six representatives.
Under the multimember plurality formula, each voter casts a single
nontransferable vote (SNTV) for one candidate, regardless of the
number of seats to be filled.

This system is highly unusual—until the enactment of electoral
reforms in early 1994, Japan and Taiwan were the only countries
employing the SNTV formula in national elections (Rigger 1994, 31).
In contrast, most multimember plurality systems allow electors to

cast multiple votes, and candidates are elected in order of their share
of the vote until all seats in the delegation have been filled. Under
Japan's SNTV formula there is no rank ordering of candidates, nor are
there the "rounds" of voting used in elections for Australia's House of
Representatives.

Japan's SNTV formula also differs from proportional representation
multimember voting systems. For example, unlike the preference voting system employed in Italy prior to political reform, voters in Japan
cannot cast a separate party vote. The ballot lists only individual candidates, and the voter selects one. Nor is Japan's voting system comparable to the single, transferable vote formula used in elections for
Ireland's Dail, in which voters rank individual candidates rather than
voting for a party list. Votes for candidates running for the Japanese
Lower House cannot be transferred to other candidates from the
same party in the event that the voter's preferred candidate already
has sufficient votes to win a seat.

Japan's SNTV formula holds significant consequences for candidate
endorsement decisions and strategies for vote allocation among the
multiple candidates from the same political party. As noted earlier,
the LDP, in order to perpetuate its hegemonic position, fielded multiple candidates in virtually every electoral district. Given the paucity
of financial support from party and factional sources and the futility
of stressing policy distinctions among competing conservative candidates, aspiring LDP legislators had no choice but to create a personal
base of support; thus the proliferation of *kōenkai*. The number of
political organizations (*seiji dantai*) registered with the Ministry of
Home Affairs increased nearly 250 percent between 1976 and 1988
(Iwai 1990, 81). But rivalry among LDP candidates in multimember
districts does not in itself account for the boom in *kōenkai*. Rather,
the main impetus was a 1975 revision to the Political Funds Control
Law (PFCL) that imposed contribution limits on individuals, corporations, and political organizations. Annual donations by a citizen or
a corporate entity were limited to ¥10,000 per political party and
¥1 million per political organization or fund maintenance organization
(*shikin kanri dantai*—e.g., the LDP's Peoples' Political Association);
political organizations could contribute no more than ¥1 million to
another political organization. Because there was no limit on the num-

ber of political organizations to which a donor could contribute, candidates and donors could circumvent the spirit of the law through multiple political organizations linked to a single candidate. Some senior LDP legislators have come to oversee networks of as many as three hundred separate personal support organizations.

Another useful loophole in the PFCL concerns fundraising parties: Candidates are not required to report the proceeds of these parties as long as a registered political organization sponsors the event. Political fundraisers, it is worth noting, did not become a conspicuous facet of Japanese political life until after the 1975 revision of the PFCL. It is not unusual for these festive gatherings to require an attendance fee of ¥50,000 or more per participant, and some fundraisers draw more than 30,000 people. There is pressure for corporations to purchase large blocs of tickets to these functions, and even government officials often feel compelled to purchase tickets. Over the course of several years, for example, prefectural bureaucrats in Miyagi Prefecture siphoned enough public money from faked travel vouchers to purchase nearly ¥10 million in tickets to fundraisers organized on behalf of Governor Honma and other local LDP candidates (*Asahi shinbun*, 28 Nov. 1993). In 1988 the Recruit scandal forced the LDP to declare a policy of "self-restraint" with regard to political fundraisers. For several years, fewer fundraising parties were held. By 1991, however, the fundraisers were becoming larger and more frequent.

Beyond all these technically legitimate funding schemes, vast sums of unreported political funds have been delivered into the coffers of LDP candidates. As illuminated by the Recruit scandal, some candidates gained preferential access to preflotation shares of corporate stock, which they sold for a handsome unreported profit. Politicians have also raised money by having paper companies under their control purchase tracts of land in areas about to acquire special zoning designation; when the land values soar, the politician disposes of the property for a sizable profit.

According to a senior executive of a large general contractor, almost all governors accept illegal contributions. With regard to former Miyagi Governor Honma, the official said: "It is pitiable to be arrested for taking [a mere] ¥20 million. Virtually all governors do it. A first-term governor who takes ¥20 million is relatively clean. Some first-termers take in ¥1 billion, and, in the case of four-termers, the take can be as high as ¥5 billion" (K. Matsumoto et al. 1993).

Changing the Rules of the Electoral Game

Japan's current electoral institutions have their roots in the Election Law of 1889, the nation's first attempt at parliamentary democracy. This law created a system of plural voting in small-sized districts, the majority of which elected a single-member delegation.[14] SNTV first arrived in Japan in 1900 with a package of major revisions that also established a secret ballot and districts that elected as few as one representative or as many as thirteen. A driving force behind the reforms of 1900 was the oligarch Yamagata Aritomo, who feared that SNTV in small districts might permit a political party to grasp an absolute majority of parliamentary seats, thus challenging the autonomy of the state bureaucracy in policymaking. The extension of suffrage to all adult males in 1925 ushered in the first incarnation of Japan's unique system of SNTV in middle-sized districts. In 1945, as part of the package of sweeping reforms intended to democratize a defeated Japan, the U.S. Occupation imposed a conditional plural vote system in large districts. When independents and candidates of the Communist Party did better than expected in the 1946 election, the Occupation authorities reluctantly acceded to pressure from conservative parties to restore the SNTV system in middle-sized districts.

The electoral district boundaries created in 1947 survived with only cosmetic revisions for over forty years. During that period, however, the portion of the population residing in rural areas dropped from two-thirds to less than one-third. By the early 1980s the inequality between the most overrepresented and the most underrepresented districts reached levels approaching five-to-one, generating a welter of court cases and appeals.[15] In 1986, in response to a Supreme Court ruling that set the maximum disparity at three-to-one, the parliament passed the "plus eight, minus seven" law. This reform added one seat to each of the eight most underrepresented districts, and took one away from the seven most overrepresented districts. The tinkering sufficed to bring the results of the 1986 general election under the court-mandated maximum disparity, but the 1990 election produced a discrepancy of 3.18-to-1 and set off a new wave of lawsuits.

The single event that pushed the issue of reform high on the national agenda was the Recruit Cosmos scandal, which forced the resignation of Prime Minister Takeshita in April 1989. The magnitude of the scandal and the LDP's disastrous showing in Upper House elections that summer forced the party's leadership to promise an attack on institutionalized political corruption. The viability of both the Kaifu and the Miyazawa administrations was explicitly dependent on the enactment of electoral reform. The Sagawa scandal brought an additional impetus for change as it toppled kingmaker Kanemaru and led to the fracturing of the Takeshita faction in late 1992. Due to intraparty discord, the LDP's four leaders declared on 15 June that the party would not endorse a meaningful reform bill. Three days later, a parliamentary vote of no-confidence in the Miyazawa cabinet was passed as a result of the strategic defection of Ozawa and his followers. The July 1993 general elections left the LDP far short of an absolute majority, and, on 9 August, eight parties combined to form the Hosokawa cabinet, the first non-LDP cabinet since 1955. The coalition government vowed to "smash the union of the legislators, bureaucrats, and industrialists," "grant importance to the interests of consumers," and "enact a political reform bill by year's end." Opinion surveys taken in early September gave the Hosokawa cabinet a 70 percent approval rating, the highest in the postwar era.

The path to the passage of a reform bill, however, remained steep and treacherous. On 18 October, the Lower House passed a reform package sponsored by the Hosokawa cabinet, but the package was defeated in the Upper House, primarily owing to the defection of some Socialist legislators. The following January, when all appeared to be lost, a joint committee, composed of ten members from each house, agreed on a package of reform bills. Most importantly, the agreement called for the creation of a Lower House electoral system based on 300 single-member districts and 200 proportional-representation districts divided into eleven regional blocks. The accord also modified the PFCL to allow candidates to maintain one organization for the purpose of receiving donations of up to ¥500,000 a year for the next five years from corporate and other donors.

Construction Friction
and the Phantom Party

The rise of career politicians, the "footless" character of the LDP as a party, the importance of *kōenkai*, the ballooning cost of a political career, and the SNTV formula—all these factors underlay the strong ties between LDP legislators and the construction industry.

The institutionalization of bartering political favors for campaign contributions in Japan bears a striking resemblance to the system in Italy, particularly in earlier times under the hegemonic hand of the Christian Democrats. As an Italian party leader boasted, "Christian Democracy is the party of government, and as such exercises a clear monopoly of power, of the opportunities for acquiring and exercising it, and, more importantly, of its distribution in Italian society" (La Palombara 1987, 16). While an aide to a veteran LDP legislator asserts, "We have run the country for more than a quarter of a century. When people want a bridge or a road built in their district, they come to us, not the socialists" (*San Francisco Chronicle*, 20 Dec. 1988).

In the Japanese case, as in Italy, the electoral institutions provided incentives for corrupt behavior. Under the SNTV system of electing multimember delegations, a political party seeking to establish and maintain parliamentary hegemony had to run multiple candidates in almost every district. In addition, the campaign finance laws created a powerful incentive for prospective career politicians to fashion intricate networks of personal support organizations and elaborate conduits to channel campaign contributions.

Career politicians also knew that their prospects for reelection depended heavily on their ability to provide supporters with tangible policy benefits. Over time, these MPs, especially those running under the LDP's banner, became more concerned with the politics of particularism and less concerned with ideological issues or national economic priorities. A similar observation has been made regarding members of the U.S. Congress, who have become increasingly attentive to constituency service: "The growth of an activist federal government . . . stimulated a change in the mix of congressional activities. Specifically, a lesser proportion of congressional effort is now going into programmatic activities and a greater proportion into pork-barrel and casework activities" (Fiorina 1977, 46).

As Prime Minister Takeshita prepared to depart for the United States, he knew that any proposal for significant change in the public works procurement process was guaranteed to incur staunch resistance from various elements within the LDP. Nor was this opposition confined to the voracious appetite for pork on the part of the rank-and-file membership of his own party. As we will see, among the fiercest supporters of the status quo were the leaders of the LDP's elaborate organizational apparatus.

Four

Factioneers, Tribalists, and the LDP's Construction Caucus

On 5 January 1988, one week before Prime Minister Takeshita's scheduled departure for the summit meeting with President Reagan, U.S. Trade Representative Clayton Yeutter announced a ban on the participation of Japanese construction firms and their overseas affiliates in federally funded public works. The ban, effective 30 December 1987, cast a shadow over the summit meeting, which ultimately did nothing to ameliorate the mounting bilateral discord. And shortly after USTR Yeutter's announcement, Alaska's Senator Frank Murkowski called for legislation that would ban Japanese firms' participation in America's private-sector construction. Representative Pete Stark of California introduced a bill denying tax depreciation and the use of tax-exempt bonds in projects employing Japanese construction firms. But the Japanese government ministries balked at making new concessions. Former Transport Minister Hashimoto Ryūtarō articulated what many were thinking: "I am against going to the bargaining table with the United States to beg for forgiveness. . . . Japan should not be forced to take action under such intimidation" (*Japan Times*, 13 Jan. 1988).

Meanwhile, a new player had quietly entered the construction fray. At Takeshita's request, Deputy Chief Cabinet Secretary Ozawa Ichirō had secretly begun sounding out personnel at the American Embassy in Tokyo in order to create a framework for future negotiations

(Krauss 1989, 29–30). In March, Ozawa would travel to Washington to seek a settlement.

Ozawa, despite his relative youthfulness and lack of experience in international negotiations, was perhaps the ideal candidate to hammer out a resolution to the construction friction. As a member of the LDP's construction tribe, he had an expansive network of personal connections that included elites in both the construction industry and the public works bureaucracy. As a rising power in the Takeshita faction—the largest and most influential of the LDP's factions at the time—Ozawa occupied a strategic position within the ruling party. And as the protégé of Kanemaru Shin (the "don of all dons" in public works) and the husband of Takeshita's sister-in-law, Ozawa held the confidence of Japan's two most powerful politicians. In addition, Ozawa's parliamentarian father had served a term as construction minister during the Yoshida cabinet, while Ozawa's father-in-law was president of a major general construction company.

Thus Ozawa had risen to the top rungs of the LDP's construction tribe, and during the LDP's era of hegemony, it was the "politics of factions and tribes" (*batsuzoku seiji*), rather than strong party organization, that shaped the LDP (Tanaka 1985). In many ways, the puzzle of Japanese politics under LDP dominance resembles that of Italian politics under Christian Democrat rule: How could a party so factionalized and unstable maintain a system of dominance for so long? Despite predictions of the inevitable extinction of factionalism, the LDP factions had become more entrenched over time, and the LDP of the early 1990s bore more resemblance to a loose coalition of warring factions than to a coherent, unified political party.

This chapter explores the LDP's factions and its "policy tribes"— those groups of legislators who wielded considerable influence within particular policy subgovernments—and their relation to the organizational structures of the LDP. The analysis focuses on the sources of intraparty factionalism, the incentives for factional affiliation, and the enigmatic ways in which the construction tribalists influenced the politics of public works.

Factions and Political Clientelism

Factions have been described as the "primary unit," the "central force," and the "real actors in intraparty politics" in postwar Japanese politics, and the LDP has been described as a "federation of factions" united for purposes of campaign and legislative strategy, rather than a unified national party.[1] Matsuyama Yukio, former editor of the *Asahi Shinbun*, told an audience at Harvard University in 1991 that the defining feature of LDP rule was "government by, for, and of the factions." And, we must add, a defining feature of the LDP factions is that they were "non-ideological conduit[s] of particularism" (Ramseyer and Rosenbluth 1993, 59).

In seeking to explain the persistence of factionalism in the LDP, some scholars have looked to aspects of Japanese culture and tradition. Recently, however, other scholars have emphasized the role of political institutions in creating an incentive structure conducive to legislative factions. This debate merits further attention.

Advocates of the culturalist view argue that factionalism derives from aspects of Japanese culture and tradition. The patron-client ties and "quasi-familial relationships" spawned by the Confucian sense of obligation and group loyalty receive particular emphasis.[2] The following brief quotations illustrate this approach:

The old concepts of loyalty, hierarchy, and duty hold sway in them [the factions]. And the [legislator] feels very comfortable when he steps into this world.

(Thayer 1969, 41)

All the fulminations against factionalism would seem to be based on criteria drawn from other political cultures about how political parties might be organized internally.

(Baerwald 1986, 17)

[The root of the LDP's factions] is the continuing ethos of patrimonial relations from Japan's feudal past and the tendency of all large Japanese organizations to structure themselves internally . . . into vertically divided competitive groups.

(Johnson 1990b, 78)

TABLE 3. *The Evolution of the LDP's Factional Lineages, 1956–1993*

1956	1957	1962	1970	1980	1986	1987	1990	1993
Ex-Ogata	Ishii	Ishii	Ishii					
Ex-Yoshida		Ikeda	Maeo	Ōhira	Suzuki	Miyazawa	Miyazawa	Miyazawa
		Satō	Satō	Tanaka	Tanaka	Takeshita	Takeshita	Obuchi
								Hata
	Kishi	Kishi	Kawashima	Shiina				
		Fukuda	Fukuda	Fukuda	Abe	Abe	Abe	Mitsuzuka
		Fujiyama						
	Ōno	Ōno	Funada	Funada				
			Murakami	Murakami				
Hatoyama	Ishibashi							
	Kōno	Kōno	Mori	Sonoda				
			Nakasone	Nakasone	Nakasone	Nakasone	Watanabe	Watanabe
	Miki	Miki	Miki	Kōmoto	Kōmoto	Kōmoto	Kōmoto	Kōmoto

SOURCE: Adapted from Tomita et al. (1986).

Three major difficulties, however, hamper the culturalist explanations. First, none of the studies clearly define "culture." All one can deduce is that culture is a vague yet ubiquitous entity that somehow shapes political behavior. Thus culturalist arguments remain mired tautologically. To say that Japanese legislators organize themselves into factions primarily because their identity as Japanese people dictates that they do so only leaves us to wonder why Japanese culture generates this particular pattern of behavior.

Second, if Japanese culture and tradition effect political factionalism, how does one explain the trend toward fewer and larger factions over the past forty years?[3] And how does one account for the increase over time in the number of LDP legislators who became members of factions?

Third, if Japan's political culture spawns intraparty factionalism, why do not similar patterns abound in all of Japan's political parties? Neither the Komeitō, the Communist Party, or the Socialist Party, to name but three, have the kind of nonideological factions that the LDP has.

Thus Japan's culture and social structure cannot account for the roots of LDP factionalism. Instead, we must look to how the factions served the needs of both the LDP's backbenchers and bosses. As we will see, Japan's political institutions provided ample incentives for factional affiliation and loyal factioneer behavior. The demise of the factions has long been predicted, based on the premise that the party would supplant the factions, or that modernization would plow under such feudalistic vestiges as factions, or that the rise of the policy tribes would render factionalism obsolete (see, e.g., Masumi 1988, 301). But the factions, despite obstacles, have evolved and endured. The five major factions of the 1990s grew out of the Kishi, Ikeda, Satō, Ōno, Kōno, and Miki factions from the LDP's early days (see Table 3). Although individual leaders came and went with regularity, the rank-and-file generally remained within a particular factional lineage for their entire political careers.

It is well known that the LDP factions supplied their members with official party endorsements, campaign funds, and placement in political posts. But the role of factions as constituency service networks has received less attention. Let us look briefly at these benefits.

Candidate Endorsement
and Campaign Support

Factions play a central role in candidate endorsement. "If you don't join a faction, you can't become an LDP legislator" (in Honzawa 1990, 60). In order to maintain a parliamentary majority, the LDP had to endorse more than one candidate in nearly every Lower House district. The presence of conservative independents, many of whom joined the party upon election, further compounded the intraparty competition for a finite pool of conservative voters. In the majority of cases, both officially endorsed candidates as well as conservative independents maintained undisguised ties to a specific faction. To reduce wasted candidate funds and campaign support, the principle of a single faction member per district emerged. Between 1958 and 1980 factional duplication in districts diminished radically, although the rate of multiple endorsees increased slightly during the 1980s (Reed and Bolland forthcoming).

Endorsements are largely determined by the relative numerical strength of the respective factions. In preparation for an election, senior members of the factions, in rough proportion to the respective size of those factions, establish and head an Election Policy Headquarters. The candidate endorsements, however, are determined by the Election Management Committee, composed of lieutenants from each faction. Generally speaking, standing incumbents receive first priority in the allocation of party endorsements. Second priority goes to hereditary politicians and promising candidates with a solid base of constituent support. Former public works bureaucrats, with their ties to the electorally powerful construction industry, are viewed as attractive candidates with a high probability of securing election. As might be expected, hotly contested interfactional battles over candidate endorsements are common (Honzawa 1990).

Factions also provide sundry forms of campaign support for their members. For example, faction leaders and senior factioneers frequently give speeches and attend campaign rallies on behalf of "their" candidates. Faction leaders call upon their nationwide networks of contacts and campaign contributors to supply infrastructural support for junior factioneers. Affiliation with the faction headed by Tanaka

Kakuei, and later by Takeshita Noboru and Kanemaru Shin, afforded the attractive benefit of especially aggressive campaign support provided by senior faction members.

Political Funds

Factions also provide candidates with political funds. The faction boss usually disburses at least ¥2 million to each junior factioneer twice annually, during midsummer and at year's end. At election time, the basic unit of disbursement reaches the ¥10 million range. The larger the faction, the larger the financial burden for the faction boss, and the greater the temptation for raising money by dubious means. Kanemaru Shin, the chairman of the Takeshita faction, kept $50 million on hand in his personal vault.

In the wake of the public outrage over "money-power politics" in the mid-1970s, fundraising became increasingly decentralized. Whereas faction leaders supplied an estimated one-third of campaign funds for their members in the 1960s, by the early 1990s they provided only about 5 to 7 percent.[4] Electoral differences among the LDP's five main factions decreased markedly in this trend toward decentralized fundraising (Cox and Rosenbluth 1993). Because the financial burden borne by factions decreased and the electoral fortunes of their members equalized, affiliation with one particular faction mattered less to an LDP backbencher. Nonetheless, the factions differed with regard to other important electoral incentives, including the allocation of political posts.

Allocation of Posts

During the LDP's era of dominance, the party's factions determined who occupied which political post and for how long.[5] It was impossible to obtain a cabinet ministership or an appointment to a top party leadership post without the backing of a faction, and since these posts brought tangible electoral rewards, legislators knew their political futures depended on joining the right faction. Over time, a disproportionate share of specific posts went to members of particular factional lineages. From 1955 to 1992, for example, nearly half of the coveted agriculture minister portfolios went to members of factions in the Kishi lineage. Other such ministerships with long factional lineage included foreign affairs, also dominated by the Kishi lineage; finance and transport, both of which had a strong Satō lineage hue, and construction, dominated by the Satō and the Kōno lineages.[6]

Between 1955 and 1993 key posts in the public works subgovernment were the property of the Satō lineage. When Tanaka Kakuei, a former contractor with strong ties to MOC, assumed leadership of the Satō faction in 1972, he quickly recognized the potential political benefits of installing his followers in construction-related posts. Tanaka's fabled "Plan to Remodel the Japanese Archipelago," which boosted construction investment to nearly one-quarter of the gross national product, further enhanced these benefits. From July 1972 until September 1976, all six construction ministers belonged to the Tanaka faction. Among other things, this bonanza of public works spending launched Kanemaru Shin on his ascent to the top of the public works subgovernment, a position he held from the mid-1980s until his arrest and resignation in 1992. But Tanaka's desire to dominate the commanding heights of the subgovernment did not end there. Between 1967 and 1980 ten of the thirteen parliamentary vice-ministers of construction were members or "shadow affiliates" of the Tanaka faction, while several others headed PARC's Construction Division (see Appendix C).

Tanaka also actively encouraged retiring MOC bureaucrats to descend into second careers in elective politics. Thanks largely to his efforts, nearly two of every three former MOC officials elected to seats in the national parliament joined the Satō lineage. The case of Chūma Tatsui highlights the strong ties between the Tanaka faction and MOC. In 1976, Chūma's appointment interrupted a succession of six consecutive construction minister appointees from the Tanaka faction. Soon after his appointment, a group of reporters supposedly heard Chūma, a member of the archrival Fukuda faction, say: "An intolerably large number of [Construction Ministry] officials are in cahoots with the Tanaka faction. If clear evidence [of favoritism] comes to light, they will be cut down!" He specifically vowed to "cut down" Tawara Takashi, then director of the Kyūshū Regional Construction Bureau, who had allegedly promised to "turn an attentive ear" toward any request from a member of the Tanaka faction (Jin et al. 1981, 184). In the end, however, Chūma failed to carry out his vow, and Tawara eventually descended into a second career in elective politics. Naturally, he chose to join the Tanaka faction.

Constituency Service Networks

For the neophyte backbencher feverishly attempting to build a stable support base before the next election, the distant hope of grasping an influential political post offers no immediate benefit. Rather, the neophyte has to concentrate on providing services to voters and campaign contributors: securing jobs for constituents, escorting "petition groups" (*chinjōdan*) to the appropriate government agency, and furnishing supporters with subsidies, tax breaks, favorable regulatory treatment, and various structural policy benefits. Unfamiliar with Nagatachō's bewildering ways and lacking contacts in the government bureaucracy, LDP backbenchers logically turned to a faction boss or a senior party leader for assistance in providing these services.

Such was the case with Satō Bunsei, a long-time LDP MP from Ōita Prefecture. When MOC issued a new five-year plan canceling a long-anticipated stretch of expressway through his district, Satō was understandably distressed. Although he was an established legislator with experience as a cabinet minister, Satō had no reputation for significant sway within the public works subgovernment. Thus he turned to his faction boss, Nakasone Yasuhiro, the prime minister at the time. Soon, funding for the expressway was restored. This prompted an upper official at MOC to grumble about "political roads" (Nihon keizai shinbunsha 1983, 137–38). Perhaps Takeshita Noboru put it best when he said: "politics is roads and roads are politics" (*dōro izu seiji, seiji izu dōro;* in Itasaka 1987, 75).

Because certain factions flowed from lineages with disproportionate sway over specific subgovernments, voters and, especially, campaign contributors, naturally favored one faction's candidate over another's. All things being equal, construction contractors, realtors and developers, and anyone with a vested interest in improving the local infrastructure would have reason to support a candidate backed by a faction in the Satō lineage. For example, Takeshita faction candidates in the 1990 general election could rely on the reputations and power networks of seven former construction ministers, ten former parliamentary vice-ministers of construction, and a pair of former heads of the Construction Division of the LDP's Policy Affairs Research Council—not to mention the ten retired construction ministry officials, including four former administrative vice-ministers, who were then members of the faction. No other faction rivaled the Takeshita faction in the number of members tied to the public works establishment. Although the efficacy of the Satō lineage in providing electoral benefits is moot, a widespread perception of its disproportionate power resources prevails (Hirose 1981, 159; Jin et al. 1981, 180).

In the same way that the structures of the U.S. Congress meet the electoral needs of its members, LDP factions came into being and thrived because they served the electoral needs of the factioneers (Mayhew 1974, 81). For backbenchers, factions provide party nominations, political funds, and political posts. Factional affiliation also affords access to senior legislators, the so-called policy tribalists, with reputed influence over specific policy subgovernments. Ties to influential policy tribalists imply access to constituency service networks. A look at the benefits of membership in the LDP's construction tribe will serve to illustate the incentives for becoming a policy tribalist.

The Construction Tribe

The policy tribalists (*zoku giin*) are those LDP legislators who have "a considerable amount of influence in a particular area of government policy and enough seniority in the party to have influence on a continuing basis within the ministry responsible for that policy area" (Curtis 1988, 114).[7]

The LDP's first policy tribe, the public works tribe, was formed in 1956 when Tanaka Kakuei led a walkout of parliamentarians from a policy deliberation meeting (Campbell 1977, 119). Over time, the number of tribes grew to about a dozen: construction, commerce and industry, agriculture, fisheries, transport, welfare, labor, education, posts and telecommunications, finance, national defense, and foreign affairs. Each tribe also has a number of branches. Within the construction tribe, for example, there are tribal branches corresponding to the various MOC bureaus; hence, a road tribe, river tribe, housing tribe, and so forth. Moreover, officials at the sub-bureau level at MOC recognize the dam tribe, the parks tribe, and the sewage tribe. In the late 1980s, for instance, Watanabe Eiichi was esteemed as a "big boss" in the dam tribe, while Tamura Hajime had the singular distinction of being recognized as *the* kingpin among sewage tribalists. From the perspective of public works bureaucrats, these distinctions are important when it comes time to lobby for budget allocations and policy proposals.

Policy tribalists are the most influential legislators in any given subgovernment. Some observers believe that the expertise and influence acquired as a result of long years of service in a specific policy area enable the LDP's policy tribalists to "match and even dominate" their peers in the government bureaucracy (Schoppa 1991, 79). In addition, tribalists act as brokers in transactions involving the LDP and specific government agencies. This role often extends to the mediation of sectionalist turf wars between government ministries as well as fighting alongside bureaucratic allies in such disputes (Johnson 1989). Furthermore, tribalists play a leading part in shaping and securing passage of policy and budget proposals. In late August, the most hectic stage of compiling ministerial budget proposals, tribalists become the focal point of the "root binding" efforts of government bureaucrats eager to secure larger allocations for their ministry or bureau. In the compilation of the 1987 budget, for example, each bureau chief, deputy chief, and section director in the MOC was assigned to contact about twenty LDP parliamentarians during a period spanning several days in late August. Special care was taken to secure the acquiescence of key members of the construction tribe, particularly its "big bosses" (pers. interview).

Construction tribalists make their presence felt in decisions concerning public works projects. "In return for their donations from the industry," one observer notes, "members of the LDP's construction tribe are expected to use their contacts with the ministries handling public works to help decide which companies win major projects or, more usually, how business will be shared . . . between the major players" (*Far Eastern Economic Review*, 16 June 1988, 58). Members of the LDP's construction tribe are seen as the most authoritative articulators of the "voice of heaven" in the *dangō* system of allocating public works contracts, and tribalists play a key role in prioritizing the major projects competing for appropriations. In this respect, the tribalists serve as gatekeepers—individuals who determine the allocation of scarce resources—and, thus, are responsible for the perpetuation of patterns of privilege and deprivation.

Naturally, construction tribalists win handsome political contributions from construction firms in exchange for this preferential policy influence. Former Construction Minister Kōnō Ichirō and his "favored contractor policy" (*gyōsha yūsen seisaku*) elevated influence-peddling to a shadowy art form. Contractors were expected to make monetary gifts in exchange for priority designation to bid on public works projects. To get an audience at Kōno's personal residence, a one-time supplicant recalled having first to pay a "shoe removal fee" (*kutsunugidai*) to Kōno's assistant. Once inside the door, a contractor paid a "floor cushion fee" (*zabutondai*) and a "something-or-other fee" (*nantokadai*) before Kōno himself deigned to make an appearance (Asano et al. 1977, 28; Kasumi 1993, 149).

Former Prime Minister Tanaka fashioned a nationwide system of illegal kickbacks in exchange for political meddling in the allocation of public works projects (Johnson 1986). As the investigation in the *zenekon* scandal revealed, the country's largest general contractors gave letter grades to construction tribalists and gauged their political contributions accordingly. For example, one large general contractor reportedly presented biannual "gratitude gifts" to some eighty influential politicians (*Asahi shinbun,* 23 Sept. 1993). Kanemaru Shin was singled out for special distinction: his A-plus grade (actually "SA," presumably to denote "Special A") brought him gifts of ¥10 million at midsummer and at year's end. Seven other construction tribalists were awarded A grades (entitling them to biannual gratuities of ¥5 million). Even those squeaking by with Ds received two installments of ¥1 million each year.

It appears that the LDP policy tribalists' increased store of policy expertise afforded them a more significant role in the policymaking process than their predecessors had enjoyed. Virtually all outside observers agree that the policy tribalists used their know-how "in the service of ever-more-effective policy plunder—gathering more resources for their constituents and favored industries" (McCubbins and Noble 1993, 8). Certainly, the construction tribalists' influence seemed substantial enough to construction contractors to warrant enormous, and often illegal, political contributions.

The Shadow Cabinet

The LDP's Policy Affairs Research Council (Seimuchōsakai, or PARC) was a training ground for aspiring policy tribalists. During the heyday of single-party hegemony, PARC was the "stage," the "shadow cabinet" or "second government," for policy drama (Inoguchi and Iwai 1987, 20 and 27–28). In most policy domains, PARC played a greater policymaking role than did the Diet's committees and subcommittees. Beginning in fiscal year 1960, government ministries submitted their budget proposals to PARC before reporting to the Ministry of Finance (McCubbins and Noble 1993, 15). From their strategic vantage point on the council, the LDP's policy tribalists could affect policy and budget proposals at the earliest stages. Before a bill was submitted for deliberation in the Diet, a complex bargaining process from within PARC had shaped its content (see Figure 3).

As with other components of the LDP's organization, PARC evolved from predecessor entities (Fukui 1970, 30). PARC's prototype emerged around 1918 as a sort of "shadow cabinet" within the Constitutional Government Party (Kenseitō). Originally, it granted the party influence over the bureaucratically dominated policy process. Although PARC performed essential functions for the LDP as a whole, it served primarily to help members pursue their goals. Legislators pursuing ideological goals could find like-minded colleagues in, for instance, PARC's deliberative councils for education and defense policy. Yet, for the majority of "foot soldiers" in the LDP's parliamentary contingent, PARC was a convenient vehicle for achieving reelection.

Certain PARC divisions (*bukai*), investigation committees (*chōsakai*), and special committees (*tokubetsu iinkai*) attracted more members than others. Generally, an LDP legislator can belong to a maximum of three divisions (and an unlimited number of investigation and special committees). Divisions with consistently sparse membership

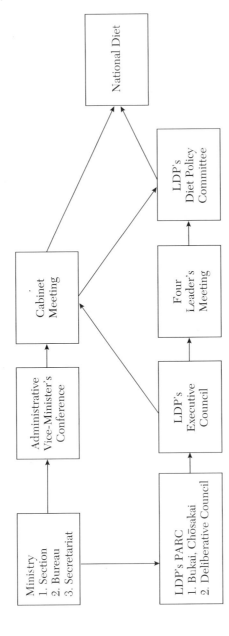

Figure 3. The LDP's Organization and the Legislative Process

include cabinet, labor, local administration, foreign affairs, justice, science and technology, and environment; the larger divisions include transport, communications, and social affairs. However, the "three noble houses" (*go-sanke*)—commerce, agriculture, and, the largest of all, construction—always draw the largest membership (Itasaka 1987, 1). The magnetic appeal of these divisions, however, did not appear until around 1967, amid a decline in the LDP's popularity at the polls.[8]

The disparity in the size of PARC's divisions derives from the perception that tangible electoral rewards accompany membership in certain divisions. Given the small and relatively unorganized domestic interest groups concerned, the cabinet, foreign affairs, and justice divisions attract few members. Although ideologically attractive to some, defense and education also draw relatively few members. In contrast, members of the commerce division claim numerous small retailers as their constituents, while those in the agricultural division appeal to the powerful farm lobby. Legislators in the construction division accomplish two goals simultaneously: garnering votes from six million construction workers and campaign contributions from a generous industry.

The legislators chairing PARC's commerce, agriculture, and construction divisions have, on average, fared better among swing voters in the election following their appointment as chair. No such benefit has accrued to the chairs of the education, local administration, or cabinet divisions.[9] For good reason, then, the chairships of the three noble houses became highly coveted, and the occupants of these posts were referred to as "cabinet ministers within the party."

The Enigma of Japanese Pork

To what extent do the LDP's construction tribalists actually deliver the bacon to their home districts? If the LDP's construction tribalists do, in fact, funnel public works projects into their prefectures, then one would anticipate a positive correlation between positional influence and increases in public works spending. To examine this matter, I constructed a multivariate regression model to analyze data for the period from 1964 to 1988 (see Appendix D).

The results of the analysis suggest that the LDP's construction tribalists do not funnel public works projects to their home prefectures, although public works spending does increase slightly beginning in the third year after the appointment of a local legislator to the post of construction minister. Still, the influence of construction tribalists in delivering pork to their home districts is much less than one might have expected.

In this regard, the politics of public works in Japan is enigmatic. Certain prefectures consistently garner higher per capita harvests of public construction allocations; while others reap consistently smaller relative yields. For extended periods, Niigata, Hokkaidō, and Shimane ranked near the top for per capita public construction spending, while Tokyo, Saitama, and Osaka consistently found themselves at or near the bottom of the rankings.[10] The stability of these rankings leads one to wonder whether supposedly influential legislators exaggerate their power, so as to lure construction contractors into making large contributions, or, instead, whether construction tribalists dole out pork in even more particularistic ways, such as preferential treatment in zoning decisions, land acquisition, and bidder designation.

The most plausible explanation is that construction tribalists use their influence to ensure the funding of projects most dear to particular firms, and they see to it that contracts go to those firms that make substantial political contributions. Tribalists pay particular attention to protecting the budgets of certain planned projects, knowing that the "complex understandings" of the *dangō* system often help determine the disposition of contracts years in advance. Thus, the designated bidder system encourages tribalists to meddle in decisions about projects reserved for firms outside the tribalist's district. For example, Kanemaru Shin allegedly pressured Governor Takeuchi to award the ¥200-million construction of the Oyama Dam in Ibaraki Prefecture to a joint venture of Tobishima Corporation and Kajima Corporation. Takeuchi's "voice of heaven" apparently produced the desired outcome, and Taisei Corporation, the original predetermined low bidder, was awarded the contract for a rock-crushing plant connected with the dam. Not coincidentally perhaps, approximately twenty of the country's largest general contractors, including Tobishima and Kajima, each funneled as much as ¥20 million a year in illegal contributions into Kanemaru's war chest.[11] With these generous contributions, contractors hoped to enlist Kanemaru's reputed influence in allocating public works contracts.

The Bounties of Credit-Claiming

To improve their chances at the polls, legislators the world round practice credit-claiming, acting to promote the impression that they are "personally responsible" for the government having taken a particular course (Mayhew 1974, 57).[12] Logically, credit-claiming should face steep obstacles in Japan's multimember electoral district system, because voters cannot easily determine which legislator delivered a given project. Yet the deeply entrenched systems of political clientelism in both Japan and Italy belie this logic.

Candidates in Japanese election campaigns frequently claim credit for roads, bridges, railway lines, and parks. "I delivered that bridge over there," "I brought in this road" are commonly heard boastings at election time. An MP who delivered an expressway is a "road representative," an assemblyman who brings a bridge to the prefecture becomes a "bridge representative," and a town councilor who secures cement covers for gutters lining neighborhood streets is dubbed a "ditchboard representative." Kanemaru Shin boasted to his supporters in Yamanashi that "to say that I was involved in the construction of 99 percent of bridges in this prefecture wouldn't be incorrect" (in Marshall with Toyama 1992, 37). A popular vehicle for credit-claiming is the *kōenkai* newsletter. A typical newsletter might carry a headline proclaiming the government's decision to build a dam in the district and include photographs of the hardworking representative arguing the merits of the proposed project before key cabinet officials and government bureaucrats.

Over time, many conservative legislators have augmented their power resources through credit-claiming. During the early decades of prewar parliamentary democracy, Hoshi Tooru was among the first politicians to use pork-barrel politics effectively. Hara Kei fashioned a system whereby public spending served the interests of the Seiyūkai party. In the early postwar years, former Prime Minister Yoshida Shigeru's "one-man road," a stretch of asphalt running from Tokyo to

Oiso (where, perhaps not coincidentally, Yoshida's estate was located) and ending in Hakone, exemplified such a system. Ōno Banboku, an LDP faction boss, secured a bullet train stop for a small town in his native Gifu Prefecture, and future Prime Minister Fukuda accomplished a similar feat with a railway stop at a small town in Gunma Prefecture. In addition to getting a local bridge named for him, Kanemaru brought a ¥200-billion project for a test line for a magnetic levitation bullet train to Yamanashi Prefecture.

But, without question, Tanaka Kakuei, dubbed the "Emperor of the Construction Ministry," was the greatest practitioner of pork-barrel politics. Among other things, Tanaka delivered to Niigata two superexpressways, a bullet train line (with three stops in small towns in his own district), a university and a technopolis, and an atomic power plant. Tanaka's reign also brought a number of schools, cultural halls, hospitals, public housing complexes, roads, bridges, tunnels, dams, and river improvement projects to Niigata. The pièce de resistance was a tunnel that "liberated" Shioya Village and its sixty households from its traditional wintertime isolation—at a cost of ¥12 billion, or ¥20 million per household. As a resident of the prefecture observed, "When superexpressways and a bullet train took shape and appeared right before our eyes, we realized just how wonderful Mr. Tanaka is" (Fukuoka 1985, 200).

Among the most powerful of the "mini-Tanakas" is Amano Kōsei, a long-time member of the LDP's construction tribe and chief of the public works subgovernment during the late 1980s. Elected to the Lower House in 1958, the same election that launched the parliamentary careers of Takeshita and Kanemaru, Amano felt obliged to become a construction tribalist because of Fukushima's undeveloped infrastructure. He took his first steps toward becoming a tribalist as a three-term member of the Fukushima Prefectural Assembly, when he labored to construct a track-and-field stadium and, later, railway lines and roads. Thanks to his discipleship under faction boss Kōno Ichirō, Amano established strong connections to the construction industry. By the mid-1970s, incumbency in a succession of construction-related posts gave him even stronger ties to the construction bureaucracy. Amano claimed credit for channeling a number of public works projects, including the so-called Amano interchange in Motomiya, into the prefecture, and he presided over and claimed sole credit for a 20 percent increase in the 1987 public works budget, the first increase since the "ice age" in public construction spending in the late 1970s.

A final example concerns the influence of construction tribalist Nakamura Kishirō. In March 1992 MOC's Road Deliberation Council designated 6,111 kilometers of prefectural roadways as national roadways. One excluded stretch of pavement was an 18-kilometer roadway in Ibaraki Prefecture. Beginning in 1986, signals from MOC concerning the possibility of redesignation alerted residents of the neighboring areas. In March 1990, though, Nakamura was appointed acting chairman of the LDP's Road Research Council. A local politician who visited Tokyo to make a direct appeal reported that Nakamura had claimed that he, Kanemaru Shin (then chairman of the Road Research Council), and Takeshita Noboru would decide the redesignation of prefectural roadways. It so happened that the mayor of a town along the roadway supported one of Nakamura's LDP rivals in Ibaraki's Third District. In November 1991 the residents of another roadway town obtained over 10,000 signatures in support of redesignation. Unfortunately, the town stood solidly in the support bases of Nakamura's two LDP rivals in the district. "Because the local leaders along the roadway did not belong to his support group," argues a disappointed local politician, "Mr. Nakamura became annoyed" and blocked the decision. Even MOC officials admit that, despite a logical case for redesignating the status of the roadway, Nakamura so strongly opposed it that the zealous enthusiasm of the local residents could not alter the ruling (*Asahi shinbun*, 14 Mar. 1993).

Nevertheless, it is important not to exaggerate the influence of the LDP's construction tribalists. Even influential construction tribalists humbly plead for public works projects on occasion, and public works bureaucrats sometimes disregard explicit orders from their political overlords. A former Finance Ministry bureaucrat turned parliamentarian estimates that the Finance Ministry decides about nine-tenths of the public works budget, leaving MOC and the construction tribe to "play" for the remainder (pers. interview). An upper official of MOC estimated that tribalists influence only about 5 percent of decisions involving the allocation of public works projects (pers. interview). Thus policy tribalists "work with bureaucrats in the bureaucrats' system. They have not provided new channels for the LDP to put into effect policies reflecting broader, national interests that do not fit well into the bureaucracy's segmented world" (Schoppa 1991, 104). In the final analysis, members of the LDP's construction tribe owe their influence to their ability to work with the public works bureaucrats.

Tiptoeing Toward Resolution

After arriving in Washington on 26 March, Ozawa held a series of talks with U.S. officials, among them Commerce Secretary William Verity and USTR Clayton Yeutter. The Americans demanded guaranteed access for U.S. firms to major private-sector projects, while the Japanese side insisted upon retaining its designated bidder system. Four days later, they reached an accord that allowed U.S. companies to participate in seven large-scale public works projects and to apply "transparent" procedures to the construction of a new headquarters for Nippon Telegraph and Telephone Company and the Trans–Tokyo Bay Expressway. (These seven projects included work on Haneda Airport, redevelopment of Tokyo Bay, Yokohama's Minato Mirai 21, Hiroshima Airport, Akashi Strait Bridge, Ise Bay Expressway, and Kansai Cultural and Academic Research City.) In addition, the accord created liaison points for foreign firms wishing to submit tenders and extended the submission of pre-tender cost estimates to sixty days (*Japan Times,* 31 Mar. 1988). Because of his influence and personal connections, Ozawa earned much of the credit for the Major Projects Agreement. That the accord ultimately failed to diminish the trade friction only highlights Japan's deeply rooted domestic resistance to market liberalization.

The American assault upon Japan's long-secluded construction fortress called attention to the role played by the LDP's factions and policy tribes in the politics of public works. As we have seen, the intraparty factions served the needs of their members, providing them with essential electoral resources (e.g., party nomination, campaign funds, and political posts) and offering members a collegial setting for seeking support and trading favors needed to fulfill the demands of constituency service. Even after a faction leader steps down, most factioneers remain within the faction, and the factional lineages come to dominate certain subgovernments.

Between 1955 and 1993 the LDP's construction tribalists controlled vast legislative power in Japan's public works subgovernment. But instead of using their influence solely to funnel public works projects into their home districts, the LDP construction tribalists largely used their regulatory clout to ensure that particular construction firms were favored in the awarding of public works contracts. Of course, they did not ignore constituency service; as we have seen, the low ideological differentiation among rival LDP candidates in the SNTV system required career politicians to grant constituency service high priority. As Ōno Banboku once observed, "A monkey that falls from a tree is still a monkey, but a legislator who falls in an election is merely human" (Inoguchi and Iwai 1987, 139–40). From the perspective of an LDP backbencher, membership in the construction tribe, with the promise of increased voter support and political funds and connections to the public works bureaucracy, offered a chance to escape such a mortal end.

Given the electoral benefits of public works, LDP politicians naturally resisted foreign pressure to open the construction market, which would have meant forfeiting invaluable electoral advantages. At the root of the construction friction, then, one finds institutional incentives for the factioneering and tribalism. It was neither Japanese culture nor Japanese traditions that produced the "politics of factions and tribes," but rather such institutions as the SNTV and the system of campaign financing.

Conclusion

Change and Inertia in the Politics of Japanese Public Works

Even as Ozawa and Yeutter were shaking hands and smiling for photographers at the conclusion of the negotiations that produced the Major Projects Agreement (MPA), the Japanese mass media were already predicting the onset of a second round of construction friction. A dark cloud of doubt and cynicism hung over the Japanese construction establishment. As Sako Hajime, then chairman of the Japan Federation of Construction Contractors, asserted: "The Japan-U.S. construction issue has been settled. It's over. The Japanese market is now open. But they [American firms] have no real intention of coming here. We can no longer accept the criticism that our market is still closed just because they are not willing to enter it" (*Japan Times,* 12 May 1988).

At least in the short run, Sako's prophesy proved correct: more than a month after the accord, no American firm had applied for permission to enter the Japanese market. Meanwhile, the fears of the Japanese construction establishment regarding an onslaught of other foreign competitors, particularly South Korean firms, quickly materialized. By late August, eleven Korean firms—among them, Samsung Construction and Hyundai Engineering and Construction—had applied to MOC, causing a Japanese executive to predict, "South Korean contractors will be a grave threat to us if they bring in cheaper wage construction workers from their own country" (*Japan Times,* 27 Aug. 1988).

By the first anniversary of the MPA, American frustration over the lack of progress in gaining access to the Japanese market had grown. The risk of conducting business in an uncharted market, coupled with the enormous expenses of setting up shop in an expanding bubble economy, dissuaded all but nine U.S. firms from establishing a presence in Japan. While Overseas Bechtel, Schal Associates, and Tishman Realty and Construction had managed to gain a toehold in the Japanese market, American resentment began to mount because the U.S. firms were relegated to the status of minor junior partners in joint ventures with Japanese contractors.[1] A U.S. construction company executive charged: "Japan has given a small portion of the pie to American firms to avoid basic reform of industry practices, bid-rigging and collusive relations among political, government, and industry circles" (Shimizu 1989). Japan's tendering system continued to attract criticism for impeding foreign access. For example, despite an accomplished record in construction markets around the world, Overseas Bechtel was judged unqualified to bid on a project connected with the ¥1.14-trillion Trans–Tokyo Bay Highway.

A second round of construction friction erupted in the fall of 1989. One source of concern in Washington was the gaping bilateral trade imbalance, to which the "construction gap" was a contributor: During 1989, U.S. construction firms reportedly performed $65 million in work in Japan, compared to $2.6 billion garnered by Japanese firms in the U.S. construction market. So the U.S. government turned its attack to the "structural impediments" blocking fair access and competition in the Japanese market. These barriers included a distribution system capable of effecting a 300 percent mark-up between the import agent and the customer; *keiretsu* groupings that excluded overseas suppliers and blocked unwanted mergers and acquisitions; and restrictions against large retail stores that might stock imported products. Also singled out for censure were the *dangō* system of bid-rigging, Japan's weak enforcement of its antimonopoly law, and the light penalties for violations of that law.

The criticism of the *dangō* system focused on an illegal cartel, composed of 140 Japanese contractors, that had rigged bids on contracts for work at the U.S. Naval Base at Yokosuka between 1984 and 1987.[2] A hidden microphone planted on a disgruntled member of the

Stars and Stripes Friendship Association (Seiyūkai) enabled the Naval Investigation Service to present the Japan Fair Trade Commission (JFTC) with irrefutable evidence of the bid-rigging operation. On 14 November, the U.S. Justice Department demanded ¥5 billion in reparations for overcharges from firms in the cartel. Meanwhile, the JFTC warned the firms and fined 70 of the companies ¥290 million for violating the antimonopoly law. For its part, MOC reprimanded 7 industry associations for not doing enough to curb bid-rigging at U.S. military bases and spanked 104 association firms by suspending their right to bid on public works projects for one to two months. In the end, 99 firms agreed to pay ¥4.7 billion in damages.

The light penalties fortified Washington's determination to press for stiffer enforcement of Japan's antimonopoly law. Scarcely two months after the Yokosuka incident, Mabuchi Construction, a leading player in the Stars and Stripes Friendship Association, won designation to bid on the construction of high-rise family housing at Camp Zama, a U.S. army base. In June 1990 MOC threatened firms caught rigging bids with suspension from bidding on public works for up to nine months, while the JFTC called for raising the maximum penalty for antitrust violations from 1.5 percent to 6 percent of illegally garnered profits. In late May of the following year, the investigation into the shady dealings of the Saitama Saturday Society first tested the JFTC's supposedly bolstered resolve. In the midst of that probe, the JFTC submitted a proposal to the LDP to increase the maximum penalty for antitrust violations from ¥5 million to "several hundred million yen." That proposal met fierce opposition from major contractors as well as influential construction tribalists. Nakamura Kishirō, then acting chairman of the LDP's Investigative Committee on Antitrust Law, was one of them. On 11 March 1994 Nakamura was arrested and charged with accepting bribes from Kiyoyama Shinji, vice-president of Kajima Corporation, in exchange for inside information about the JFTC's investigation of the Saturday Society.

As the Structural Impediments Initiative (SII) talks continued, U.S. negotiators focused their attack on Japan's underdeveloped social infrastructure. Their complaints evoked enthusiastic, if tactfully suppressed, support from Japan's public works bureaucrats and their parliamentary allies, who quickly sought to exploit the situation by formulating a new ten-year public investment plan. In the initial budget proposals compiled in May 1990, the spending ministries asked for ¥500 trillion in public investment, nearly double the amount spent on public works during the preceding decade. MOC requested ¥310 trillion for roads and other projects, while the Transport Ministry sought ¥50 trillion for airports, railways, and ports. Ultimately, the Japanese government agreed to spend a total of ¥430 trillion on public works in the 1990s.

A third round of construction friction exploded in 1993. In mid-April, a senior U.S. Commerce Department official hinted that the Clinton administration was considering establishing numerical targets for contracts received by U.S. firms in Japan's construction market (*Japan Times*, 17 Apr. 1993). On 30 April, USTR Mickey Kantor stated, "Despite years of negotiations and two trade agreements, the Japanese market remains fundamentally closed to American firms" (in Bradford et al. 1993, 6). Kantor threatened to impose sanctions within sixty days if negotiations did not produce meaningful market access. Coming in the middle of the Sagawa affair, Kantor's threat shocked an already jittery Japanese construction establishment. Even those who viewed his announcement as another instance of American bullying conceded a kernel of truth in the USTR's case.[3] As a *Yomiuri Shinbun* editorial put it, "To our regret, there are various areas in which Japan must improve. The current system is a hotbed of bid-rigging and cozy relations among politicians, bureaucrats, and members of the construction industry. The system is a strong barrier to foreign companies" (in Sanger 1993b).

Although talks in June 1993 bought the Japanese side some time, they failed to extinguish the flames. Citing "a significant and persistent pattern or practice of discrimination against U.S. products or services that results in identifiable harm to U.S. businesses," USTR Kantor reserved special censure for discriminatory barriers to Japan's construction market (in Hershey 1993). However, because of turmoil in Japanese politics—turmoil surrounding the sensational *zenekon* scandal, preparations for the Tokyo meeting of the G-7, and especially, the upcoming general elections—Kantor delayed the imposition of sanctions until 1 November. Meanwhile, in August, MOC agreed to employ "conditional open bidding" on an experimental basis for specified public works projects. When talks resumed in September, the Americans criticized Japan's negotiating tactics, rejected MOC's proposal, and demanded an across-the-board open bidding system, expansion of the MPA, strengthening of the antimonopoly law, and the adoption of criteria to measure the progress of foreign firms in gaining access to Japan's construction market.

With the USTR's deadline looming, the Japanese negotiators retreated to Tokyo to devise a plan. Any temptation to stall and press for concessions was foreclosed by the exposure of the *zenekon* scandal and the media-led campaign for institutional reform. Chiba Prefecture took action first. On 16 August the prefectural government announced that it would experiment with an open competitive bidding system. Other local governments quickly followed, including scandal-ridden Sendai City and Ibaraki Prefecture. On 8 September MOC agreed to implement conditional open bidding systems on an experimental basis for large, centrally contracted public works projects. But the expanding *zenekon* scandal and U.S. pressure soon pushed MOC even further. On 27 October Chief Cabinet Secretary Takemura Masayoshi announced the government's decision to introduce open bidding for centrally funded projects valued at or over 4.5 million IMF special drawing rights (about ¥720 million) and for projects undertaken by eighty-four public corporations valued at or over 15 million SDRs (¥2.4 million). In the case of prefectures and large municipalities, open bidding would be required for projects surpassing 15 million SDRs and for design and consultancy services on national projects exceeding 450,000 SDRs (¥72 million). Prime Minister Hosokawa predicted that the new system would bring about "historic reform with economic and social implications," and some observers estimated that the new procedures would funnel about 20 percent of national projects to foreign construction firms.

This action sufficed to persuade USTR Kantor to defer retaliatory action until 20 January in order to assess the changes. When that deadline arrived, Kantor lauded the magnitude of the concessions and expressed optimism over the potential elimination of discriminatory treatment of U.S. firms. Nevertheless, on 31 March, the USTR cited construction as one of the forty-three areas affected by unfair trading practices. With this invocation of Super 301, Japan's construction establishment had six months to institute more reforms or face possible trade retaliation. Thus, while few could have imagined it, the bilateral construction conflict continued to blaze unabated a decade after its inception.

Foreign Pressure and Domestic Change

Up until the mid-1980s foreign firms and their governments showed no interest in prying open the Japanese construction market, leaving the intricate system of clientelist exchange relations to function in relative equilibrium in a sheltered domestic arena. But in an increasingly interdependent world political economy, the existence of non-tariff barriers resonated widely and powerfully among international trade partners. Political and business leaders in the United States were frustrated by the chronic U.S. trade deficit with Japan and anxious about Japan's challenge to America's economic preeminence.[4] Efforts to "level the playing field" in Japan's construction market was but one tactic in a larger U.S. offensive to open overseas markets. The devaluation of the dollar following the Plaza Accord in 1985 only added impetus to this market access offensive.

While seemingly irrational from a short-term economic perspective, rational calculations dictated the onset of construction friction. The fact that U.S. firms possessed superior technology for the design and construction of airport terminals made the Kansai Airport a logical focal point for the aggressive unilateralism of U.S. trade monitors. Japan's lavish budget for public works intended to create an economy driven by domestic demand, was an extremely attractive target; a U.S. Commerce Department official estimated that acquiring a fair share of that market could be worth $14 billion a year to U.S. firms (Bradford et al. 1993, 7). Among the projects discussed at the onset of the bilateral friction were an $8.7-billion bridge and tunnel spanning Tokyo Bay, a $26-billion urban renewal project on Tokyo's bay front and a similar $15.2-billion project in Yokohama, $402 billion in highway construction for 1990–1995, and a master land-use plan calling for $7.6 trillion in infrastructure investments. Yet the U.S. government did not make construction a trade issue solely because of pressure from the U.S. construction industry.[5] Rather, it was "policy entrepreneurs" in the U.S. Consultate in Osaka and in Congress who placed the issue on the government's agenda (Krauss 1989).

Thus the tale of U.S.-Japan construction friction illustrates how international forces influence domestic politics and vice versa. American *gaiatsu* ("external pressure") compounded the problems of collusive action in Japan's public works domain. By dictating a deadline for action and moving the locus of decision-making to the top levels of the political order, American *gaiatsu* altered the nature of decision-making in a policy arena that had been dominated by a stable subgovernment elite. Once routine structural policymaking had been transformed into a foreign policy crisis, the Foreign Ministry, the Prime Minister's Office, and senior LDP leaders outside the construction tribe were compelled to assume new places at the bargaining table.[6]

By insisting on the eradication of exclusionary business practices, American *gaiatsu* increased the risks and the costs for Japanese firms of evading the government's antitrust watchdogs. The U.S. Justice Department's decision to seek treble damages from firms that rigged bids at the Yokosuka Naval Base gave Japanese contractors a taste of American-style antitrust enforcement. A subsequent episode involving an illegal cartel that allegedly colluded on bids for telecommunications projects at the U.S. Air Force Base at Yokota reinforced that lesson (Blustein 1993b). As part of its promise to take antitrust enforcement more seriously, the JFTC increased its investigative staff by nearly 50 percent and raised the maximum penalty for violating the antitrust law. During the 1991 fiscal year, 175 Japanese companies were penalized, more than double the previous record high, and investigators levied fines fifteen times greater than in 1990.

The new JFTC was hardly a snarling antitrust watchdog, but its expanded powers represented an additional obstacle for would-be bid-riggers. Investigations of informal industry associations obliged prospective conspirators to find new means of forging collusive accords. For example, the murky activities of the Management Harmony Society came under scrutiny in the aftermath of the Yokosuka incident. Rumored to be a pipeline for funneling political contributions and sharing public works information, the society abruptly disbanded in the summer of 1990. At the time, speculation ensued in the press that a similar fate awaited various local associations. Those speculations proved well founded in May 1991, when JFTC investigators descended upon the offices of forty-nine member companies of the Saitama Saturday Society. According to insiders, the Saturday Society had rigged bids on public works projects for many years. In May 1992, however, the JFTC suddenly dropped its investigation, allegedly because of "insufficient evidence." Forty-three of the member firms were fined a total of ¥1 billion and were banned from bidding on public works contracts for one month, and the firms' 100,000 employees were required to sign an oath forswearing future bid-rigging. Subsequent revelations suggest that Nakamura Kishirō and other LDP construction tribalists may have exerted enough influence to halt the investigation and reduce the proposed increase in the penalty for antitrust violations (*Asahi shinbun*, 16 Mar. 1994).

By prodding the Japanese side to modify the government procurement system, American *gaiatsu* helped to magnify the difficulties of delimiting conspiratorial rings and blocking spoilers. The cosmetic adjustments effected in 1988 under the Major Projects Agreement created an affirmative action program for foreign firms in the Japanese construction market. Between 1988 and 1991, American firms garnered around $400 million for construction services in Japan—but during that same period Japanese firms secured an estimated $7.5 billion in construction business in the United States. Even though the MPA was expanded to embrace forty projects, Japan refused to modify the designated bidder system until *gaiatsu* threatened severe domestic economic hardship and the unraveling political scandal began to topple high-level officials. The bursting of the bubble economy in 1991 and the onset of recession further undermined the *dangō* system's customarily stable collusive interactions, and Japanese contractors raced to outbid one another in paying off politicans in a fierce competition for government contracts.[7]

The construction affair offers three lessons about the impact of American *gaiatsu* on domestic political behavior in Japan. First, *gaiatsu* more often succeeds when the desired change serves the interests of key domestic actors.[8] Indeed, the issue of Japan's increase in public works spending, enthusiastically supported by all policy protagonists in the domestic subgovernment, was the only topic at the SII talks that elicited swift agreement, though the decision to spend ¥430 trillion on public works over the course of the 1990s fell short of the requested amount. Second, foreign pressure can alter the cost-benefit calculations of domestic actors. By prompting changes in antitrust enforcement and spotlighting murky activities, *gaiatsu* increased the already steep costs of collusive action in Japan's public works domain. Third, *gaiatsu* alone cannot dictate dramatic change in established patterns of domestic political behavior. The U.S. threat of retaliation under Article 301 transformed routine decision-making into crisis decision-making, but over the course of more than five years American pressure failed to modify the Japanese government procurement system. Modest institutional reform came only when foreign pressure capitalized on needed change in a policy domain already suffering from economic hard times and political scandal.

The Imperiled Domestic Interests

While international factors transformed Japan's construction market into a trade battlefield and influenced the timing and nature of the government's response, domestic politicial concerns pitched and protracted the conflict. As a newspaper editorial observed upon the announcement of the MPA, "The key to the settlement of the [construction] issue was how to adjust conflicting interests on the domestic front, mainly those within the ruling Liberal Democratic Party, between government departments and between the government and the industries involved" (*Japan Times*, 11 Apr. 1988). And, as Chief Cabinet Secretary Takemura asserted, domestic political concerns, rather than American *gaiatsu*, motivated the government's decision to implement an open bidding system for certain categories of public works projects (*Asahi shinbun*, 7 Nov. 1993).

Market liberalization most directly threatened the interests of the domestic construction industry, with its six million workers, over half a million firms, and politically potent industry associations. Having long relied on the *dangō* system for a stable income and a "fair share" of the market—a mutual insurance system against insolvency— Japan's contractors had reason to oppose any suggestion to open the public construction market to foreign competition. Liberalization was especially terrifying for the welter of subcontractors and small-scale firms. Although somewhat less vulnerable, the internationally competitive industry giants also resented the imposition of *gaiatsu* to gain special concessions for U.S. firms. Having labored to establish a profitable presence in overseas markets, many large firms were loath to concede to an affirmative action program for foreign competitors.

The construction imbroglio also imperiled the interests of Japan's public works bureaucrats. MOC officials perceived the relentless efforts of the United States to pry open the Japanese market as an encroachment upon a hallowed domestic bailiwick. The technocrats who wielded virtual monopoly control over the design phase of public works projects felt especially threatened. The public works bureaucrats knew that changes in the government procurement system would subvert their promotional and postretirement security, for the designated competitive tendering system was the linchpin in a clientelist system in which contractors rewarded helpful retiring government bureaucrats with posts suited to their descent from heaven.

In addition, the construction friction threatened the secure livelihood of Japanese legislators, particularly members of the long-dominant LDP. Over time, career politicians had come to dominate the LDP's legislative contingent, and they prized their links with construction industry constituents. Reforming government procurement policies would undermine the delicate system of "honest graft" through which a percentage of revenues from public works contracts were funneled back into the coffers of influential legislators. The prospect of construction contracts being granted to foreign firms also jeopardized the opportunities for constituency service and credit-claiming so important to legislators' electoral success. Most at risk were the construction tribalists and the intraparty factions whose influence came from their reputed sway over public works decisions.

Bound by ties of mutual self-interest, legislators, government officials, and contractors were willing to endure great hardship to protect the corrupt bidding system. This "union of political, bureaucratic, and business worlds" (*sei-kan-zaikai no yuchaku*) operated in an environment conducive to institutionalized political clientelism, a milieu that afforded a safe haven for bid-rigging and the economically inefficient allocation of public resources. The relentless quest for a secure livelihood bound these political actors into a concrete triangle. Yet, as an editorial in *Asahi Shinbun* pointed out, "Pernicious politicians and contractors can easily weather criticism from within, but it is not so easy to sidestep the issue when the bidding system so intimately connected with *dangō* becomes the target of foreign pressure" (7 Apr. 1993).

Growth with Clientelism

For more than forty years Japan maintained economic efficiency and high growth rates in its internationally competitive sectors alongside glaring inefficiency in many domestic sectors. Although clear signs of disquietude appeared in the mid-1980s, a delicate symbiotic balance characterized interactions between the two distinct policy regimes: Expansion of the developmental state required the stable political environment and social quiescence of the clientelist state. Meanwhile, the legitimacy of the clientelist state, with its concomitant particularism, corruption, and inefficiency, depended upon the economic growth and rising standard of living generated by the developmental state.

Partly by design and partly by default, the developmental state was largely insulated from the gluttonous clientelist networks. Policymaking for the strategic sunrise industries—unlike policymaking for agriculture, small business, and public works—rarely entailed palpable distributive benefits. State-led development, dictated by international imperatives during Japan's early industrialization, left a legacy of segregating strategic policy from structural policy in high-growth sectors. But for the clientelist state to sustain itself, it had to channel distributive benefits to pivotal claimants—to the elites—rather than to the general public. Among the groups consistently excluded from the inner sanctums of policymaking were organized labor, consumers' and taxpayers' groups, and residents of large urban areas.[9] As the wealth generated by high-speed growth enhanced the material prosperity of the citizenry, the appeal of mass-based, ideological rallies for mobilizing partisan support gradually lost their luster, further stabilizing Japan's policymaking environment.[10]

Because of the rural bias of the LDP's support base, peripheral and relatively low-income segments of the population benefited disproportionately from the Japanese economic miracle. The residents of large cities, who received rather small payoffs in policy benefits in return for their tax burden, suffered the most. While Japan's city dwellers coped with an inferior urban infrastructure, residents of the rural hinterland were treated to a brimming barrel of political pork. Robin Hood–like, the tribalists performed "a vital function for the system, redistributing income from the rich sectors to the poor ones and ensuring that high-speed growth did not benefit one group to the exclusion of others" (Johnson 1986, 20). With the benefits accruing to business interests, political clientelism under protracted single-party dominance acted as a proxy for social welfare expenditures. (At least until the mid-1970s, Japan ranked at or near the bottom among advanced industrialized countries in such expenditures.)

A second factor helps to explain the anomaly of economic growth within a clientelist political order. In addition to promoting the broad consultation and interaction that characterized government-business relations in Japan, a deeply entrenched system of informal structures and practices bound public- and private-sector elites together. Out of this grew a pervasive corruption "so highly organized and . . . so much a part of the extra-legal ways of the Japanese system that most citizens . . . do not recognize it for what it is, but accept it as part of the system" (van Wolferen 1989, 136). A general contractor, gazing in horror at the unfolding *zenekon* scandal remarked: "Was what we were doing really illegal?" (*Asahi shinbun,* 21 Oct. 1993). As long as standards of living continued to rise, systematized corruption legitimized the status quo. The cumulative effect of the corruption scandals beginning in the late 1980s revealed the materialist covenant that bound special interests, incumbent and retired government officials, and candidates for elective office in a passionate embrace.

In the structural policy market, questions of who go what, when, and how depended on who wielded the greatest political influence. Particularly during the era of high-speed economic growth, when Japan had a relatively underdeveloped social welfare system, officially sanctioned inefficiency abounded in those policy arenas in which the redistributive effect served as a proxy for social welfare policy. Although the social welfare system improved dramatically, rice growers, construction contractors, and shopkeepers continued to reap formal

and informal government protection in spite of high rates of inefficiency and declining rates of improvement in labor productivity.[11]
With regard to public works, a cordoned-off domestic market enabled
the growth of an oversized and relatively inefficient domestic construction industry. Here, American *gaiatsu* helped create a focal point
for mass-media criticism, which rallied public disenchantment over
the domestic costs of Japan's "structural impediments." And, further
reinforcing a widespread sense of deprivation, the SII talks spot-
lighted the backwardness of Japanese infrastructure vis-à-vis other advanced countries.

Pork-barrel politics, however, sustained the LDP's protracted legislative hegemony. The money that poured into the coffers of the LDP
and its factions essentially covered the cost of an insurance premium
for maintaining stable rule under a one-party dominant regime:

The LDP, maintaining its monopoly of power, succeeded in making the
economy grow through the expansion of exports. This provided sufficient
financial resources to enable the party to follow a policy of distributive politics. Constituency service was provided by appropriations that poured into
the election districts. This in turn enabled the party to secure a majority of
seats in the National Diet and thus perpetuate its rule. . . . In this way, a
stable system that linked politics and the economy came into being.

(Kyogoku 1987, 23)

This arrangement helped to insulate Japan's strategic policy market
from partisan demands that might have sidetracked developmental
goals. By satisfying greedy self-interested politicians, bureaucrats, and
special interests, political clientelism served an important systemic
function.

In this way, the political requisites of the developmental state dove-
tailed with the dysfunctional clientelist system. The maladies of "part
versus whole" and "constituency versus nation" contributed to the equitable distribution of national economic wealth that legitimized Japan's steep and painful developmental trajectory to the front ranks of
industrialized countries. A seamless web of mutual interactions connected a system of institutionalized corruption with a government-
business partnership founded upon extensive bargaining and cross-
fertilization. In sum, insofar as the inefficient allocation of public
resources sustained the LDP's protracted hegemony, the dysfunctions

of a political clientelist order served essential functions in maintaining developmental capitalism.

Another Japanese Export?

Japan's economic success leads one to wonder if its model for growth with clientelism is exportable. In answering this question, we cannot ignore two principal peculiarities of modern Japanese history. First is the legacy of institutionalized political rule in a developmental state, a regime in which an elite civil bureaucracy asserted itself in policymaking and in calculating the national budget. The centralized state that emerged in the latter half of the nineteenth century posed steep obstacles to partisan meddling in the budget or in industrial policy.[12] Second, the carefully controlled extension of suffrage ensured bureaucratic dominance over civil society and expedited state patronage of favored groups and individuals. The timing and sequence of these developments was significant for Japanese economic growth. At least until the mid-1970s, the state bureaucracy managed to maintain a strategic role in economic policymaking, while political clientelism was basically confined to structural policy arenas. In this regard, the case of Japan contrasts markedly with Italy, where, under the *blocco storico,* a constituency created for partisan patronage emerged before one formed for bureaucratic autonomy could take shape (Shefter 1977, 441–46). Simply stated, the sequence of these two developments left Japan with an elite, meritocratic, and activist state bureaucracy, while Italy emerged with an overstaffed, patronage-ridden, and unesteemed corps of civil servants recruited in disproportionate numbers from the backward south.

In light of these historical differences in politico-economic structure, the Japanese model cannot easily be duplicated by other advanced industrialized democracies. The broader range of salient interests, the greater empowerment of consumers and other nonproducer interest groups, and the weaker position of government officials (as compared with elected politicians) in the policymaking process—all make replication impossible. In addition, the calls for political reform in many advanced liberal democracies of North America and Western Europe challenge the prospects for emulation of the Japanese model. The United States, with its laissez-faire economic ideology, stringent antitrust codes, and vocal consumers' and taxpayers' lobbies, appears particularly unsuited. Even in Italy, where systemic dualism characterizes the politico-economic order, it would be difficult to replicate the Japanese experience. Fashioning an elite and truly meritocratic state bureaucracy without any vestige of patronage from key industrial sectors would also pose a challenge.

While Japan's domestic political and economic structures more closely resemble those of developing countries, successful emulation in those countries is unlikely as well. Comparable systems operate in South Korea and Taiwan, and some of the structures and conditions for emulation exist in Singapore, Malaysia, and Thailand, but the majority of developing countries in Asia, Africa, and Latin America have high levels of income inequality as well as unrestrained patronage and political corruption. Moreover, the world political economy is no longer hospitable to protectionism. During the first three decades of the postwar period, the heyday of Pax Americana, countries like Japan were allowed to protect domestic industries and sectors to create a stable capitalist world economy to contain the "communist menace." But the collapse of communism in Eastern Europe has eliminated the rationale for conservative solidarity and for American support of conservative regimes in countries such as Japan and Italy. Indeed, steep international opposition will challenge any attempt to replicate the Japanese model in today's increasingly intolerant world political economy, riddled with conflicting trends toward higher levels of interdependence and rising demands for aggressive unilateralism.

In sum, the Japanese model does not appear exportable: the economic, political, and social costs of transplanting and sustaining it in toto are too high.

How Institutions Matter

Although all democratic polities exhibit sporadic instances of collusion in public works, among advanced countries only Italy can rival Japan in the systematic and pervasive nature of such activity. Under the guise of a political party, the LDP, a federation of warring factions whose candidates battled ruthlessly against one another, dominated the legislative arena for nearly four decades. While pork-barrel politics and the "personal vote" abound in other polities, the degree and prevalence of these phenomena under LDP rule contradict a central assumption of comparative political wisdom, that pork-barrel activity is lower in systems featuring multimember legislative districts. Surprising as well is how little "bacon" influential LDP legislators brought back to their home prefectures.

If we are to understand these patterns, the question is not *whether* institutions matter—they obviously do—but rather, *how* the institutional rules of the game limit courses of action and create incentives and disincentives for certain modes of behavior. In the politics of public works, the pivotal institutions in Japan are the government procurement system, the civil service employment system, and the electoral system; in addition, the political party system affects the structure of the policymaking process and the interactions among political elites.

As we have seen, the government procurement system, by limiting the pool of bidders to ten "qualified" firms, simplifies the complex task of apportioning the costs and benefits of collusive action, it reduces the colluders' transaction costs and bars entry by outsiders. In this way, the system creates a rationale for trade associations—and, on occasion, the organized underworld—to enforce the selective incentives that sustain illicit arrangements. Since firms must be designated in order to bid, there is ample incentive for contractors to construct mutually beneficial bridges to government officials and politicians. In return for their expertise and access to confidential government information, retired bureaucrats earn lucrative second careers with construction firms. And in return for invoking the "voice of heaven" in the allocation of public works contracts, influential politicians receive campaign support and political money from grateful contractors. The competition among firms seeking to outbid one another for the services of ex-bureaucrats and influential legislators inflates the cost of public construction and increases the likelihood of political corruption. In an already collusion-prone industry like construction—with its lumpy demand and high levels of government procurement—lax enforcement and weak penalties for antitrust violations are powerless to discourage price-fixing cartels.

The civil service employment system conditions the behavior of government beaucrats and their interactions with special interests and legislators. Because the majority of government bureaucrats in Japan retire between the ages of 50 and 55, they must "descend from heaven" into second careers in the private sector, quasi-governmental entities, and elective politics. *Amakudari* thus blurs the boundary between public and private realms even more so than the revolving-door phenomenon in U.S. Pentagon procurement. In Japanese public construction, the need to secure *amakudari* landing spots prompts particularistic consideration in designating bidders and in affording strategic leaks of confidential information to firms employing former bureaucrats. The lifetime employment and *amakudari* systems also offer fierce disincentives for would-be whistle-blowers. Since the postretirmenent prospects of government officials relate directly to the level and prestige of their final posting in the bureaucracy, officials do whatever it takes to secure promotion. To that end, bureaucrats build bridges of mutual benefit to legislators whose influence might be instrumental in securing passage of budget proposals, in greasing promotional wheels, and in securing attractive *amakudari* landing spots. In return for these services, bureaucrats assist in the preferential allocation of public works contracts, advance information to bolster credit-claiming, and offer various forms of informal campaign support. The civil service employment system thus promotes dubious behavior in supposedly impartial public administrators.

Electoral institutions affect the way legislators interact with voters and campaign contributors, government bureaucrats, and other legislators. Owing to the single, nontransferable vote, for example, LDP candidates were always competing against one another for the conservative vote in multimember disticts. This arrangement fostered a strong particularistic orientation in which candidates competed to provide services to personal constituents as they downplayed ideology and policy issues (Grofman, forthcoming). The combination of intra- and interparty competition drove LDP candidates to barter with special interest groups, offering access and favorable policy treatment in exchange for reliable blocs of votes and substantial political contributions. In such contests, hereditary politicians had the advantage over newcomers, who had to create their personal constituencies from scratch. In addition, competition among LDP candidates at the district level created a rationale for intraparty factions, which assisted in securing party endorsement, campaign funds, political posts, and constituency services. Furthermore, the SNTV system enhanced the importance of money in politics, and Japan's decentralized campaign finance law rewarded those candidates who built the most complex financial support networks.

Finally, the political party system put a distinctive spin on the behavioral patterns of self-seeking actors. Hegemonic party regimes tend to produce higher degrees of elite cohesion and stability, fewer effective veto points, and more selective interest group access than do polities governed by multiparty coalitions or party governments (Weaver and Rockman 1993, 18). In both Japan and Italy, protracted single-party rule granted disproportionate weight to the interests of governing party candidates and fostered institutionalized links between the dominant party, its support groups, and the state bureaucracy. "As far as the party affiliation of the deputy is concerned," observed an Italian bureaucrat, "the only party that counts at the moment in public administration is Christian Democracy. We find little need to pay attention to the demands or the threats of the other political parties, or their representatives, or their deputies" (LaPalombara 1987, 319). Japanese government bureaucrats have voiced similar views, calling the LDP "the party" (*tō*), as if a single-party dictatorship ruled Japan. Nearly four decades of single-party dominance enabled the institutionalization of information pipelines to the government bureaucracy, and through these lines policy benefits were funneled to the LDP's key support groups and denied to its opponents. In both Japan and Italy, protracted single-party hegemony enabled a de facto shift of influence over policymaking away from parliamentary committees and into the deliberative organs and factions of the ruling party.

In sum, the institutionally determined rules of the public works game in Japan produced a routinized system of bid-rigging, rampant bureaucratic turf wars, electoral rivalries among partisan colleagues, intraparty factionalism, and enigmatic pork-barrel politics. The synergistic interaction of several critical institutions gave shape and substance to a concrete triangle of legislators, bureaucrats, and contractors. Therefore, meaningful reform in this policy domain would have to address all the institutions that channel the self-interested behavior and interactions of the central political actors. Indeed, the steadfast Japanese resistance to U.S. pressure to pry open the domestic construction market, as well as the reform crisis that hastened the LDP's collapse, derived from a recognition of the vital interests served by these institutions.

Wrecking Ball or Face-Lift?

Japan's existing institutions could not harness the particularism, corruption, and inefficiency that arise when political clientelism takes precedence over the general welfare. In 1993 international and domestic factors combined to topple the LDP's legislative hegemony and pave the way for institutional reforms. The end of the cold war deprived the LDP of the scant ideological glue of anticommunism, and deteriorating economic conditions promoted dissatisfaction among voters and important business interests. Meanwhile, a succession of sensational political scandals made it impossible for LDP leaders to continue to resist policial reform.

The fall of the Berlin Wall in November 1989, signaling the end of cold war ideology, jolted mainstream conservative parties like the Christian Democrats in Italy and the LDP in Japan.[13] With the dissolution of the Soviet Union and the collapse of communist regimes throughout Eastern Europe, the Christian Democrat and LDP candidates lost their tenuous ideological ties to their respective parties. For both parties, a distaste for communism and a general avowal of capitalist democracy had been the only common ideological denominators. The end of the cold war also allowed the United States to reevaluate its support of conservative regimes in Western-bloc countries. The Central Intelligence Agency had once funneled clandestine funds to prop up the LDP, but now the Clinton administration felt the American interests would be better served by an open show of support for opposition parties advocating political reform.

Clear signs of domestic unrest had appeared in Japan during the mid-1980s. Soaring land prices drove the cost of home ownership far beyond the means of the average urban salaried worker. A growing gap between haves and have-nots divided a society that had long perceived itself as a monolithic middle class. Taxpayers and consumers recognized the high cost of policies created to protect domestic interest groups—such as rice farmers, small shopkeepers, and construction contractors—and they complained that their standard of living and the country's level of infrastructure development were not as high as they should be. The expression "rich Japan, poor Japanese" gained popularity. Somewhat surprisingly, given the widespread repugnance for American *gaiatsu*, public opinion polls showed that almost half of the Japanese people supported most or all of the U.S. government's demands in the SII talks (*Nihon keizai shinbun*, 27 Mar. 1990). In addition, the maturation of vital industries reduced the demand for government intervention, while a pronounced gap emerged between the needs and expectations of internationally active firms and those with domestic spheres of interests. The turbulence caused by the bursting of the bubble economy and the onset of economic recession also undermined the political status quo (Ishi 1993; Wood 1992).

Against this backdrop, an unprecedented succession of corruption scandals broke, in Japan and abroad.[14] Scandals were nothing new in Japan: between 1975 and 1993 there was roughly one major political corruption exposé a year. As it happened, however, two of the most sensational—the Recruit scandal and the Sagawa affair—broke in the wake of the international and domestic turbulence described above. The combined effect of an unpopular sales tax, opposition to agricultural liberalization, and the Recruit scandal contributed to the LDP's stunning setback in the 1989 Upper House elections, in which the party lost its absolute majority of seats. The LDP's precarious position in the Upper House obliged both the Kaifu cabinet and the subsequent Miyazawa cabinet to focus intensively on reform. As the intervals between scandals shortened and the extent of the exposés broadened, the LDP could no longer pay lip service to reform. The party's leadership would actually have to attempt to do something.

Nevertheless, no one background factor was sufficient to motivate fundamental institutional reform in Japan—or in Italy, for that matter. The Berlin Wall had fallen and Eastern Europe's communist regimes had collapsed, but cold war tensions persisted in East Asia.[15] Although the economic turbulence that began in the late 1980s might have heightened fears of voter reprisal in Japan and Italy, both the LDP and the Christian Democrats had survived similar challenges in the past. And while the Sagawa and *zenekon* scandals and the *Mani Pulite* investigations were highly sensational and involved major political leaders, both regimes had weathered countless corruption incidents. What was distinctive was the unprecedented magnitude of the Italian scandal and the quick succession of the major Japanese scandals. Moreover, while the Italian electorate cast out the Christian Democratic rascals, the LDP emerged from the 1993 elections with one more seat than it had at the time the elections were called. That is to say, the fall of Japan's Liberal Democrats, which paved the way for the creation of a non-LDP coalition of reformers, was not dictated by disgruntled voters.

While diverse factors contributed to the timing of the collapse of single-party hegemony and paved the way for political reform in Italy and Japan, the ultimate force for change was structural.[16] The need for massive infusions of money to maintain the LDP's largest faction ultimately dictated the fall of Kanemaru and the subsequent fracturing of the Takeshita faction, which triggered the end of the LDP's legislative hegemony. Kanemaru's mythical political clout had enabled him to charge off-scale rates for his brokerage services in the allocation of distributive policy benefits, but once it became clear that Kanemaru was doomed, Ozawa Ichirō and his followers had to distance themselves from their mentor to preserve their own political future. So they broke off from the Takeshita faction and established the Reform Forum 21, with Hata Tsutomu as its titular head. When the LDP failed to agree on a meaningful electoral reform bill, Ozawa left the party altogether and created the Shinsei Party.

The collapse of the LDP's legislative hegemony was dictated by the success of Ozawa's party and the other "new parties" in the July 1993 elections, and the establishment of a flimsy non-LDP coalition held together by a vague consensus concerning the need for electoral reform. Had Ozawa and his followers chosen to remain in the fold, the LDP would have prolonged its mastery of the parliamentary realm. And had the LDP's leadership correctly perceived Ozawa's desperate desire to protect and enhance his political power, steps could have been taken to keep him and his followers from defecting. In the end, the LDP could not agree on a political reform bill because the career politicians, who had labored arduously to construct personal support networks, opposed institutional reforms that threatened their incumbency.

The enabling conditions for political reform in Italy and Japan were thus broadly similar. The deaths of their respective hegemonic regimes were caused by political trichinosis, contracted from decades of doling out ever-increasing quantities of pork. This rapacious appetite for pork and the pervasive clientelist structures in both polities were the accumulated product of rational strategies adopted by politicians, bureaucrats, and corporate officials to manipulate the institutional rules of the game for maximum benefit. The end of the cold war, economic hard times, and corruption scandals involving major political figures—these played a part, but structural imperatives eventually made conditions ripe for reform. And in both polities, exposés involving systematized clientelism—especially in government procurement and public works—generated widespread condemnation and demands for reform. No matter how self-serving their respective motives, the vocal endorsement of institutional reform on the part of established powerbrokers like Bettino Craxi and Ozawa Ichirō reinforced the mounting pressures for change. The fall of the Christian Democrats and the LDP resulted from the inability of the respective political systems to harness the spiraling ante and ever more costly by-products of systematized political clientelism.

Implications for Reform

Beginning in the summer of 1993, each of the key institutions in Japan's public works domain experienced some reform within a matter of months. Though these reforms were, at best, only partial, and though it is too soon to gauge their full effects, some signs of change have already appeared.

By the spring of 1994, all but two prefectures and all but one of the twelve largest municipalities either had introduced conditional open-bidding procedures for large-scale public works projects or had taken steps to implement such procedures on an experimental basis (*Asahi shinbun*, 2 May 1994). For example, nearly one-third of the sixty-eight firms competing to construct a park in Kōbe City submitted bids under the minimum acceptable price. The losers in the bidding for a riparian project in Miyagi Prefecture accused the winner of "dumping" (ibid., 9 and 14 Feb. 1994). About ¥456 million separated the high and low bids submitted by twenty-two joint ventures vying for a tunnel project in Ibaraki Prefecture. In the case of a highway tunnel project in Kagawa Prefecture, the lowest bid among the twenty-eight competing firms came from a Tokyo-based firm that had not been designated to bid in the original round (ibid., 1 Dec. 1993 and 14 Feb. 1994). An editorial in the *Asahi Shinbun* commented, "Contractors with no previous record are jumping into the fray and winning contracts, competition to submit the low bid is intensifying, and a succession of contractors are submitting bids below the minimum acceptable price. This state of affairs would have been inconceivable in the era of designated bidding" (14 Feb. 1994). Indeed, the changed environment prompted the chair of the Japan Federation of Construction Contractors to call for "self-restraint" in curbing excessive competition among firms vying to submit the low bid. MOC has even contemplated a policy to restrain price-dumping in an industry long characterized by inflated bids (ibid., 22 Feb. and 4 Mar. 1994).

Other changes have included the appearance of new actors at the credit-claiming podium. For example, Socialist Party MP Koshiishi Azuma actually preceded an LDP rival in claiming credit for the construction of a segment of the Trans-Chūbu Highway through Yamanashi Prefecture (ibid., 6 Feb. 1994). Naturally, such events rarely occurred during the era of LDP hegemony. Moreover, MOC's new policy of self-restraint in the securing of postretirement posts for its upper officials has produced some results. At a press conference in March 1994, Construction Minister Igarashi Kōzō announced that in 1993 fewer than 20 MOC officials descended into positions with construction firms, compared with 145 individuals the previous year. And, breaking with tradition, no upper officials assumed positions with large-scale general contractors. According to Deputy Vice-Minister Ban Noboru, the self-restraint policy obliged MOC's 1993 contingent of descending angels to commence second careers outside the construction industry or, in some cases, to opt for outright retirement (ibid., 22 Mar. 1994).

Nonetheless, although the reforms of 1993 and early 1994 marked the most concentrated and significant instance of institutional transformation since the early stages of the U.S. Occupation, they have not eradicated all vestiges of the old order. The 1993 general elections toppled the LDP from the commanding heights of the legislative realm, but former LDP legislators claimed the most powerful posts in the ephemeral cabinets of Hosokawa Morihiro and Hata Tsutomu, and Ozawa replaced Kanemaru as the shadow ruler in these "non-LDP" cabinets. Reminiscent of the "opening to the left" policy of Italy's Christian Democrats in the 1960s, the LDP became the dominant coalition partner in the administration of Socialist Prime Minister Murayama Tomiichi in June 1994.[17]

While the rules of the electoral game were significantly altered, the Hosokawa cabinet had to offer concessions in order to secure a compromise with the LDP. The LDP had its way with regard to donations from organizations and corporations, and, more importantly, the LDP dictated the number of single-seat districts. As a local contractor cynically observed, "Even if the LDP loses power, nothing will change" (ibid. 19 Aug. 1993). Italians, too, began to question the possibility of real change, given that Silvio Berlusconi reportedly once controlled many of the politicians arrested in the *Mani Pulite* operation. In the wake of the investigations, bribe-filled envelopes (*bustarelle*) have continued to change hands.[18] For meaningful change to take place, elected politicians will need good reasons to refuse bribe-filled envelopes or, for that matter melon boxes filled with cash. In the case of Japan, under an electoral order in which three-fifths of the legislative seats are to be chosen by a single-vote formula that encourages clientelism, the best way to curtail such corruption is to reduce the cost of pursuing a political career by enforcing strict limits on campaign contributions and by increasing public financing for political parties.

Despite the introduction of a conditional open bidding system in the allocation of large-scale public works contracts, the procurement system for small and medium-scale public works projects has not been modified. Instances of bid-rigging have occurred even in projects using supposedly open bidding procedures.[19] In the words of a major construction company official, "The reform [of the bidding system] is nothing but a cheap trick to deceive the general public, and it's ridiculously silly. This will not cause *dangō* to disappear" (ibid., 21 Oct. 1993). As a local contractor mused, "*Dangō* will continue just as it did under the designated bidder system" (ibid., 25 Sept. 1993). Many recall that the anti-*dangō* media campaign in the early 1980s forced the disbanding of the corrupt Construction Fellowship Society, which subsequently reemerged as the equally corrupt Management Harmony Society (ibid., 22 Aug. 1990). And bid-rigging continued to take place even in the midst of the JFTC investigation into the activities of the Saitama Saturday Society (ibid., 10 May 1992). To minimize the by-products of bid-rigging, Japan will have to initiate open, competitive bidding procedures for all public works and be vigilant in enforcing painful penalties for antitrust violations.

Predictably, MOC's promise to exercise self-restraint has not put an end to the practice of government bureaucrats descending into sinecures with construction firms and agencies that allocate public works contracts. The promise, a partial and temporary measure, was made just as arrests of MOC officials were anticipated in the *zenekon* scandal. Although some MOC officials were questioned in the *zenekon* investigations, none was arrested or prosecuted. Once the sensational exposés and intense media scrutiny faded, public works bureaucrats again enjoyed postretirement sinecures as their deferred compensation for less-than-lucrative careers in the government bureaucracy. Piecemeal reforms cannot curb the social costs associated with a practice as deeply rooted as *amakudari:* what are needed are stricter regulations concerning the reemployment of ex-officials in firms that receive public contracts and an increase in the retirement age for government officials.

Entrenched patterns of elite behavior die hard: "Although wholesale change in formal rules may take place, at the same time there will be many informal constraints that have great survival tenacity because they still resolve basic exchange problems among the participants, be they social, political, or economic" (North 1990, 91). Meaningful reform requires more than cosmetic changes in the rules of the game; it demands overhauling the key institutions that provide incentives for particular patterns of behavior among the political elite. It also demands that elites develop the will and the stamina to enforce the letter as well as the spirit of the new rules. As long as the old patterns of behavior continue to perform essential functions for the political elite, those patterns will endure.

Appendixes

Appendix A

Chronology of Trade Friction and Scandal in Japanese Construction, 1985–1994

1985
12 April   Official of U.S. Consulate in Osaka asks that U.S. firms be permitted to bid on projects at the Kansai International Airport (KIA)
May   U.S. government formally requests that American firms be allowed to bid on KIA projects
July   Ministry of Transport announces that foreign firms will not be disadvantaged in designation decisions concerning bidding on KIA projects
December   Kansai International Airport Corporation (KIAC) nominates only Japanese firms to bid on a levee for an artificial island at KIA

1986
24 June   Senator Frank Murkowski (R-Alaska) demands that the USTR Clayton Yeutter launch an investigation according to section 301 of the Trade Law
26 July   Commerce Secretary Malcolm Baldridge receives promise from Prime Minister Nakasone to open a seminar for foreign firms to explain bidding procedures for KIA projects
5 September   South Korea's Construction Minister visits Japan to petition for access for Korean firms; President Chun makes similar request at meeting of heads of state held in Seoul on 21 September
8–9 October   KIAC convenes seminar for foreign firms

1987

21 January   Bechtel signs contract to enter joint venture with six
                    Japanese companies to supervise the design phase of the
                    terminal at KIA

18 March   Senator Murkowski introduces proposal to revise Airport
                    Law

30 April   U.S. House of Representatives passes omnibus provision
                    to Trade Law that includes retaliatory measures against
                    Japanese construction firms

1 May   Prime Minister Nakasone promises President Reagan
                    that Japan will eliminate discriminatory practices in its
                    construction market

30 June   U.S. Senate unanimously adopts a bill excluding Japa-
                    nese firms from federally funded airport projects

25 September   Bechtel granted metropolitan contractors license

29 October   U.S. Senate approves Senator Murkowski's amendment
                    by a 96-1 vote

4 November   Bilateral talks involving business interests on participa-
                    tion in KIA projects

16 November   U.S. points to bid-rigging on public works as a "structural
                    impediment" to fair trade

1 December   Senator Murkowski sends letter to USTR Yeutter de-
                    manding invocaton of Section 301

4 December   U.S. House of Representatives votes 399-17 to ban Japa-
                    nese firms from participating in federally funded public
                    works; two weeks later the bill passes the Senate

22 December   Brooks-Murkowski Amendment inserted into annual
                    Expenditure Law

1988

5 January   Effective 30 December 1987, USTR bans Japanese
                    firms from federally funded public works

22 January   Senator Murkowski threatens to seek retaliatory leg-
                    islation against Japanese firms in private-sector con-
                    struction

25 January   Representative Pete Stark (D-Calif.) introduces bill that
                    would effectively exclude Japanese firms from private
                    construction projects

17–19 February   High-level bilateral talks on construction end in failure

25 February   Trade Policy Study Group recommends invocation of
                    Section 301

2–8 March   Bilateral talks on construction end without resolution

3 March   Washington, D.C., Transit Authority rejects Kajima

	Corporation's bid (result of Brooks-Murkowski Amendment); similar action taken against Kajima in Houston on 25 March; low bid by Kumagai Gumi for a public works project in San Francisco rejected on 11 May
22–29 March	Bilateral talks produce Major Projects Agreement (MPA), signed on 25 May
25 March	French design selected for KIA terminal
21 April	Omnibus trade bill passes the House and, on 27 April, the Senate; bill sent to President Reagan on 13 May; vetoed on 24 May
15 August	Fluor Daniel granted contractors license
6 September	First meeting of MPA monitoring commission
24 November	Contract for Minato Mirai, one of the special projects set aside in the MPA, granted to a joint venture that includes Schal Associates
8 December	Japan Fair Trade Commission orders payment of fines in Yokosuka Naval Base bid-rigging incident

1989

25 May	Suggestion to undertake talks on "structural impediments"; agreement reached at summit on 14 July
4–5 September	First meeting of Structural Impediments Initiative (SII) talks
29 September	Senator Murkowski sponsors a rider to a bill banning firms involved in the Yokosuka Naval Base bid-rigging incident from participating in U.S. federally funded public works
20 December	Bechtel wins contract for Haneda Airport

1990

| July/August | Dissolution of the Management Harmony Society |
| November | KIAC bypasses AEG Westinghouse for people-mover contract |

1991

3 April	U.S. Department of Justice announces possible action against foreign collusion
25 April	Bilateral construction talks; USTR Carla Hills gives 30-day ultimatum under threat of Super 301
2 June	U.S.-Japan Construction Market Agreement signed (expands list of specially designated projects from 17 to 34)

1992

| 22 January | Los Angeles trolley war |
| 27 August | Kanemaru Shin admits receiving ¥5 billion from Tokyo Sagawa Kyūbin and resigns as LDP vice-president |

1993
6 March | Kanemaru indicted on charges of tax evasion
20–23 March | Acting upon evidence gathered in the Kanemaru probe, investigators search the offices and homes of 18 major general contractors
30 April | USTR Mickey Kantor threatens to impose sanctions if Japan does not more fully open its construction market to American firms within 60 days
June | Bilateral talks to review progress on construction-related issues; U.S. demands replacement of the designated bidding system with an open bidding system
29 June | Sendai Mayor Ishii Tooru arrested on charges of receiving ¥100 million in bribes from four general contractors
30 June | Clinton administration formally identifies Japan as a country that discriminates against U.S. construction firms; imposition of sanctions deferred until 1 November 1993
18 July | In general elections, LDP loses its absolute majority in the Lower House
19 July | Sanwa Town Mayor Oyama arrested on charges of receiving a ¥14-million bribe from a general contractor
23 July | Ibaraki Governor Takeuchi arrested on charges of receiving ¥10 million from a general contractor
9 August | Hosokawa cabinet formed
September | Bilateral talks on construction
27 September | Miyagi Governor Honma arrested on charges of receiving a ¥20-million bribe from a general contractor
October | Chief Cabinet Secretary Takemura announces that an open bidding system will be put in place for large-scale public works projects and consultancy contracts; USTR Kantor defers retaliatory action until 20 January

1994
January | USTR Kantor includes construction in a list of 43 areas in which impediments block fair trade in Japanese markets
11 March | Member of Parliament Nakamura arrested on charges of improper use of the powers of office
31 March | USTR Kantor cites problems in access to Japan's construction market as one of 43 areas affected by unfair trading practices; threat of Super 301 looms

Appendix B

Administrative Vice-Ministers of Construction, 1948–1994

	Date of Appointment	Background	Bureau
Iwasawa Tadazō	10 July 1948	Technician	Road
Nakata Masami	1 Mar. 1950	Generalist	Economic°
Inaura Shikazō	22 July 1952	Technician	
Ishiba Jirō	18 Nov. 1955	Generalist	Secretariat
Yoneda Masafumi	1 June 1958	Technician	River
Shibata Tatsuo	16 Dec. 1958	Generalist	Secretariat
Yamamoto Saburō	1 Nov. 1961	Technician	River
Yamamoto Tatsuo	23 July 1963	Generalist	Secretariat
Yamanouchi Ichirō	18 Oct. 1963	Technician	River
Maeda Kōki	7 Jan. 1965	Generalist	Secretariat
Onouchi Yukio	11 Nov. 1967	Technician	Road
Shimura Seiichi	5 June 1970	Generalist	Secretariat
Sakano Shigenobu	9 June 1972	Technician	River
Otsuru Atsushi	1 Aug. 1973	Generalist	Secretariat
Takahashi Kuniichirō	16 July 1974	Technician	Road
Takahashi Hiroma	11 June 1976	Generalist	Secretariat
Inoue Takashi	23 May 1978	Technician	Road
Awaya Toshinobu	17 July 1979	Generalist	Secretariat
Inada Yutaka	10 June 1981	Technician	River
Maruyama Yoshihito	15 June 1982	Generalist	Secretariat

	Date of Appointment	*Background*	*Bureau*
Takahide Hidenobu	16 June 1984	Technician	City
Toyokura Hajime	1 Oct. 1985	Generalist	Secretariat
Inoue Shōhei	10 Jan. 1987	Technician	River
Takahashi Susumu	12 Jan. 1988	Generalist	Secretariat
Suzuki Michio	27 June 1989	Technician	Road
Makino Tōru	3 July 1990	Generalist	Secretariat
Mitani Hiroshi	26 June 1992	Technician	Road

° Nakata was chief of the General Affairs Bureau, the organizational predecessor of the Economic Affairs Bureau.

Appendix C

Construction Ministers, 1955–1994

	Date of Appointment	*Cabinet*°	*Party (Lineage)*
Baba Motoharu	22 Nov. 1955	Hatoyama C	LDP (Ogata)
Nanjō Tokuo	23 Dec. 1956	Ishibashi	LDP (Kishi)
Nemoto Ryūtarō	10 July 1957	Kishi A	LDP (Kōno)
Endō Saburō	12 June 1958	Kishi B	LDP (Kishi)
Murakami Isamu	18 June 1959	Kishi C	LDP (Ōno)
Hashimoto Tomisaburō	19 July 1960	Ikeda A, B	LDP (Satō)
Nakamura Umekichi	8 Dec. 1960	Ikeda B, C	LDP (Kōno)
Kōno Ichirō	18 July 1962	Ikeda D, E	LDP (Kōno)
Koyama Osanori	18 July 1964	Ikeda F	LDP (Kōno)
Setoyama Mitsuo	3 June 1965	Satō A	LDP (Kōno)
Hashimoto Tomisaburō	1 Aug. 1966	Satō B	LDP (Satō)
Nishimura Eiichi	3 Dec. 1966	Satō C	LDP (Satō)
Hori Shigeru	25 Nov. 1967	Satō D	LDP (Satō)
Tsubokawa Shinzō	30 Nov. 1968	Satō E	LDP (Satō)
Nemoto Ryūtarō	14 Jan. 1970	Satō F	LDP (Satō)
Nishimura Eiichi	5 July 1971	Satō G	LDP (Satō)
Kimura Takeo	7 July 1972	Tanaka A	LDP (Satō)
Kanemaru Shin	22 Dec. 1972	Tanaka B	LDP (Satō)
Kameoka Takao	25 Nov. 1973	Tanaka C	LDP (Satō)
Ozawa Tatsuo	11 Nov. 1974	Miki A	LDP (Satō)

	Date of Appointment	*Cabinet*°	*Party (Lineage)*
Kariya Tadao	9 Dec. 1974	Miki A	LDP (Satō)
Miki Takeo	15 Jan. 1976	Miki A	LDP (Miki)
Takeshita Noboru	19 Jan. 1976	Miki A	LDP (Satō)
Chūma Tatsui	15 Sept. 1976	Miki B	LDP (Kishi)
Hasegawa Shirō	24 Dec. 1976	Fukuda A	LDP (Kishi)
Sakurauchi Yoshio	28 Nov. 1977	Fukuda B	LDP (Kōno)
Tokai Motosaburō	7 Dec. 1978	Ōhira A	LDP (Kishi)
Watanabe Eiichi	9 Nov. 1979	Ōhira B	LDP (Satō)
Saitō Shigeyoshi	17 July 1980	Suzuki A	LDP (Satō)
Shiseki Ihei	30 Nov. 1981	Suzuki B	LDP (Kishi)
Utsumi Hideo	27 Nov. 1982	Nakasone A	LDP (Satō)
Mizuno Kiyoshi	27 Dec. 1983	Nakasone B	LDP (Ikeda)
Kibe Yoshiaki	1 Nov. 1984	Nakasone C	LDP (Kōno)
Etō Takami	28 Dec. 1985	Nakasone D	LDP (Kōno)
Amano Kōsei	22 July 1986	Nakasone E	LDP (Kōno)
Ochi Ihei	6 Nov. 1987	Takeshita A	LDP (Kōno)
Okonogi Hikosaburō	27 Dec. 1989	Takeshita B	LDP (Kōno)
Noda Takeshi	3 June 1989	Uno	LDP (Kōno)
Harada Shōzō	10 Aug. 1989	Kaifu A	LDP (Ikeda)
Watanuki Tamisuke	28 Feb. 1990	Kaifu B	LDP (Satō)
Otsuka Yūji	29 Dec. 1990	Miyazawa A	LDP (Kōno)
Yamasaki Taku	5 Nov. 1991	Miyazawa B	LDP (Kōno)
Nakamura Kishirō	12 Dec. 1992	Miyazawa B	LDP (Satō)
Igarashi Kōzō	9 Aug. 1993	Hosokawa	Japan Socialist
Morimoto Kōji	28 Apr. 1994	Hata	Kōmeitō
Nosaka Kōken	30 June 1994	Murayama A	Japan Socialist

° After the system employed in Satō and Matsuzaki (1986).

Positional Influence and the Pork Barrel: A Multivariate Regression Model

I constructed a multivariate linear regression model to test the assumption that a legislator's positional influence correlates positively with increased public construction expenditures in his or her home prefecture. The dependent variable in the regression is the appraised annual value of total public construction started per prefecture as measured in per capita terms (as reported in a monthly sample made by the Ministry of Construction). Specifically, the analysis sought to determine whether public works spending increased in the home prefectures of the construction minister, the head of PARC's construction division, the prime minister, and retired high-level officials of the Ministry of Construction. To control for the possibility that a positive correlation might accompany the appointment of a legislator to *any* major post, the analysis also included individuals appointed to the supposedly "pork-less" positions of foreign minister, labor minister, and head of PARC's labor division. To account for the potential gap between the time of appointment and the delivery of distributive policy benefits, "lags" of one through five years were incorporated.

Aside from these positional influence factors, three additional political variables were used. First, the number of Lower House legislators per capita—a measure used to determine whether the relatively "overrepresented" prefectures reap a proportionately larger harvest of public construction expenditures than do the "underrepresented" prefectures. Second, the number of LDP MPs per capita—used in a similar vein; notably, the LDP tends to attract strong support from rural districts, many of which have experienced a net decrease in population since the last significant reapportionment in 1947. Third, a measure of whether public construction expenditures tended to increase during years with general elections for the Lower House—intended to test the popular assumption that the LDP tried to boost government spending on construction during election years essentially in order to "buy" voter support.

Five independent demographic and economic variables were also incorporated into the model: (1) annual estimates of population were factored in to determine how public construction spending responds to changes in the population of the prefectures; (2) the aggregate value of manufactured goods shipments—to see whether increased business activity accompanies expanded public works spending; (3) per capita income; (4) per capita agricultural income; and (5) increases in per capita payments of national taxes—to see if these were rewarded with a proportionate expansion of public construction spending.

The regression analysis focuses on the period from 1964 to 1988 and proceeds down two pathways. The first set of regressions involve data on all of Japan's forty-seven prefectures except Okinawa, which did not revert to Japanese control until 1972. Including the lag effects, the analysis involves a total of nearly 60,000 data points. The second set of regressions contains most of the relevant variables for the nine prefecture-wide districts (*zenkenku*)—Fukui, Yamanashi, Shiga, Nara, Tottori, Shimane, Tokushima, Kōchi, and Saga—districts in which legislators' positional influence and the possible impact of positional influence on credit-claiming are clearer than in prefectures that house more than one electoral district. However, all the prefecture-wide districts are located in the rural hinterland, where LDP candidates generally cast a disproportionately long shadow, and thus these prefectures are not representative of all prefectures.

The regression analyses suggest that the share of the variance explained by the political variables—including the positional influence factors—is markedly less than much of the received wisdom would have it. While public works spending increases in the prefectures represented by legislators serving as construction minister beginning in the third year following their appointment, the size of the increase is not as high as might have been anticipated. Likewise, there was no statistically significant positive correlation either for legislators appointed to the prime ministership or for those appointed to the head of PARC's construction division (except in the case of the data concerning the nine prefecture-wide districts). Similarly, the results do not sustain the widespread belief that the districts of retired Construction Ministry officials are showered with increased public works spending following their election.

These results are preliminary, and a full test of these relationships would require additional analysis. For example, it may be that legislators in positions of influence in the public works subgovernment exercise their influence not to funnel projects into their districts but instead to ensure that specific projects are awarded to particular firms, possibly firms that have contributed funds to their political war chest. Further research is also needed to account for the informal influence of powerful individuals such as Kanemaru Shin, long reputed to be "the don of all dons" in Japan's public works subgovernment.

Notes

Introduction

1. In 1965 Potashnick Construction, a Missouri firm, was awarded a major public works contract for a project in Shizuoka that was part of the Tōmei Expressway linking Tokyo and Nagoya, but Potashnick pulled out of the project, citing financial difficulties and problems with Japanese subcontractors.

2. See, among others, Johnson et al. (1989), Magaziner and Hout (1981), Okimoto (1989), Patrick and Rosovsky (1976), Yamamura (1982), and Zysman (1983). For a preliminary version of the argument I present in this section, see Woodall (1992). My notion of dual economic policy markets was shaped by the insightful works of Lowi (1964, 1972), Ripley and Franklin (1987), and Huntington (1961).

3. Whether Japan's economic miracle was realized because of or in spite of heavy, continuing state intervention is beyond the scope of the analysis here. The question is at the heart of the debate between the so-called revisionists and empirically oriented economists and political scientists; for example, compare Johnson (1982, 1990a), Johnson et al. (1989), and Tyson (1993), with Beason and Weinstein (1994) or Calder (1993). For a discussion of the nature and limitations of Japan's high-growth industrial policy, see Yoshikawa and Woodall (1985, esp. 693–701). Inoue (1993, 10–18) provides a succinct overview of the array of Japanese industrial policy tools. Vogel (1993) offers an insightful analysis of the defense-related spin-ons of Japanese commercial technology in contrast to the commercial spin-offs of U.S. defense technologies.

4. Calder (1993, 183–95) presents an instance of private-sector defiance in the case of Kawasaki Steel. Samuels and Whipple (1989, esp. 276–80) assess MITI's abortive attempts to develop a commercial aircraft industry.

5. On this point I concur with Katzenstein's (1985, 19–20) view concern-

ing the "smart-state" thesis. While the developmental state has not always been sufficiently farsighted or swift to anticipate which industries to target and how to develop them, its wide-ranging and activist role presents an iron-clad case against the mythical notion of unfettered competition as the engine of Japanese economic growth.

6. Describing the politics of commercial R&D programs in the United States, Banks et al. point out, "With rare exceptions, programs are conceived and designed in executive branch agencies by professional civil servants who are dedicated to the mission of their organization" (1991, 54). "A member of Congress," these authors reason, "viewing the uncertainties of the distributive consequences of [a commercial R&D program], should prefer to take his or her share of the pig in a more prosaic and safer form, such as federal construction projects" (75).

7. According to data collected by the Organization for Economic Cooperation and Development (reprinted in Keizai kōhō sentaa 1994, 71), the 1992 index for producer subsidy equivalents (in which higher values denote higher levels of government assistance) for agricultural products in Japan was 71, compared to 47 for the European Community and 28 for the United States. The 1992 index for consumer subsidy equivalents (in which larger negative figures denote greater consumer burdens) for agricultural products in Japan was − 52, compared with − 40 for the European Community and − 19 for the United States. Between 1960 and 1990, however, the contribution of agriculture to Japan's GDP fell from 9 percent to less than 2 percent, and whereas 26 percent of Japan's workforce had been employed in agriculture in 1960, by 1990 that figure had dropped to 6 percent (MAFF data reprinted in *Japan Almanac* 1992, 110).

8. Other advocates of the bureaucratic-dominance thesis include Pempel (1974); Baerwald (1974); Johnson (1975); Campbell (1977); Inoguchi (1983); van Wolferen (1989, 1993). Arguing the legislative-dominance thesis are Muramatsu and Krauss (1984); Pempel (1987); Inoguchi and Iwai (1987); McCubbins and Noble (1993). In the middle ground are Satō and Matsuzaki (1986). Samuels (1987) and Calder (1993) both emphasize the central role of the private sector in policymaking, depicting the private-sector elites as formidable bargaining opponents and, on occasion, as domineering actors in the politics of policymaking.

9. Berger and Piore (1980) present an insightful analysis of the nature, casues, and functions of industrial dualism. Clark (1979) and Dore (1973) assess the contours of the Japanese case.

10. In contrast, McCubbins and Noble (1993) expend so much effort disproving the "abdication" thesis—the notion that the legislature abdicates control over policy choices to the bureaucracy—that they ignore the contributions of the bureaucracy.

11. Lowi (1964, 677–715; 1972, 298–310). Clausen (1973) and Ripley and Franklin (1987) also contribute important insights to this school of thought.

12. Ramseyer and Rosenbluth (1993) and McCubbins and Noble (1993) adopt this approach, and it leads the latter to argue that Japanese bureaucrats "act from a script written and directed by politicians and parties" (12). However, there is nothing in principal-agent theory that dictates that the legislators, rather than government bureaucrats, play the role of principal in the policymaking process.

Chapter One

1. An official of the U.S. Embassy in Tokyo described this episode to me. Krauss (1989) also mentions the incident.

2. The defining phrases quoted in this paragraph are from T. Maeda (1988, 16); Cutts (1988, 48); "Dangō" (1983, 67); *Kensetsugyō wa ima* (1980, 91); Taoka (1982, 338); Uchiyama (1982, 32–39); Watanabe (1982, 272); *Los Angeles Times* (26 Apr. 1991); K. Maeda (1990, 85). See Woodall (1993a) for a preliminary version of the argument presented in this section.

3. This incident is described in Kōsei torihiki iinkai (1990, 33–36), "Gojūgo-oku-en" (1989), and *Yomiuri shinbun* (Osaka ed., 21 June 1989). On the heels of the cease-and-desist order, an editorial in *Asahi Shinbun* (6 Oct. 1989) commented, "The [American] demand has come as a great shock to the Japanese construction industry, which has continued to do business in a climate where fixing bids is considered commonplace."

4. For examples of such lists, see Erickson (1969, 84); Haar (1983, 14); Hay and Morris (1991, 75–80); Kuhlman (1969, 69).

5. Data in this section are drawn from *Kensetsu gyōkai gurafu* (1989, 1994); Ministry of Construction; Economic Planning Agency; Kensetsu Keizai Kenkyūjo (Research Institute on Construction and Economy).

6. According to the official government scheme, construction firms are grouped into three categories: general contractors (*zenekon*), specialized contractors, and equipment installers. The cornerstone of the industry are the general contractors—grouped into twenty-eight subcategories—some of which are backed by retinues of up to four layers of subcontractors. In the mid-1980s, over one-third of licensed construction contractors were classified as general contractors, while the remainder were firms specializing in wood building (21.6 percent), specialized work (25.7 percent—e.g., asphalt, dredging and reclamation, and electrical projects), and equipment installation (17.8 percent); *Kensetsu sangyō handobukku* (1987, 17).

7. For profiles of the Big Six, see T. Maeda (1988, 55–66, 144–152, 156–167). Data on the size of these firms are from *Japan Company Handbook*

(1994). T. Maeda (149–52 and 168–81) also profiles the "quasi-large-scale" contractors in the second tier of *zenekon*.

8. Such contacts among competitors were the basis of a price-fixing ring in the U.S. electrical equipment industry in the early 1960s: "Getting together with competitors was looked on as a way of life, a convention, 'just as a manager's office always has a desk with a swivel chair.' It was considered easier to negotiate market percentages than to fight for one's share, less wearing to take turns on rigged bids than to play the rugged individualist" (Smith 1963, 175).

9. On the issue of self-enforcement, see, for example, Stigler (1964, 44–61); Asch (1969, 64); Hay and Kelley (1974, 77); Scherer and Ross (1990, 245).

10. Wolff and Howell (1992, 57) argue that lax antitrust enforcement can be viewed as a facet of Japan's trade policy: "Weak antitrust enforcement has made possible the 'privatization of protection'—the *de facto* protection of the domestic market on a sector-by-sector basis by private groups through restrictive distribution arrangements, import-regulating cartels, pressures on customers and distributors, and similar measures."

11. A former member of a government advisory committee claims that eliminating bid-rigging and payoffs would reduce the cost of public works by half (Jin et al. 1981, 194). Former Transport Minister Ishihara Shintarō believes that price-fixing inflates the cost of public construction in Japan by 40 percent (Ishihara and Morita 1989). Maeda Kunio, a scholar who has written widely on the construction industry, calculates that *dangō* results in projects costing 30 to 40 percent more than necessary (in Kasumi 1993, 146–47). The situation is comparable to the state of affairs in Italy, as described by a senior Treasury Minister there: "In effect, much of Italian enterprise has functioned with a system of hidden taxation, in the form of bribes and kickbacks they [contractors] had to pay for any public contract" (*New York Times*, 25 Mar. 1993).

12. The cost of certain construction tools and materials, such as metal tools and lumber, are higher in Japan than in the United States, but these differences account for only a fraction of the overall disparity. T. Satō (1992) analyzes cross-national differences in private-sector construction costs: If one sets per-square-foot costs in the U.S. at 100, then costs in Canada are 126, costs in typical European countries are in the 101 to 135 range (except for Finland, 161, and the U.K., 226), while costs in Japan are 274.

Chapter Two

1. On the motives of bureaucrats, see, for example, Niskanen (1971, 36, 38–39); Simon (1976, 110–11); Downs (1967, 81–88); Johnson (1989, 8). In

Japan, the allure of elite social status and a sense of national service also drive the actions of state officials. As Johnson observes, "The ancestors of the modern Japanese bureaucrats are the *samurai* of the feudal era." A career in the central bureaucracy—particularly the economic ministries, such as finance or MITI—continues to "attract the most talented graduates of the best universities in Japan, and the positions of higher-level officials in these ministries are . . . considered the most prestigious in the country" (1982, 20 and 36). Moreover, in interviews I conducted, a wide range of current and former bureaucrats expressed patriotism and a commitment to the general welfare that exceeded mere lip service. During these interviews, MOC officials emphasized the desire to achieve nationwide "balance" in decisions concerning the allocation of public resources. Given their lower salaries relative to former university classmates employed in the private sector, myopic material self-interest could not be the only goal of Japanese government bureaucrats.

2. On the politicization and reputation of MOC, see Ramseyer and Rosenbluth (1993, 124); Okimoto (1989, 202); Calder (1988, 153–54, 190–91, and 292); Marshall with Toyama (1992, 37); Kanryō kikō kenkyūkai (1978, 46–47); Kusayanagi (1975, 154); Saitō (1978, 89).

3. Ōhashi went on to serve ten terms in the Lower House of the Diet, representing his native Shimane. As for the "Gang of Four"—Miyashige Mamoru, Kōno Tsutomu, Katō Yutaka, and Wada Tsutomu—each proceeded to enjoy a successful career at MOC. S. Matsumoto (1974, 139), Johnson (1982, 59–60), and Kanryō kikō kenkyūkai (1978, 27) discuss this matter.

4. Kato (1992) shows how Finance Ministry officials shaped agendas and persuaded politicians of the merits of a consumption tax. For examples from MITI, see Johnson (1982). One of the MITI episodes involved a protracted tug-of-war between Tanaka Kakuei and Fukuda Takeo in seeking to promote the careers of officials within the ministry sympathetic to their respective interests. Another case concerned pressure that led to the resignation in 1993 of a bureau chief, Naitō Masayuki, who had approved the "gilded promotion" of a junior official. It so happened that the junior official was the son of the administrative vice-minister, and the promotion took place immediately prior to the junior official's resignation from MITI in order to run in the 1993 Lower House elections.

5. Nishioka (1988) provides a detailed description of the events summarized here. Contemporary newspaper accounts include *Asahi shinbun* (5 Dec. 1951; Tokyo ed., 3 Apr. 1952; Tokyo ed., 4 June 1953); *Nihon keizai shinbun* (19 June 1951, 27 Aug. 1951); *Mainichi shinbun* (13 Mar. 1959); *Yomiuri shinbun* (3 Dec. 1948, 27 Dec. 1952); *Shakai taimusu shinbun* (14 Mar. 1953).

6. Chalmers Johnson (1974) was among the first scholars to recognize the political importance of *amakudari;* my analysis drew inspiration from his

work. The findings presented here are based on data concerning the post-retirement fates of 114 former upper-level officials (bureau chief and above) who served between 1948 and 1988. The postretirement fates of noncareer civil servants is far more harried: "Having no real authority or law-making power, these retired officials are obliged to grow old in a 'second life' making the rounds with résumé in hand" (S. Matsumoto 1974, 151). See also Kanryō kikō kenkyūkai (1978, 151), and Yamamoto (1975, 140–41).

7. *Amakudari hakusho* (1985, 138) provides information about the post-retirement reemployment pathways for officials of selected ministries:

Reemployment Post	*Construction*	*Transport*	*Agriculture*
Public corporation	46	29	73
Industry association	56	177	633
Private sector	146	220	635
Elective politics	14	6	15
Academic positions	9	4	61
Miscellaneous	4	47	——
Unclear	23	43	316
Total	298	526	1,733

8. Despite the striking parallels and differences between *pantouflage* and *amakudari*, I am unaware of any in-depth comparative analysis of their origins and functions. For example, in contrast to the one-way street taken by Japanese bureaucrats, French government officials need merely take a leave of absence from the civil service in order to run for elective office. Criticism surrounds the practice in both countries. The statement of a French observer (cited in Cohen 1969, 198) applies equally well to Japan: they "decide everything among themselves behind a curtain of opaque 'technicity,' in clandestine meetings where agreements are too easily reached among civil servants who have already *pantouflés* (moved into private firms) and civil servants who would like to *pantoufler*." The term *pantouflé* (literally "bedroom slippers") refers to how high civil servants slip back and forth from lifetime appointments in the *grand corps* to high-placed private-sector jobs. I am grateful to David Wilsford for insights.

9. For example, an official posted to MOC's Road Bureau discovered that the de facto strongman in the area of road administration was not the incumbent bureau chief but, rather, a retired director of the bureau and (and former vice-minister of construction) who exercised "cloistered rule" from the post of president of the Japan Highway Corporation.

10. Jin et al. (1981, 198–99); *Asahi shinbun* (13 Sept. 1993). Between 1974 and 1984, among the "descending angels" who landed at the five public corporations under MOC jurisdiction, over 40 percent were former MOC officials (*Amakudari hakusho* 1985, 161):

	Former Agency of "Old Boys"		
Public Corporation	*MOC*	*MOF*	*Other*
Housing	21	5	8
Japan Highway	13	5	13
Metropolitan Highways	5	2	7
Water Resources	8	2	16
Hanshin Superhighway	9	0	13
Total	56	14	57

By comparison, only 28 officials of these public corporations rose to their position through internal promotion during this time period.

11. Thirty-eight MOC officials descended into national elective politics between 1950 and 1994:

	Date Elected	*Diet Chamber*	*Party*	*Factional Lineage*
Awaya Toshinobu	1986	Lower	LDP/Shinsei	Satō
Fujiwara Setsuo	1960	Lower	LDP	Kishi
Imai Isamu	1972	Lower	LDP	Ikeda
Inaura Shikazō	1956	Upper	LDP	Satō
Inoue Shōhei	1989	Upper	LDP	Satō
Inoue Takashi	1980	Upper	LDP	Satō
Ishiba Jirō	1974	Upper	LDP	Satō
Ishii Keiichi	1993	Lower	Kōmeitō	——
Iwasawa Tadayasu	1950	Upper	Jiyūtō/LDP	——
Jinnouchi Takao	1988	Upper	LDP	Satō
Kamijō Katsuhisa	1974	Upper	LDP	Ikeda
Koga Issei	1990	Lower	LDP/Shinsei	Kishi

(*continued*)

	Date Elected	Diet Chamber	Party	Factional Lineage
Koga Raishirō	1971	Upper	LDP	Satō
Kutsukake Tetsuo	1986	Upper	LDP	Satō
Maeda Takeshi	1986	Lower	LDP/Shinsei	Satō
Majima Kazuo	1992	Upper	LDP	Satō
Masuoka Kōji	1977	Upper	LDP	Satō
Matsushita Tadahiro	1993	Lower	LDP	Satō
Matsutani Sōichirō	1992	Upper	LDP	Satō
Mochizuki Kunio	1974	Upper	LDP	Satō
Nagata Yoshio	1992	Upper	LDP	Satō
Nakata Masami	1952	Lower	Jiyūtō	——
Nemoto Takumi	1993	Lower	LDP	Ikeda
Norota Hōsei	1977	Lower	LDP	Satō
Onimaru Katsuyuki	1967	Upper	LDP	Kōno
Ozawa Kyūtarō	1953	Upper	Jiyūtō/LDP	Kishi
Sakano Shigenobu	1974	Upper	LDP	Satō
Sawada Issei	1962	Upper	LDP	Kishi
Shimizu Yasuo	1992	Upper	LDP	Satō
Shiojima Dai	1983	Lower	LDP	Satō
Takeuchi Fujio	1971	Upper	LDP	Satō
Tawara Takashi	1979	Lower	LDP	Satō
Ueda Minoru	1968	Upper	LDP	Satō
Ueno Kōsei	1992	Upper	LDP	Kishi
Yamamoto Sachio	1963	Lower	LDP	Satō
Yamanouchi Ichirō	1968	Upper	LDP	Ikeda
Yokouchi Shōmei	1993	Lower	LDP	Satō
Yoneda Masafumi	1959	Upper	LDP	Satō

12. The 1980 Upper House election, in which two MOC former vice-ministers won seats, clearly illustrates the Construction Machine's success in directing the vote in each administrative jurisdiction (Jin et al. 1981, 188):

MOC Jurisdiction	Inoue Takashi	Sakano Shigenobu
Hokkaidō Development Agency	76,691	3,285
Tōhoku Regional Bureau	240,455	1,331
Kantō Regional Bureau	179,029	121,510
Hokuriku Regional Bureau	144,788	48,266
Chūbu Regional Bureau	21,365	162,449
Kinki Regional Bureau	178,150	13,917
Chūgoku Regional Bureau	86,239	2,811
Kyūshū Regional Bureau	24,764	227,518
Okinawa Development Agency	2,179	12,304

Chapter Three

1. The zenith of Christian Democratic dominance came in 1948, when the party won nearly 49 percent of the popular vote and 53 percent of the seats in the Chamber of Deputies. However, that was the only time the party came close to reaping half of the popular vote and commanding an absolute majority in the Chamber of Deputies. In contrast, during the height of LDP dominance in the late 1950s and early 1960s, the party secured almost 60 percent of the popular vote and over 63 percent of Lower House seats. For comparative electoral data, see Gorvin (1989).

2. On the rise of career politicians worldwide, see King (1981, 249–85); Sartori (1967, 156–73); Hancock (1972); Jackson (1988); Polsby (1968).

3. This point is argued in Masumi (1985, 3–26; 1988, 288); Yamaguchi (1985); Curtis (1988, 229–32 and passim); Hirose (1983, 54); Kyōgoku (1987, esp. 245–89).

4. I use "hereditary parliamentarian" to denote a parliamentarian whose parent, parent-in-law, grandfather, uncle, or sibling has served in the national Diet. Aoki (1980, 64–93) uses a broader definition of the term.

5. The occupational routes that bring LDP legislators to the Diet vary from election to election, but the preponderance of hereditary politicians among LDP backbenchers (including independents and New Liberal Club candidates who later joined the LDP) has tended to increase since the late 1950s. Throughout the 1980s, roughly 40 percent of LDP backbenchers were hereditary politicians. (Below, the total number of LDP backbenchers is shown in brackets after the election year; data from various years of *Kokkai benran, Jinji kōshinroku, Asahi senkyo taikan, Seikan yōran*).

	Former Officials	Former Local Politicians	Former Staffers	Hereditary Politicians
1958 [30]	5	12	4	7
1960 [33]	14	14	6	6
1963 [41]	6	12	13	15
1967 [35]	10	8	10	15
1969 [45]	10	17	12	18
1972 [37]	10	14	13	11
1976 [61]	16	20	23	20
1979 [38]	8	12	12	16
1980 [25]	5	10	10	11
1983 [33]	10	13	11	12
1986 [47]	12	17	19	20
1990 [53]	17	21	21	20

And the preponderance of hereditary politicians among LDP leaders has markedly increased since the late 1960s. (The total number of LDP leaders is shown in brackets after the period of the cabinet.)

	Former Officials	Former Local Politicians	Former Staffers	Hereditary Politicians
1955–57 [53]	17	5	4	4
1958–60 [53]	22	5	4	5
1960–62 [55]	27	7	4	4
1963–65 [56]	23	4	6	6
1966–67 [59]	28	8	6	7
1968–71 [61]	27	10	7	10
1972–73 [65]	22	10	10	8
1974–76 [67]	20	13	9	19
1976–78 [67]	20	18	16	16
1979–81 [64]	18	15	17	24
1982–84 [64]	19	12	21	24
1985–87 [63]	15	17	24	33
1989 [61]	12	22	30	37
1990–91 [62]	12	19	21	31

6. According to Masumi (1985, 385), *kōenkai* became prevalent among conservative parliamentary candidates at the time of the general election of 1958. In the 1960 election, Masumi believes, candidates running under the banner of the Socialist party followed suit, and by 1963, candidates for local political office had organized *kōenkai* as well. See also Allinson (1980, 114–16 and passim); Yonemoto (1987, 234); Iyasu (1984, 152); Thayer (1969, 88). The pioneering work of Curtis (1971) supplies much of our understanding of *kōenkai*.

7. On Kanemaru's *kōenkai*, see Yonemoto (1987, 223, 227, 234); "Kai no kuni" (1991); *Yomiuri shinbun* (18 and 28 Mar. 1993); *Asahi shinbun* (28 Mar. 1993); *Nihon keizai shinbun* (24 Mar. 1993).

8. On the functions of *kōenkai*, see Thayer (1969, 102); Curtis (1988, 157); Iyasu (1984, 152, 177); Matoba (1986, 165); Tomita et al. (1986, 260).

9. On constituency service, see Masumi (1988, 292); Okuno (1978, 72); Thayer (1969, 94); Hirose (1981, 257); Matoba (1986, 163).

10. Norota Hōsei, Futada Kōji, Satō Takao, and Muraoka Kanezō benefited from this support. These *kōenkai* were disbanded in the midst of the *zenekon* scandal, which intensified in the wake of the July 1993 general elections.

11. Ishikawa and Hirose (1989, 141–42); and Iwai (1990, 127). By way of comparison, the nonelection-year expenses for an aspirant to the Lower House are roughly four times the amount spent by a typical candidate for the U.S. House of Representatives in 1988. During those U.S. elections, candidates spent $274,000, on average, although the average winning candidate spent $388,000 (Magelby and Nelson 1990).

12. Two surveys, one by the Utopia Research Group (reported in Iwai 1990, 126) and one by *Tokyo shinbun* (30 May 1992; reprinted in Fukuoka 1993, 103), on the sources of political financing present roughly similar results:

Amounts (in thousands of yen)

Source	Utopia Survey	Tokyo Shinbun Survey
Public financing	¥18,800 (15%)	¥23,800 (18%)
Party and faction	¥10,376 (8%)	¥19,906 (15%)
Political contributions and *kōenkai*	¥54,342 (43%)	¥61,210 (46%)
Fundraising parties	¥20,407 (16%)	¥13,154 (10%)
Loans	¥15,143 (12%)	¥6,101 (5%)
Other	¥7,468 (6%)	¥9,611 (7%)
Total	¥126,536	¥133,782

13. The demographic factors are discussed in Curtis (1971, 127–29) and Masumi (1985, 385). Mackie and Rose (1982, 406–12) provide a succinct discussion of the basic features of electoral systems worldwide.

14. Under the 1889 Election Law, votes were cast for a plurality of candidates and 257 districts elected a total of 300 representatives. The system was based on an "open ballot" (not a secret ballot), in which the only eligible voters were males 25 years of age or older who paid at least ¥15 in direct taxes. For an overview of the evolution of Japan's electoral institutions up to the mid-1980s, see Soma (1986, esp. 21–41 and 206–44).

15. In 1947 the disparity between the most overrepresented and the most underrepresented districts was 1.51-to-1; by the mid-1980s, the disparity had grown to 5.12-to-1. Relevant data are presented in Tonedachi (1994, 73) and Kawamura and Matsui (1993, 10).

Chapter Four

1. See, for example, Scalapino and Masumi (1962, 18); Benjamin and Ori (1981, 65); Baerwald (1986, 46–47); Ike (1972, 81–83); Iyasu (1984, 115 and 118); Ward (1967, 65 and 68–69).

2. Nakane (1970) and Stockwin (1982, 35–39) argue this point. Culturalist views also inform the pioneering work of Scalapino and Masumi (1962); for example: "In part, it [factionalism] is the product of deeply rooted cultural forces that contribute to a 'Japanese-type organizational model,' a structure built on the basis of loosely federated leader-follower familial-type units" (100). Other analyses in the cultural mode include Totten and Kawakami (1965); Farnsworth (1966); Ishida (1971); Curtis (1971, 1988); Thayer (1969); Baerwald (1986); and Johnson (1990b), though he had earlier made a case against "national character" explanations (1982, 7–9).

3. Kohno (1992) raises a similar question. For example, in 1956 the LDP comprised eight "army divisions" and one "regiment." By the mid-1960s, five main factions had emerged. Reed and Bolland (forthcoming, 10–19) argue that the SNTV in middle-sized districts, which elect on average four representatives, holds the key to the recent stability of a five-factioned LDP, because the effective number of candidates in a district tends to be one greater than the number of open seats.

4. The estimate for the 1960s is from Totten and Kawakami (1965). Estimates for the 1990s are from the Utopia Survey and a survey taken by the *Tokyo shinbun,* reprinted respectively in Iwai (1990, 126) and Fukuoka (1993, 103). The effects of decentralization and the revisions of the Political Fund Control Law were frequently mentioned in the interviews I conducted; see also Iwai (1990, 106–9) and Kohno (1992, 368–69).

5. The allocation of posts took three fundamental forms. Sometimes a

party president would reward "mainstream" factional allies by allocating posts on the basis of the numerical "power balance" that prevailed at the time. On other occasions, to promote intraparty goodwill, the president would distribute posts in roughly equal numbers to all factions. At yet other times, posts were allocated on the basis of simple seniority ranking (Satō and Matsuzaki 1986, 63–67).

6. The dominance of one or two factions in various political posts between 1955 and 1992 is illustrated by the following data:

| | | *Percentage of Posts Filled by* | |
| | | *Any One* | |
	No. of Posts	*Faction*	*Two Factions*
Cabinet ministership			
Construction	42	35.7	69.0
Foreign Affairs	40	40.5	64.3
Finance	41	38.1	61.2
Transport	42	35.7	61.9
Agriculture	42	42.9	61.9
Health and Welfare	42	28.6	57.1
Home Affairs	42	28.6	54.8
Labor	42	26.2	52.4
Justice	42	28.6	52.4
Party leadership			
Secretary General	42	45.2	69.0
Executive Council chair	42	38.1	59.5
PARC chair	42	38.1	52.4

7. Noteworthy among the numerous studies of the roles and functions of the LDP's policy tribes are Inoguchi and Iwai (1987); Itasaka (1987); Nihon keizai shinbunsha (1983); Park (1986); Satō and Matsuzaki (1986); Schoppa (1991); Yuasa (1986). But whereas Yuasa maintains that appointment to the chairmanship of a PARC division in itself entails tribalist status (11–12), Satō and Matsuzaki (264) as well as Inoguchi and Iwai (154–64 and 293–304) contend that appointment to particular party and cabinet posts in a policy area determines which legislators become tribalists. Schoppa (1991, 79) calls the LDP's tribalists "cliques of Diet members with special influence in specific policy areas."

8. The change can be deduced from the increase in the membership of the *bukai* and the number of LDP parliamentarians affiliated with the corresponding standing committees in the Diet's Lower House (Inoguchi and Iwai 1987, 136–37). Between 1955 and 1975, the number of PARC divisions and committees roughly tripled (Satō and Matsuzaki 1986, 263; *Seikan yōran* 1991, 488–91):

	Divisions	Investigation Committees	Special Committees	Total
1955	15	3	14	32
1965	15	18	45	78
1975	17	29	46	92
1985	17	31	61	109
1991	17	33	50	100

Membership in PARC divisions also rose sharply (Fukui 1987; Satō and Matsuzaki 1986; *Jiyūminshutō seimu chōsakai meibo* various years):

PARC Division	1955	1971	1980	1986	1988
Cabinet	6	51	38	39	45
Local Administration	6	61	42	48	56
National Defense	6	47	43	54	53
Justice	6	32	33	36	37
Foreign Affairs	6	52	37	46	43
Finance	8	87	61	73	61
Education	8	73	61	74	73
Social	8	75	80	95	94
Labor	6	41	42	48	43
Agriculture	8	156	149	178	152
Fisheries	6	62	60	68	66
Commerce	8	92	114	154	128
Transport	8	87	68	82	80
Communications	8	59	64	81	82
Construction	8	127	132	183	178
Science & Technology	——	6	29	37	36
Environment	——	5	30	36	36

9. For example, consider the changes in the swing vote for PARC division heads from 1955 to 1991, where "swing vote" is defined as the candidate's percentage of the vote in the election following appointment to the specified post minus the percentage in the election before appointment. (These calculations include only legislators representing Lower House districts.)

PARC Division	N	Swing Vote	Positive Swing	Negative Swing
Education	22	−4.42%	10	12
Local Administration	22	−4.14	6	16
Cabinet	25	−2.31	10	15
Agriculture	17	5.54	10	7
Construction	23	5.95	14	9
Commerce	23	6.02	12	11

10. For example, the average annual rank among Japan's 47 prefectures from 1966 to 1989 for selected prefectures was: Hokkaidō (3.2), Niigata (4.4), Shimane (10.6), Tokyo (28.7), Osaka (39.2), and Saitama (40.2). For 1975 to 1989 the average annual ranking was: Hokkaidō (3.6), Niigata (4.9), Shimane (4.6), Tokyo (34.9), Osaka (46.5), and Saitama (41.5).

11. *Asahi shinbun* (28 Mar. 1993); *Yomiuri shinbun* (28 Mar. 1993). Other alleged instances of Kanemaru's farflung influence include construction of the Tokyo Trans-Bay Tunnel and a parking structure in Yokkaichi City (*Asahi shinbun*, 10 Apr., 29 Aug., 15 Nov. 1993).

12. Sources for the following discussion of credit-claiming in Japan include Hirose (1981, 57); van Wolferen (1989, 193, 305); Wakata (1986, 69); Inoguchi and Iwai (1987, chap. 2). For discussions of credit-claiming by politicians in the United States, Italy, and elsewhere, see Mayhew (1974, 52–53); Johannes and McAdams (1987, 537); Walston (1988, 233).

Conclusion

1. Overseas Bechtel and a group of nine Japanese firms were awarded a ¥90-billion contract to perform work on Haneda Airport. Schal Associates secured 6 percent of an ¥18-billion project—jointly undertaken with a group of Japanese contractors—to construct a hotel and conference hall as part of Yokohama's "Minato Mirai 21." Meanwhile, Tishman Realty and Construction broke into the private sector market by winning a contract to work on a hotel in Osaka. Other U.S. companies that established a presence in Japan

included Fluor Daniel, the Ralph M. Parsons Company, Turner Construction, Morrison Knudsen, and Hellmuth, Obata, and Kassabaum.

2. Details of the incident are provided in "Gojūniman" (1989); *Mainichi shinbun* (23 Apr. 1990); Peterzell (1990); *Sandei mainichi* (3 Dec. 1989); *Shūkan bunshun* (3 Dec. 1989, 28).

3. For example, *Asahi shinbun* (25 Oct. 1993) reported the results of a study conducted by the Management and Coordination Agency: of the 139 government agencies and public corporations surveyed, one third employed a designated bidding system and did not publicly disclose bidding results, and about half employed qualifying standards that disadvantaged foreign firms.

4. Woodall (1993b, 38–42) offers an overview of the nature and consequences of these international structural changes. Kennedy (1987, 525 and passim) and, especially, Nye (1990) discuss the nature and implications of the relative decline in U.S. hegemony. Bhagwati uses the term "diminished giant syndrome" to describe the psychological effects of this decline in the United States; see Bhagwati and Patrick (1993, 11).

5. One U.S. Commerce Department official admitted that the construction industry had not applied as much pressure as desired to reinforce the government's stance in the construction talks. That official attributed this reticence to the fact that the larger U.S. firms feared losing token projects in the Japanese market and the smaller firms lacked political clout (Bradford et al. 1993; see also Setzer and Krizan 1993).

6. The construction case thus affirms Putnam's thesis (1988) concerning the "synergistic strategies" by which a foreign negotiator can manipulate conditions in his counterpart's domestic polity. Building upon Putnam's work, Schoppa (1993, 372) argues that "by transforming a narrow domestic issue into one with implications for an important bilateral relationship . . . foreign pressure can expand elite-level participation as previously uninvolved bureaucratic agencies, senior party leadership, and interests groups come to have a stake in dealing with the problem." Moreover, the threat of U.S. retaliation under Section 301 produced an air of crisis and anxiety in Tokyo. Elevating the dispute to a crisis almost ensured the participation of Japanese officials at the highest level: "crisis decisions in foreign policy are made by an elite of formal, official office-holders" (Lowi 1967, 301). In the negotiations that produced the Major Projects Agreement in 1988, for example, the key decision-makers were Prime Minister Takeshita Noboru and Ozawa Ichirō, his specially selected chief negotiator.

7. With the economic decline in 1991, private construction investment in Japan decreased, and government spending on public works helped cover the difference, rising from 26.4 percent of total construction investment in 1990 to 34 percent in 1992. Nevertheless, Japan's largest general contractors

continued to suffer due to the decline in overseas construction activity. In particular, the collapse of real estate prices in many parts of the United States, reduced demand for office space (especially in places like California, where flows of military funds were drying up), and the effects of economic recession resulted in fewer orders for the Japanese construction firms. Many of these firms incurred losses on assets they had acquired at vastly inflated prices prior to the U.S. recession.

8. A similar point is made by Schoppa (1993, 373 and passim). Based on an analysis of Japanese financial politics, Rosenbluth (1989, 53 and 94), argues that "foreign diplomatic pressure is effective only when market forces have already altered domestic costs and benefits or when there is a perceived threat of retaliation." Similarly, Bayard and Elliott (1995) found that U.S. market-opening initiatives were particularly effective when they meshed with the interests of domestic Japanese groups that shared American interests.

9. Apter and Sawa (1984); Ishikawa and Hirose (1989, 65–120); Pempel (1979); Steinhoff (1988); Taylor (1983); van Wolferen (1989, 65–81, 159–80 and passim).

10. See, for example, Curtis (1988, 229–32); Kyōgoku (1987, 245–89); Masumi (1985, 1:3–26).

11. On the situation in agriculture, see Hayami (1990); Hillman and Rothenberg (1988); Van der Meer and Yamada (1990).

12. The fact that the bureaucratic elite erected barricades does not mean that the prewar developmental regime was completely insulated from partisan meddling. Elected politicians did influence the making of structural policy, such as budgetary and locational decisions concerning public works; see Akita (1967); Duus (1968); Mikuriya (1980); Najita (1967); Scalapino (1953); Woodall (1990). The essential point is that elected politicians played a decidedly minor role in the forging of policies for strategic industries and sectors, particularly in the prewar era and during the first three decades after World War II.

13. Various writers cite the end of the cold war as a contributing factor in the fall of ruling parties in Japan, Italy, Canada, Germany, and Venezuela; see, for example, Inoguchi (1993); Martin (1993); Schorr (1993).

14. At the outset of the 1990s, major political corruption scandals rocked Japan, Italy, India, Brazil, Venezuela, and the United States; less sensational scandals appeared in Germany, Spain, France, and Britain. Now that the West is no longer fixated on containing the communist menace, Daniel Bell (1993, 18) theorizes, "democratic political corruption has become one of the surpassing political issues. The bipolar world dominated by the Communist-capitalist dichotomy has been replaced by a politically unitary one, divided by corrupt and clean."

15. Remnants of the cold war survive in the tensions on the Korean pen-

insula, the dispute between Japan and Russia concerning sovereignty over the Southern Kuriles, and the persistence of Marxist-Leninist regimes in China, North Korea, and Vietnam.

16. I concur with Odawara's assessment (1993, 32): "What destroyed Kanemaru was the Sagawa Express scandal's exposure of his skillful wielding of backroom power as lubricated by illicit funds and unscrupulous connections. More disturbing, however, is that nothing was accidental about this affair; corruption is deeply imbedded in factional politics."

17. The policy of "opening to the left" was approved at the Christian Democratic congress held in Naples in 1962, and became a necessity in the wake of the party's poor showing (and the Communist Party's stellar performance) in elections the following year. Under this policy, the Christian Democrats repeatedly relied upon the Socialist Party as a coalition partner or as the supplier of external support in numerous Christian Democrat–dominated cabinets from 1963 through 1992.

18. For example, 80 percent of the eight hundred industrialists surveyed by Pino Arlacchi stated that the *bustarelle* continued to change hands even after the *Mani Pulite* probe. Although the investigation apparently resulted in slight improvement (85 percent of those polled admitted that bribes were necessary to win public contracts prior to the crackdown), 13 percent said that nothing had changed. Arlacchi's findings are discussed in "Still Crooked" (1994).

19. For instance, bid-rigging allegedly occurred in March 1994 under open bidding procedures in the allocation of the contract to construct a pavilion to honor those who died in World War II. The low bid of ¥5 billion was submitted by a joint venture headed by Takenaka Corporation, the only member of the Big Six not implicated in the *zenekon* scandal. Tenders were accepted only from A-rank firms as determined by MOC's Kantō Regional Construction Bureau. Although there were thirty such firms, the need to exchange information among firms in order to form joint ventures allegedly facilitated the successful bid-rigging; *Asahi shinbun* (19 Mar. 1994).

References

Akita, George.
    1967.   *The Foundations of Constitutional Government in Modern Japan.* Cambridge: Harvard University Press.

Allinson, Gary D.
    1980.   "Opposition in the Suburbs." In Kurt Steiner, Ellis S. Krauss, and Scott C. Flanagan, eds., *Political Opposition and Local Politics in Japan,* 95–130. Princeton: Princeton University Press.

Amakudari hakusho [White paper on amakudari]. Various years. Tokyo: Seifu kankei tokushu hōjin rōdō kumiai sōgo kyōgikai.

Amano Kōsei.
    1986.   *Yukai ni watatta jigujagu jinsei* [Zig-zagging pleasantly through life]. Fukushima: Amano Kōsei.

Amsden, Alice.
    1989.   *Asia's Next Giant: South Korea and Late Industrialization.* New York: Oxford University Press.

Anchordoguy, Marie.
    1989.   *Computers Inc.: Japan's Challenge to IBM.* Cambridge: Council on East Asian Studies, Harvard University.

Aoki Kōyō.
    1980.   "Kokkai e no michi: shinjin giin to seshū giin" [Pathway to the Parliament: New faces and hereditary parliamentarians]. In Naka Hisarō, ed., *Kokkai giin no kōsei to henka* [Composition and changes in Diet parliamentarians]. Tokyo: Seiji kōhō sentaa, 64–93.

Apter, David E., and Nagayo Sawa.
    1984.   *Against the State: Politics and Social Protest in Japan.* Cambridge: Harvard University Press.

Archer, J. C.

1983.   "The Geography of Federal Fiscal Politics in the United States of America: An Exploration." *Environment and Planning C: Government and Policy* 1:377–400.

Asahi senkyō taikan [Asahi election survey]. Various years. Tokyo: Asahi shinbun senkyō honbu.

Asano Chiaki, Ninagawa Masao, Takeuchi Naokazu, and Watanuki Jōji.

1977.   "Dokengyō ni nottoreta chihō seiji—oshoku kyōdōtai o baiyō suru mekanizumu" [Construction industry riding rough shod over local government: The mechanism for cultivating a corrupt partnership]. *Asahi jaanaru*, 21 January, 26–35.

Asch, Peter.

1969.   "Collusive Oligopoly: An Antitrust Quandary." *The Antitrust Law and Economics Review* 2:53–68.

Ashworth, William.

1981.   *Congress, Lobbies, and the American Pork-Barrel System.* New York: Hawthorn/Dutton.

Auerbach, Stuart.

1986.   "Japan Accused of Unfair Tactics." *Washington Post*, 6 June.

Baerwald, Hans H.

1974.   *Japan's Parliament: An Introduction.* New York: Cambridge University Press.

———.

1986.   *Party Politics in Japan.* Worchester, Mass.: Allen and Unwin.

Banks, Jeffrey S., Linda R. Cohen, and Roger G. Noll.

1991.   "The Politics of Commercial R&D Programs." In Linda R. Cohen and Roger G. Noll, eds., *The Technology Pork Barrel*, 53–76. Washington, D.C.: The Brookings Institution.

Bayard, Thomas O., and Kimberly Ann Elliott.

1995.   *Reciprocity and Retaliation in U.S. Trade Policy.* Washington, D.C.: Institute for International Economics.

Beason, Richard, and David E. Weinstein.

1994.   "Growth, Economies of Scale, and Targeting in Japan." Harvard Institute of Economic Research Disussion Paper #1644.

Beck, Melinda.

1982.   "Highway Robbery." *Newsweek*, 2 August.

Bell, Daniel.

1993.   "The Old War." *New Republic*, 23 August, 18–21.

Benjamin, Roger, and Ori Kan.

1981.   *Tradition and Change in Postindustrial Japan: The Role of the Political Parties.* New York: Praeger.

Berger, Suzanne, and Michael J. Piore, eds.

1980.   *Dualism and Discontinuity in Industrial Society.* Cambridge: Cambridge University Press.

Bhagwati, Jagdish, and Hugh T. Patrick, eds.

1993.   *Aggressive Unilateralism: America's 301 Trade Policy and the World Trading System.* Ann Arbor: Univ. of Michigan Press.

Blustein, Paul.

1993a.   "Rigged Bids and Painful Revelations." *Washington Post,* 9 May.

———.

1993b.   "Trustbusters on the Dango." *Washington Post,* 14 May.

Bradford, Hazel, Debra K. Rubin, and Jeff Barber.

1993.   "U.S. Getting Tough with Japan." *Engineering News-Record,* 17 May, 6–7.

Brooks, Roger A., ed.

1990.   *Opening Japan: The Construction Market.* Washington, D.C.: The Heritage Foundation.

Cain, Bruce E., John A. Ferejohn, and Morris P. Fiorina.

1987.   *The Personal Vote: Constituency Service and Electoral Independence.* Cambridge: Harvard University Press.

Calder, Kent E.

1988.   *Crisis and Compensation: Public Policy and Political Stability in Japan, 1949–1986.* Princeton: Princeton University Press.

———.

1993.   *Strategic Capitalism: Private Business and Public Purpose in Japanese Industrial Finance.* Princeton: Princeton University Press.

Campbell, John Creighton.

1977.   *Contemporary Japanese Budget Politics.* Berkeley: University of California Press.

———.

1989.   "Democracy and Bureaucracy in Japan." In Takeshi Ishida and Ellis S. Krauss, eds., *Democracy in Japan,* 113–37. Pittsburgh: University of Pittsburgh Press.

Caro, Robert A.

1974.   *The Power Broker: Robert Moses and the Fall of New York.* New York: Knopf.

Cassese, Sabino.

1993.   "Hypotheses on the Italian Administrative System." *West European Politics* 16:316–28.

Chida, Tomohei, and Peter N. Davies.

1990.   *The Japanese Shipping and Shipbuilding Industries: A History of Their Modern Growth.* London: Athlone.

Chittiwatanapong, Prasert.

 1992. "Japanese Official Development Assistance to Thailand: A Study of the Construction Industry." *Occasional Paper of the U.S.-Japan Relations Program*, Harvard University.

Clark, Rodney.

 1979. *The Japanese Company.* New Haven: Yale University Press.

Clausen, Aage.

 1973. *How Congressmen Decide.* New York: St. Martin's Press.

Cohen, Stephen S.

 1969. *Modern Capitalist Planning: The French Model.* London: Weidenfeld and Nicholson.

"Conductor of Commerce: Interview with Ishikawa Rokurō." 1988. *Journal of Japanese Trade and Industry*, 41.

Cox, Gary W., and Frances Rosenbluth.

 1993. "The Electoral Fortunes of Legislative Factions in Japan." *American Political Science Review* 87:577–89.

Curtis, Gerald, L.

 1971. *Election Campaigning Japanese Style.* New York: Columbia University Press.

 ———.

 1988. *The Japanese Way of Politics.* New York: Columbia University Press.

Cutts, Robert L.

 1988. "The Construction Issue: Japan Slams the Door." *California Management Review* 30:46–63.

"Dangō: yami karuteru" [Dangō: Shady cartel]. 1983. *Shūkan gendai*, 17 June, 67.

"Demand Grows for Alien Construction Workers." 1988. *Japan Economic Journal*, 10 December, 5.

Destler, I.M., Haruhiro Fukui, and Hideo Sato.

 1979. *The Textile Wrangle: Conflict in Japanese-American Relations, 1969–1971.* Ithaca: Cornell University Press.

"Doboku gyōkai: ima 'dangō tengoku'" [Construction industry: Now is "dangō heaven"]. 1979. *Shūkan yomiuri*, 19 August, 20–22.

Dore, Ronald P.

 1973. *British Factory—Japanese Factory.* Berkeley: University of California Press.

Downs, Anthony.

 1967. *Inside Bureaucracy.* Boston: Little, Brown.

Drew, Elizabeth.

 1983. *Politics and Money: The New Road to Corruption.* New York: Macmillan.

Duus, Peter.
  1968.   *Party Rivalry and Political Change in Taisho Japan.* Cambridge: Harvard University Press.
Ehrenhalt, Alan.
  1991.   *The United States of Ambition: Politicians, Power, and the Pursuit of Office.* New York: Random House.
Erickson, Walter B.
  1969.   "The Economics of Price-Fixing." *The Antitrust Law and Economics Review* 2:83–122.
Evans, Peter, Harold Jacobson, and Robert D. Putnam, eds.
  1993.   *Double Edged Diplomacy: International Bargaining and Domestic Politics.* Berkeley: University of California Press.
Farnsworth, Lee W.
  1966.   "Challenges to Factionalism in Japan's Liberal Democratic Party." *Asian Survey* 6:501–9.
Fenno, Richard F.
  1978.   *Home Style: House Members in Their Districts.* Boston: Little, Brown.
Ferejohn, John A.
  1974.   *Pork Barrel Politics: Rivers and Harbors Legislation, 1947–1968.* Stanford: Stanford University Press.
Fiorina, Morris P.
  1977.   *Congress: Keystone of the Washington Establishment.* New Haven: Yale University Press.
Friman, H. Richard.
  1990.   *Patchwork Protectionism: Textile Trade Policy in the United States, Japan, and West Germany.* Ithaca: Cornell University Press.
Fukai, Shigeko N.
  1990.   "Japan's Land Policy and Its Global Impact." *Occasional Paper of the U.S.-Japan Relations Program,* Harvard University.
Fukui, Haruhiro.
  1970.   *Party in Power: The Japanese Liberal Democrats and Policymaking.* Berkeley: University of California Press.
  ———.
  1987.   "The Policy Research Council of Japan's Liberal Democratic Party: Policy Making Role and Practice." *Asian Thought and Society* 34:3–30.
Fukui, Haruhiro, and Shigeko N. Fukai.
  1992.   "Election Campaigning in Contemporary Japan." Paper presented at the 44th Annual Meeting of the Association for Asian Studies, Washington, D.C.

Fukuoka Masayuki.

　1985. 　　*Nihon seiji no fūdo* [The political environment of Japan]. To-kyo: Gakuyō shobo.

———.

　1993. 　　*Seiji no koto ga wakaru hon* [Guide to understanding political matters]. Tokyo: Kanki shuppan.

Genther, Phyllis A.

　1990. 　　*A History of Japan's Government Business Relationship: The Passenger Car Industry.* Ann Arbor: Center for Japanese Studies.

Gerth, H. H., and C. Wright Mills, eds.

　1958. 　　*From Max Weber: Essays in Sociology.* New York: Oxford University Press.

Gilpin, Robert.

　1987. 　　*The Political Economy of International Relations.* Princeton: Princeton University Press.

"Gojūgo-oku-en wa doko e kieta? 'kankū dangō' no gigoku" [Whence the ¥5.5 billion? The Kansai Airport bid-rigging scandal]. 1989. *Zaikai tenbō,* September, 64–67.

"Gojūniman kensetsu gyōsha o sasaeru 'gyōkai eigyō' no riidaa tachi" [The leaders who dominate the "industry business" of the 520,000 construction contractors]. 1989. *Zaikai tenbō,* September, 68–70.

Gorvin, Ian, ed.

　1989. 　　*Elections Since 1945: A Worldwide Compendium.* Essex, England: Longman Publishing Group.

Grofman, Bernard.

　Forth-　　"SNTV: An Inventory of Theoretically Derived Propositions
　coming. 　and a Brief Review of the Evidence from Japan, Korea, Taiwan, and Alabama." In Bernard Grofman, Sung-Chull Lee, Edwin Winckler, and Brian Woodall, eds., *Elections in Japan, Korea, and Taiwan Under the Single Non-Transferable Vote: The Comparative Study of an Embedded Institution.* Ann Arbor: University of Michigan Press.

Haar, Burl W.

　1983. 　　"Collusion in the Highway Construction Industry: Economic Evidence as an Investigative Tool." Ph.D. dissertation, University of Nebraska.

Hancock, M. Donald.

　1972. 　　*Sweden: The Politics of Industrial Change.* Hinsdale, Ill.: Dryden Press.

Hasegawa Fumio and the Shimizu Group FS.

　1988. 　　*Built by Japan: Competitive Strategies of the Japanese Construction Industry.* New York: Wiley.

Hasegawa Tokunosuke.
 1990. *Tochi kaikaku no shiten* [Focusing on the land problem]. Tokyo: Tōyō keizai shinpōsha.
Hashimoto Ryūtarō.
 1988. "The Myth of Limited Access to Public Works Projects." *Liberal Star,* March, 15.
Hay, Donald A., and Derek J. Morris.
 1991. *Industrial Economics and Organization: Theory and Evidence.* 2d ed. New York: Oxford University Press.
Hay, George A., and Daniel Kelley.
 1974. "An Empirical Survey of Price Fixing Conspiracies." *Journal
 of Law and Economics* 17:13–38.
Hayami, Yujiro.
 1990. *Japanese Agriculture Under Siege: The Political Economy of
 Agricultural Policies.* London: Macmillan.
Hershey, Robert D.
 1993. "Japan Formally Accused of Bias Against U.S. Contractors."
 New York Times, 1 July.
Hibbing, John R.
 1991. "Contours of the Modern Congressional Career." *American
 Political Science Review* 85:405–28.
Hillman, Jimmye S., and Robert A. Rothenberg.
 1988. *Agricultural Trade and Protection in Japan.* London: Trade
 Policy Research Centre.
Hippo, Yasuyuki, and Tamura Saburo.
 1988. "Japan." In W. Paul Strassman and Jill Wells, eds., *The Global
 Construction Industry.* London: Unwin Hyman.
Hirose Michisada.
 1981. *Hojokin to seikentō* [Subsidies and the ruling party]. Tokyo:
 Asahi shinbunsha.

———.
 1983. "The Ingredients of LDP Success." *Japan Echo* 10:54–61.
Honda Yasuharu.
 1974. "Sekkei no dekinai genba kantoku—kensetsushō" [On-site
 overseer that cannot plan—Ministry of Construction]. *Gendai,* 184–203.
Honzawa Jirō.
 1990. *Jimintō habatsu* [LDP factions]. Tokyo: Piipurusha.
Hrebenar, Ronald J.
 1986. "The Money Base of Japanese Politics." In Ronald J. Hrebenar, ed., *The Japanese Political Party System: From One-
 Party Rule to Coalition Government,* 55–79. Boulder, Colo.:
 Westview Press.

Huntington, Samuel P.
   1961.   *The Common Defense.* New York: Columbia University Press.
Igarashi Akio.
   1986.   "Mezase Nagatachō ichibanchi" [Aiming for number one Na-
              gatacho]. *Ushio,* December, 110–25.
Iinuma, Y.
   1987.   "The Public Construction Scandal." *Tokyo Business Today,*
              February, 26–27.
Ike, Nobutaka.
   1972.   *Japanese Politics: Patron-Client Democracy.* 2d ed. New York:
              Knopf.
Inoguchi Takashi.
   1983.   *Gendai Nihon seiji keizai no kōzu* [The composition of the
              contemporary Japanese political economy]. Tokyo: Tōyō kei-
              zai shinpōsha.

———.
   1993.   "Nihon to itaria—fuhai no kōzu" [Japan and Italy: The com-
              position of corruption]. *This Is Yomiuri,* August, 76–84.
Inoguchi Takashi, and Iwai Tomoaki.
   1987.   " 'Zoku giin' no kenkyū: Jimintō seiken o gyūjiru shuyakutachi"
              [Research on policy tribesmen: The leading actors who direct
              the LDP regime]. Tokyo: Nihon keizai shinbunsha.
Inoue, Ryuichiro.
   1993.   "An East Asian Industrial Policy Model." In Ryuichiro Inoue,
              Hirohisa Kohama, Shujiro Urata, eds., *Industrial Policy in
              East Asia,* 2–27. Tokyo: Japan External Trade Organization.
Ishida, Takeshi.
   1971.   *Japanese Society.* New York: Random House.
Ishida, Takeshi, and Ellis S. Krauss, eds.
   1989.   *Democracy in Japan.* Pittsburgh: University of Pittsburgh
              Press.
Ishihara Shintarō, and Morita Akio.
   1989.   *"No" to ieru Nihon* [The Japan that can say no]. Tokyo:
              Kōbunsha.
Ishi Hiromitsu.
   1993.   "Baburu keizai to sono hōkai" [The bubble economy and its
              collapse]. *Keizai tōkei nenkan,* 14–21. Tokyo: Tōyō keizai.
Ishikawa Masumi, and Hirose Michisada.
   1989.   *Jimintō: chōki shihai no kōzō* [LDP: The structure of pro-
              tracted rule]. Tokyo: Iwanami shoten.
Itasaka Hidenori.
   1987.   *"Zoku" no kenkyū* [Research on tribes]. Tokyo: Keizaikai.

Itō Daiichi.
　1980.　　*Gendai Nihon kanryōsei no bunseki* [Analysis of the con-
　　　　　　temporary Japanese bureaucracy]. Tokyo: Tokyo daigaku
　　　　　　shuppankai.
Itō Hirokazu.
　1987.　　*Zankoku kensetsu gyōkai* [Merciless construction industry].
　　　　　　Tokyo: Eeru shuppansha.
Itō Shinji.
　1988.　　"Takeshita Faces Trade Disputes Tied to Domestic Politics."
　　　　　　Japan Times, 3 January.
Itō Yasuo.
　1978.　　"Kensetsu kanryō to 'kensetsu gyōkai' no yuchaku no kōzu"
　　　　　　[Adhesive structure between construction bureaucrats and
　　　　　　the construction industry]. *Zaikai tenbō*, December, 64–69.
Iwai Tomoaki.
　1990.　　*"Seiji shikin" no kenkyū* [Research on political funds]. Tokyo:
　　　　　　Nihon keizai shinbunsha.
Iyasu Tadashi.
　1984.　　*Jimintō: kono fushigi na seitō* [LDP: This counterintuitive
　　　　　　party]. Tokyo: Kōdansha.
Jackson, William Keith.
　1988.　　*The Dilemma of Parliament.* Wellington, New Zealand: Allen
　　　　　　and Unwin.
Japan Almanac. 1992,1993. Tokyo: Asahi shinbunsha.
Japan Company Handbook. 1994. Tokyo: Tōyō keizai.
Jin Ikkō.
　1989.　　*Daigishi no hisho: odorokubeki kengen, kane, yashin* [Assis-
　　　　　　tants of Diet members: Surprising power, money, ambitions].
　　　　　　Tokyo: Kappa Books.
Jin Ikkō, with Murakami Masaki and Itō Shin'ya.
　1981.　　"Kensetsushō no zeikin kuichirashi wa yurusenai" [Unfor-
　　　　　　givable devouring of tax monies by the Construction Minis-
　　　　　　try]. *Gendai*, February, 176–205.
Jinji kōshinroku [Who's who]. Various years. Tokyo: Jinji kōshinsho.
Jiyūminshutō seimu chōsakai meibo [Roster of the Liberal Democratic
　　　　　　Party's Policy Affairs Research Council]. Various years.
　　　　　　Tokyo: Jiyūminshutō kōhō iinkai shuppan kyoku.
Johannes, John R., and John C. McAdams.
　1987.　　"Entrepreneur or Agent: Congressmen and the Distribution
　　　　　　of Casework, 1977–1978." *Western Political Quarterly* 40:
　　　　　　535–53.

Johnson, Chalmers.

1974.   "The Re-employment of Retired Government Bureaucrats in Japanese Big Business." *Asian Survey* 14:953–65.

————.

1975.   "Japan: Who Governs? An Essay on Official Bureaucracy." *Journal of Japanese Studies* 2:1–28.

————.

1982.   *MITI and the Japanese Miracle: The Growth of Industrial Policy, 1925–1975.* Stanford: Stanford University Press.

————.

1986.   "Tanaka Kakuei, Structural Corruption, and the Advent of Machine Politics in Japan." *Journal of Japanese Studies* 12:1–28.

————.

1989.   "MITI, MPT, and the Telecom Wars: How Japan Makes Policy for High Technology." In Johnson et al., 177–240.

————.

1990a. "Trade, Revisionism, and the Future of Japanese-American Relations." In Kozo Yamamura, ed., *Japan's Economic Structure: Should It Change?* 105–36. Seattle: Society for Japanese Studies.

————.

1990b. "The People Who Invented the Mechanical Nightingale." *Daedalus* 12:71–90.

Johnson, Chalmers, Laura D'Andrea Tyson, and John Zysman, eds.

1989.   *Politics and Productivity: The Real Story of Why Japan Works.* Cambridge, Mass.: Ballinger.

"Kai no kuni de hajimaru 'Kanemaru-ha' issō" [Sweeping away the "Kanemaru faction" in the Land of Kai]. 1991. *Sandei mainichi*, 24 February, 32–33.

"Kanagawa ken gojūgo-oku-en o meguru 'nyūsatsu gigoku' o arau" [Laundering the ¥5.5-billion 'bidding corruption' in Kanagawa Prefecture]. 1982. *Shūkan posuto*, 17 September, 46–49.

Kanryō kikō kenkyūkai.

1978.   *Kensetsu zankoku monogatari* [The story of construction gluttony]. Tokyo: Eeru shuppansha.

Kaplan, David, and Alex Dubro.

1986.   *Yakuza.* New York: Addison-Wesley.

Kasumi Jirō.

1993.   "Zenekon gigoku: kanryō no hanzai" [The general contractors scandal: Crimes of the government bureaucrats]. *Bungei shunju*, November, 138–50.

Kato, Junko.
  1992.   "Tax Reform in Japan: The Influence and Strategy of Fiscal Bureaucrats." Ph.D. dissertation, Yale University.
Katzenstein, Peter J.
  1985.   *Small States in World Markets: Industrial Policy in Europe.* Ithaca: Cornell University Press.
Kawamura Toshio, and Matsui Shigeaki.
  1993.   *Shosenkyokusei-seitōhō no kiken na nerai* [The dangerous aim of single-member districts]. Tokyo: Gakushū no tomo.
Keizai kōhō sentaa. 1994. *Japan 1994: An International Comparison.* Tokyo: Keizai kōhō sentaa.
Kennedy, Paul.
  1987.   *The Rise and Fall of the Great Powers: Economic Change and Military Conflict from 1500 to 2000.* New York: Random House.
"Kensetsu gyōkai: amakudari tōshi to kensetsuzei nijūshūnen no sōkan ni mondai ari" [Construction industry: The problem of descent from heaven and the twenty trillion yen blood tax]. 1982. *Shūkan posuto,* 5 February, 178–81.
Kensetsu gyōkai gurafu [Construction industry graphs]. Various years. Tokyo: Nihon doboku kōgyō kyōkai kōhō iinkai.
Kensetsu sangyō handobukku [Construction industry handbook]. 1987. Tokyo: Kensetsu keizai kenkyūjo.
Kensetsugyō wa ima [The construction industry is now]. 1980. Tokyo: Nikkan kensetsu tsūshin shinbunsha.
Kensetsushō meikan [Ministry of Construction directory]. Various years. Tokyo: Jihyōsha.
Keohane, Robert O., and Joseph S. Nye, Jr.
  1977.   *Power and Interdependence: World Politics in Transition.* Boston: Little, Brown.
King, Anthony.
  1981.   "The Rise of the Career Politician in Britain—and Its Consequences." *British Journal of Political Science* 11:249–85.
Kohno, Masaru.
  1992.   "Rational Foundations for the Organization of the Liberal Democratic Party in Japan." *World Politics* 44:369–97.
Kohno, Masaru, and Yoshitaka Nishizawa.
  1990.   "A Study of Electoral Business Cycles in Japan: Elections and Government Spending on Construction." *Comparative Politics* 22:151–66.
Kokkai benran [Diet handbook]. Various years. Tokyo: Nihon keizai shinbunsha.

Kōsei torihiki iinkai. 1990. *Kōsei torihiki iinkai nenji hōkoku* [Annual report of the Fair Trade Commission]. Tokyo: Kōsei torihiki kyōkai.

Krauss, Ellis S.

    1989.   "Under Construction: U.S.-Japan Negotiations to Open Japan's Construction Markets to American Firms, 1985–1988." Pew Program in Case Teaching and Writing in International Affairs, Case #145, Graduate School of Public and International Affairs, University of Pittsburgh.

Kuhlman, John M.

    1969.   "The Nature and Significance of Price-Fixing Rings." *The Antitrust Law and Economics Review* 2:69–82.

Kusayanagi Daizō.

    1975.   "Kofu na nitodate basha—kensetsushō" [Old-fashioned two-wheel horse cart: Ministry of Construction]. *Bungei shunju,* February, 142–55.

Kyōgoku, Jun'ichi.

    1987.   *The Political Dynamics of Japan.* Translated by Ike Nobutaka. Tokyo: University of Tokyo Press.

Lancaster, Thomas.

    1986.   "Electoral Structures and Pork Barrel Politics." *International Political Science Review* 7:67–81.

LaPalombara, Joseph.

    1987.   *Democracy Italian Style.* New Haven: Yale University Press.

Lesbirel, S. Hayden.

    1991.   "Structural Adjustment in Japan: Terminating 'Old King Cole.'" *Asian Survey* 31:1079–94.

Levy, Sidney M.

    1993.   *Japan's Big Six: Inside Japan's Construction Industry.* New York: McGraw-Hill.

Lincoln, Edward J.

    1993.   *Japan's New Global Role.* Washington, D.C.: The Brookings Institution.

Lowi, Theodore J.

    1964.   "American Business, Public Policy, Case Studies, and Political Theory." *World Politics* 16:677–715.

    ———.

    1967.   "Making Democracy Safe for the World: National Policies and Foreign Policy." In James N. Rosenau, ed., *Domestic Sources of Foreign Policy,* 295–331. New York: Free Press.

    ———.

    1972.   "Four Systems of Policy, Politics, and Choice." *Public Administration Review* 32:298–310.

Maas, Arthur A.
1951.   *Muddy Waters.* Cambridge: Harvard University Press.
MacDougall, Terry Edward.
1988.   "The Lockheed Scandal and the High Costs of Politics in Japan." In Andrei S. Markovits and Mark Silverstein, eds., *The Politics of Scandal.* New York: Holmes and Meier.
Mackie, Thomas T., and Richard Rose.
1982.   *The International Almanac of Electoral History.* 2d ed. London: Macmillan.
Maeda Kunio.
1990.   *Nichibei kensetsu masatsu* [Japan-U.S. construction friction]. Tokyo: Nikkan shobō.
Maeda Tetsuji.
1988.   *Kensetsu* [Construction]. Tokyo: Jitsumu kyōiku shuppan.
Magaziner, Ira C., and Thomas M. Hout.
1981.   *Japanese Industrial Policy.* Berkeley: Institute of International Studies.
Magelby, David B., and Candice J. Nelson.
1990.   *The Money Chase: Congressional Campaign Finance Reform.* Washington, D.C.: The Brookings Institution.
Marshall, Andrew, with Michiko Toyama.
1992.   "The Man Who Would Be Kingmaker." *Tokyo Journal,* December, 32–39.
Martin, Jacques.
1993.   "The Godmother: Italy's Meltdown—and Ours." *The New Republic,* September, 23–28.
Masumi Junnosuke.
1985.   *Gendai seiji: 1955 ikō* [Contemporary politics: The post-1955 period]. 2 vol. Tokyo: Tokyo daigaku shuppankai.

———.
1988.   "The 1955 System in Japan and Its Subsequent Development." *Asian Survey* 28:286–306.
Matoba Toshihiro.
1986.   "Jimintō no seisaku kettei katei" [The LDP's policymaking process]. In Nakano Minoru, ed., *Nihon gata seisaku kettei no hen'yō* [Changes in the Japanese policymaking process]. Tokyo: Tōyō keizai shinpōsha.
Matsumoto Kōji, Suzuki Naoya, and Oki Kazuharu.
1993.   "Tsugi ni taihō sareru no wa dare da" [Who is next to be arrested?]. *AERA,* 11 October, 8.
Matsumoto Seichō.
1974.   "Kensetsu kanryō ron" [Theory of the construction bureaucrats]. *Bungei shunju,* February, 134–51.

Mayhew, David R.
  1974.   *Congress: The Electoral Connection.* New Haven: Yale University Press.
McCubbins, Matthew D., and Gregory W. Noble.
  1993.   "Equilibrium Behavior and the Appearance of Power: Legislators, Bureaucrats and the Budget Process in the U.S. and Japan." Unpublished manuscript.
McGill, Peter.
  1994.   "Construction and Corruption." *The American Chamber of Commerce in Japan Journal* 31:6–13.
McMillan, John.
  1991.   "Dangō: Japan's Price-Fixing Conspiracies." *Politics and Economics* 3:201–18.
Mikuriya Takashi.
  1980.   *Meiji kokka keisei to chihō keiei* [The formation of the Meiji state and local administration]. Tokyo: Tokyo daigaku shuppankai.
Minami Renpei.
  1981.   *Kensetsu gyōkai: aku no kōzu* [Construction industry: The structure of evil]. Tokyo: Eeru shuppansha.
Ministry of Construction. 1988. *From Obtaining Construction Business Licenses to Winning Contracts: A Guide to Construction in Japan.* Tokyo: Research Institute on Construction and Economy.
Murakami Yasusuke.
  1984.   *Shin chūkan taisei no jidai* [Age of the new middle mass]. Tokyo: Chūō kōronsha.
Muramatsu, Michio, and Ellis S. Krauss.
  1984.   "Bureaucrats and Politicians in Policymaking: The Case of Japan." *American Political Science Review* 78:26–146.
Myrdal, Gunnar.
  1968.   *Asian Drama: An Enquiry into the Poverty of Nations,* vol. 2. New York: Twentieth Century Fund.
Najita, Tetsuo.
  1967.   *Hara Kei in the Politics of Compromise.* Cambridge: Harvard University Press.
Nakamura Yoshimitsu.
  1982.   *Kensetsu gyōkai* [Construction industry]. Tokyo: kyōikusha.
Nakane, Chie.
  1970.   *Japanese Society.* Berkeley: University of California Press.
Nawa Tetsurō.
  1987.   "Dangōzai" [The crime of dangō]. In *Nihon daihyakka zenshū.* Tokyo: Shogakkan.

Nihon keizai shinbunsha. 1983. *Jimintō seichōkai* [LDP's PARC]. Tokyo: Nihon keizai shinbunsha.

———.

1990. *Tochi o kangaeru* [Contemplating land]. Tokyo: Nihon keizai shinbunsha.

Nikkenren nijūnenshi [Twenty-year history of the Japan Federation of Construction Contractors]. 1987. Tokyo: Nihon kensetsugyō dantai rengōkai.

Nishioka Toshirō.

1988. "'Dōro sanpō' no seitei katei: nijūnendai no dōro gyōsei o megutte" [The policy process of the "Three Road Laws": Looking at road administration, 1955–1965]. M.A. thesis, Tokyo Tōritsu Daigaku.

Niskanen, William A.

1971. *Bureaucracy and Representative Government.* Chicago: Aldine Atherton.

North, Douglass C.

1990. *Institutions, Institutional Change, and Economic Performance.* Cambridge: Cambridge University Press.

Nye, Joseph S., Jr.

1990. *Bound to Lead: The Changing Nature of American Power.* New York: Basic Books.

Odawara Atsushi.

1993. "How Factionalism Is Undermining Japanese Politics." *Japan Quarterly* 40:28–33.

Okimoto, Daniel I.

1989. *Between MITI and the Market: Industrial Policy for High Technology.* Stanford: Stanford University Press.

Okimoto, Daniel I., Haruo Sugano, and Frederick Weinstein, eds.

1984. *Competitive Edge: The Semiconductor Industry in the U.S. and Japan.* Stanford: Stanford University Press.

Okuno Hitoshi.

1978. "Kensetsu kanryō to seijika no yuchaku" [Ties between construction bureaucrats and politicians]. *Zaikai tenbō,* December, 70–79.

Olson, Mancur.

1982. *The Rise and Decline of Nations: Economic Growth, Stagflation, and Social Rigidities.* New Haven: Yale University Press.

Ōmiya Kenichirō, and Group B.

1993. *Nihon no seijika-kanryō jinmyaku chizu* [A map of the networks of Japan's politicans and bureaucrats]. Tokyo: Yūbasha.

Onis, Ziya.

1991. "The Logic of the Developmental State." *Comparative Politics* 24:109–26.

"Ōte kensetsu 'seiji buchō' ga kaita dangō nikki no shōgeki bubun" [The surprising portion of the dangō diary of a "political bureau chief" of a major contractor]. 1982. *Shūkan gendai*, 1 May, 54–55.

Park, Yung H.
    1986.   *Bureaucrats and Ministers in Contemporary Japanese Government*. Berkeley: Institute of East Asian Studies.

Patrick, Hugh T., and Henry Rosovsky, eds.
    1976.   *Asia's New Giant*. Washington, D.C.: The Brookings Institution.

Peck, Merton J., Richard C. Levin, and Akira Goto.
    1987.   "Picking Losers: Public Policy Toward Declining Industries in Japan." *Journal of Japanese Studies* 13:79–123.

Pempel, T. J.
    1974.   "The Bureaucratization of Policymaking in Postwar Japan." *American Journal of Political Science* 18:647–64.

————.
    1979.   "Corporatism Without Labor? The Japanese Anomaly." In Philippe C. Schmitter and Gerhard Lehmbruch, eds., *Trends Toward Corporatist Intermediation*, 231–70. Beverly Hills, Calif.: Sage.

————.
    1982.   *Policy and Politics in Japan: Creative Conservatism*. Philadelphia: Temple University Press.

————.
    1987.   "The Unbundling of 'Japan, Inc.': The Changing Dynamics of Japanese Policy Formation." In Kenneth Pyle, ed., *The Trade Crisis: How Will Japan Respond?* 117–52. Seattle: Society for Japanese Studies.

————.
    1990a.   "Introduction. Uncommon Democracies: The One Party Dominant Regimes." In T. J. Pempel, ed., *Uncommon Democracies: The One Party Dominant Regimes*, 1–32. Ithaca: Cornell University Press.

————.
    1990b.   "Conclusion. One-Party Dominance and the Creation of Regimes." In T. J. Pempel, ed., *Uncommon Democracies: The One Party Dominant Regimes*, 333–60. Ithaca: Cornell University Press.

Pennock, J. Roland.
    1979.   *Democratic Political Theory*. Princeton: Princeton University Press.

Peterzell, Jay.
    1990.   "Penetrating the World of Dangō." *Time*, 15 January, 48.

Polsby, Nelson W.

1968.   "The Institutionalization of the United States House of Representatives." *American Political Science Review* 62:144–268.

Posner, Richard.

1970.   "A Statistical Study of Antitrust Enforcement." *Journal of Law and Economics* 13:365–415.

Putnam, Robert D.

1988.   "Diplomacy and Domestic Politics: The Logic of Two-Level Games." *International Organization* 42:427–60.

Ramseyer, Mark, and Frances McCall Rosenbluth.

1993.   *Japan's Political Marketplace.* Cambridge: Harvard University Press.

Reed, Steven R., and John Bolland.

Forth-   "The Fragmentation Effect of SNTV in Japan." In Bernard
coming.   Grofman, Sung-Chull Lee, Edwin Winckler, and Brian Woodall, eds., *Elections in Japan, Korea, and Taiwan Under the Single Non-Transferable Vote: The Comparative Study of an Embedded Institutions.* Ann Arbor: University of Michigan Press.

Rigger, Shelley Elizabeth.

1994.   "Machine Politics in the New Taiwan: Institutional Reform and electoral Strategy on the Republic of China on Taiwan." Ph.D. dissertation, Harvard University.

Ripley, Randall B., and Grace A. Franklin.

1987.   *Congress, the Bureaucracy, and Public Policy.* 4th ed. Chicago: Dorsey Press.

Rosenbluth, Frances McCall.

1989.   *Financial Politics in Contemporary Japan.* Ithaca: Cornell University Press.

———.

1993.   "Japan's Response to the Strong Yen: Party Leadership and the Market for Political Favors." In Gerald L. Curtis, ed., *Coping with Change: Japan's Foreign Policy After the Cold War,* 137–59. Westchester: M. E. Sharpe.

Saitō Kyōhei.

1978.   "Kensetsu kanryō no jinji to jinmyaku ni miru tokui taishitsu" [Viewing the peculiar constitution through the personnel and personal connections of construction bureaucrats]. *Zaikai tenbō,* December, 86–91.

Sakakibara, Eisuke.

1991.   "The Japanese Politico-Economic System and the Public Sector." In Samuel Kernall, ed., *Parallel Politics: Economic Policymaking in Japan and the United States,* 50–79. Washington D.C.: The Brookings Institution.

Samuels, Richard J.
    1987.   *The Business of the Japanese State: Energy Markets in Com-
                 parative and Historical Perspective.* Ithaca: Cornell Univer-
                 sity Press.
Samuels, Richard J., and Benjamin C. Whipple.
    1989.   "Defense Production and Industrial Development: The Case
                 of Japanese Aircraft." In Johnson et al., 275–318.
Sanger, David E.
    1993a.   "Japan Builders Graded Politicians in Giving Cash." *New York
                 Times,* 28 March.
———.

    1993b.   "Tokyo Worried by U.S. Criticism of Curbs on Construction
                 Bidding." *New York Times,* 4 May.
Sartori, Giovanni.
    1967.   "Italy: Members of Parliament." In Giovanni Sartori, ed., *De-
                 cisions and Decision-Makers in the Modern State.* Paris:
                 UNES.
———.

    1970.   "Concept Misinformation in Comparative Politics." *American
                 Political Science Review* 64:1033–53.
———.

    1976.   *Parties and Party Systems: A Framework for Analysis.* Cam-
                 bridge: Cambridge University Press.
———, ed.
    1984.   *Social Science Concepts: A Systematic Analysis.* Beverly Hills,
                 Calif.: Sage.
Satō Seizaburō, and Matsuzaki Tetsuhisa.
    1986.   *Jimintō seiken* [LDP rule]. Tokyo: Chūō kōronsha.
Satō Takayoshi.
    1992.   "Kenchiku kosuto no nichibei hikaku" [A comparison of the
                 cost of construction in Japan and the U.S.]. *Kenchiku zasshi,*
                 August, 36–37.
Scalapino, Robert A.
    1953.   *Democracy and the Party Movement in Prewar Japan: The
                 Failure of the First Attempt.* Berkeley: University of California
                 Press.
Scalapino, Robert A., and Masumi Junnosuke.
    1962.   *Parties and Politics in Contemporary Japan.* Berkeley: Uni-
                 versity of California Press.
Scherer, F. M., and David Ross.
    1990.   *Industrial Market Structure and Economic Performance.*
                 3d ed. Boston: Houghton Mifflin.

Schoenberger, Karl.
    1989.   "Japan Tries to Stop Builder Bid-Rigging." *Asian Wall Street Journal,* 5 March, 1.
Schoppa, Leonard J.
    1991.   "*Zoku* Power and LDP Power: A Case Study of the *Zoku* Role in Education Policy." *Journal of Japanese Studies* 17:79–106.

———.

    1993.   "Two-Level Games and Bargaining Outcomes: Why Gaiatsu Succeeds in Japan in Some Cases but Not Others." *International Organization* 47:353–86.
Schorr, Daniel.
    1993.   "Political Shakedown." *New Leader,* 13 December, 4.
Seiji handobukku [Handbook of politics]. Various years. Tokyo: Seiji kōhō sentaa.
Seikan yōran [Survey of Parliament and bureaucracy]. Various years. Tokyo: Seisaku jihōsha.
Setzer, Steven W., and William Krizan.
    1993.   "U.S. Getting Tough with Japanese." *Engineering News-Record,* 230:6–7.
Shefter, Martin.
    1977.   "Party and Patronage: Germany, England, and Italy." *Politics and Society* 7:403–51.
Sheridan, Kyoko.
    1993.   *Governing the Japanese Economy.* Cambridge, England: Polity Press.
Shimizu, Kazuhiko.
    1989.   "Construction Door Still Seen as Shut." *Japan Times,* 17 May.
Shiraishi, Kojiro.
    1990.   "The Recruit Scandal and 'Money Politics' in Japan." *Occasional Paper of the U.S.-Japan Relations Program,* Harvard University.
Simon, Herbert A.
    1976.   *Administrative Behavior: A Study of Decision-Making Processes in Administrative Organization.* 3d ed. New York: Free Press.
Smith, Richard Austen.
    1963.   "The Incredible Electrical Conspiracy." *Fortune,* April, 161–224.
Soma Masao.
    1986.   *Nihon no senkyō seido* [A history of Japan's electoral system]. Fukuoka: Kyūshū daigaku shuppankai.

Steinhoff, Patricia J.
    1988.   "Protest and Democracy." In Ishida and Krauss, 171–98.
Stigler, George J.
    1964.   "A Theory of Oligopoly." *Journal of Political Economy* 72 : 44– 61.
"Still Crooked: Italy." 1994. *The Economist*, 5 February, 53–54.
Stockwin, J. A. A.
    1982.   *Japan: Divided Politics in a Growth Economy.* 2d ed. London: Weidenfeld and Nicolson.
Tanaka Rokusuke.
    1985.   *Hoshu honryū no chokugen* [Straight talk about the conservative mainstream]. Tokyo: Chūō kōronsha.
Taoka Shunji.
    1982.   "Dangō wa 'junpu bizoku' ka" [Is dangō a "pristine way of life"?]. *Bungei shunju*, December, 338–45.
Taylor, Jared.
    1983.   *Shadows of the Rising Sun.* New York: William Morrow.
Thayer, Nathaniel B.
    1969.   *How the Conservatives Rule Japan.* Princeton: Princeton University Press.
Thompson, Dennis F.
    1993.   "Mediated Corruption: The Case of the Keating Five." *American Political Science Review* 87 : 369–81.
Togawa Isamu.
    1961.   *Seiji shikin: seikai no chika suidō o saguru* [Political funds: Exploring the political world's subterranean waterway]. Tokyo: Rōzuruho shinsho.
"Tokken kanryō amakudari no kōzō: kensetsushō no jittai" [The structure of amakudari for privileged bureaucrats: The situation in the Ministry of Construction]. 1982. In *Amakudari hakusho,* 79–96.
Tomita, Nobuo, Akira Nakamura, and Ronald J. Hrebenar.
    1986.   "The Liberal Democratic Party: The Ruling Party of Japan." In Hrebenar, ed., 235–82.
Tonedachi Masaaki.
    1994.   "Ippyō no omomi" [The weight of a single vote.] *AERA,* 20 May, 70–73.
Totten, George O., and Kawakami Tamio.
    1965.   "The Functions of Factionalism in Japanese Politics." *Pacific Affairs* 38 : 109–22.
Tyson, Laura D'Andrea.
    1993.   *Who's Bashing Whom? Trade Conflict in High-Technology Industries.* Washington, D.C.: Institute for International Economics.

Uchiyama Shōzō.
    1982.   *Dangō mondai e no shiten* [Focusing on the dangō problem].
                Tokyo: Toshi bunkasha.
Upham, Frank K.
    1989.   "Legal Regulation of the Japanese Retail Industry: The Large
                Retail Stores Law and Prospects for Reform." *Occasional Pa-
                per of the U.S.-Japan Relations Program.* Harvard University.

    ———.
    1993.   "Privatizing Regulation: The Implementation of the Large-
                Scale Retail Stores Law." In Gary D. Allinson and Yasunori
                Sone, eds., *Political Dynamics in Contemporary Japan,* 264–
                94. Ithaca: Cornell University Press.
Van der Meer, Cornelius L. J., and Saburo Yamada.
    1990.   *Japanese Agriculture: A Comparative Economic Analysis.*
                London: Routledge.
Van Wolferen, Karel G.
    1989.   *The Enigma of Japanese Power: People and Politics in a State-
                less Nation.* New York: Knopf.

    ———.
    1993.   "Japan's Non-Revolution." *Foreign Affairs* 72:54–65.
Vogel, Steven K.
    1993.   "The Power Behind Military 'Spin-Ons': The Military Impli-
                cations of Japan's Commercial Technology." In Wayne Sand-
                holtz, Michael Borrus, John Zysman, Ken Conca, Jay Stowsky,
                Steven Vogel, and Steve Weber, eds., *The Highest Stakes: The
                Economic Foundations of the Next Security System,* 55–80.
                London: Oxford University Press.
Wade, Robert.
    1990.   *Governing the Market: Economic Theory and the Role of
                Government in East Asian Industrialization.* Princeton:
                Princeton University Press.
Wakata, Kyoji.
    1986.   "Electoral Mobilization in Kansai and California." *Kansai
                University Review of Law and Politics* 7:31–104.
Walston, James.
    1988.   *The Mafia and Clientelism: Roads to Rome in Post-War Cala-
                bria.* London: Routledge.
Ward, Robert E.
    1967.   *Japan's Political System.* Englewood Cliffs, N.J.: Prentice-Hall.
Watanabe Shōichi.
    1982.   "'Dangō' ni miru Nihon-teki keiei no genten" [The origin of
                Japanese management as seen in "Dangō"]. *Chūō kōron keiei
                mondai:* 270–76.

Watanuki Jōji.
    1967.   *Nihon no seiji shakai* [Japan's political society]. Tokyo: Tokyo daigaku shuppankai.

———.
    1991.   "Social Structure and Voting Behavior." In Scott C. Flanagan, Shinsaku Kohei, Ichiro Miyake, Bradley M. Richardson, and Joji Watanuki, eds., *The Japanese Voter*, 49–83. New Haven: Yale University Press.

Weaver, R. Kent, and Bert A. Rockman.
    1993.   "Assessing the Effects of Institutions." In R. Kent Weaver and Bert A. Rockman, eds., *Do Institutions Matter?* 1–41. Washington, D.C.: The Brookings Institution.

Wilson, Rick K.
    1986.   "An Empirical Test of Preferences for the Political Pork Barrel: District Level Appropriations for River and Harbor Legislation, 1889–1913." *American Journal of Political Science* 30:729–54.

Wolff, Alan William, and Thomas R. Howell.
    1992.   "Japan." In Thomas R. Howell, Alan William Wolff, Brent L. Bartlett, and Michael Gadbaw, eds., *Conflict Among Nations: Trade Policies in the 1990s*, 45–144. Boulder, Colo.: Westview Press.

Wood, Christopher.
    1992.   *The Bubble Economy: The Japanese Economic Collapse*. New York: Sidgwick and Jackson.

Woodall, Brian.
    1990.   "Pork Barrel Politics in Japan: Trade Friction, Public Works, and the Triadic Syndicate, 1955–1988." Ph.D. dissertation, University of California at Berkeley.

———.
    1992.   "The Politics of Land in Japan's Dual Political Economy." In John O. Haley and Kozo Yamamura, eds., *Land Issues in Japan: A Policy Failure?* 113–48. Seattle: Society for Japanese Studies.

———.
    1993a.   "The Logic of Collusive Action: The Political Roots of Japan's Dangō System." *Comparative Politics* 25:297–312.

———.
    1993b.   *Japan's Changing World Role: Emerging Leader or Perpetual Follower?* New York: The Japan Society.

Yakuin shikihō [Quarterly bulletin on company officials]. 1993. Tokyo: Tōyō keizai shinpōsha.

Yamaguchi Yasushi.
  1985.   "Sengo Nihon no seiji taisei to seiji katei" [The political system
            and policy process in postwar Japan]. In Miyake Ichirō, Ya-
            maguchi Yasushi, Muramatsu Michio, and Shindō Eiichi, eds.,
            Nihon seiji no zahyō: sengo yonjūnen no ayumi [Coordinates
            of Japanese politics: Forty years of postwar change]. Tokyo:
            Yuhikaku sensho.
Yamamoto Nobuo.
  1975.   "'Jisankin tsuki mukoiri' to iu Kensetsushō amakudari jinji
            no kai" [Construction Ministry personnel and amakudari: A
            "dowried bridegroom"?]. *Shūkan yomiuri*, 15 March, 138–
            41.
Yamamura, Kozo, ed.
  1982.   *Policy and Trade Issues of the Japanese Economy: American
            and Japanese Perspectives.* Seattle: University of Washington
            Press.
Yonemoto Kazuhiro.
  1987.   "Shūhyō to rieki haibun o ninau kōenkai ga chi de chi o arau
            seisoshi o enshutsu shita" [The kōenkai that shoulder the votes
            and benefit distribution that produce blood feuds]. In Ishii
            Shinji, ed., *Jimintō to iu chie* [Wisdom known as the LDP],
            222–37. Tokyo: Jikku shuppan.
Yoshida Shin'ichi.
  1984.   *Dokyumento jichitai oshoku: Fukushima-Kimura ookoku no
            hōkai* [Documenting corruption in local autonomy: The col-
            lapse of the Kimura kingdom in Fukushima]. Tokyo: Asahi
            sensho.
Yoshikawa, Aki.
  1987.   "The Japanese Challenge in Biotechnology: Industrial Policy."
            Berkeley Roundtable on the International Economy Working
            Paper #29.
Yoshikawa, Aki, and Brian Woodall.
  1985.   "The 'Venture Boom' and Japanese Industrial Policy: Promot-
            ing the Neglected Winners." *Asian Survey* 25:692–714.
Yoshino, Kaye N.
  1993.   "The Development of High Technology Industries in Japan:
            The Case of High Definition Television." M.A. thesis, Har-
            vard University.
Yuasa Hiroshi.
  1986.   *Kokkai "zoku giin"—Jimintō seichō to kasumigaseki* [The
            Diet's policy tribesmen: LDP's PARC and Kasumigaseki]. To-
            kyo: Kyōikusha.

Zaikai tenbō shuzai gurupu.

　1978.　　　"Kensetsu kanryō: 'amakudari' ichiran" [Construction bureau-
　　　　　　crats: A glimpse at amakudari]. *Zaikai tenbō*, December,
　　　　　　56–63.

Zysman, John.

　1983.　　　*Governments, Markets, and Growth*. Ithaca: Cornell Univer-
　　　　　　sity Press.

Index